Africa since 1940

The Past of the Present

Second edition

Africa since 1940 is the flagship textbook in Cambridge University Press's New Approaches to African History series. Now fully revised to include the history and scholarship of Africa since the turn of the millennium, this important book continues to help students understand the historical process out of which Africa's position in the world has emerged. A history of decolonization and independence, it allows readers to see just what political independence did and did not signify, and how men and women, peasants and workers, religious and local leaders sought to refashion the way they lived, worked, and interacted with each other.

Covering the transformation of Africa from a continent marked by colonization to one of independent states, Fred Cooper follows the "development question" across time, seeing how first colonial regimes and then African elites sought to transform African society in their own ways. He shows how people in cities and villages tried to make their way in an unequal world, through times of hope, despair, renewed possibilities, and continued uncertainties. Looking beyond the debate over what or who may be to blame for Africa's recurrent crises, he explores alternatives for the future.

Frederick Cooper is Professor of History at New York University. Author and coauthor of a number of books on the history of Africa and of empires, his recent books include *Citizenship between Empire and Nation: Remaking France and French Africa* (2014) and *Citizenship, Inequality, and Difference: Historical Perspectives* (2018). His books have won prizes from the American Historical Association, the African Studies Association, and the World History Association. He has conducted research in both East and West Africa, has taught at Harvard University and the University of Michigan, and has been a visiting professor in France.

New Approaches to African History

Series Editors
Judith Byfield, *Cornell University*
Martin Klein, *Professor Emeritus, University of Toronto*

Editorial Advisors
William Freund, *Emeritus Professor, University of Kwazulu-Natal*
Richard Roberts, *Stanford University*
Didier Gondola, *Indiana University-Purdue University, Indianapolis*
Derek Peterson, *University of Michigan*
Kenda Mutongi, *Massachusetts Institute of Technology*
Elisabeth McMahon, *Tulane University*
John Thornton, *Boston University*

New Approaches to African History is designed to introduce students to current findings and new ideas in African history. Although each book treats a particular case and is able to stand alone, the format allows the studies to be used as modules in general courses on African history and world history. The cases represent a wide range of topics. Each volume summarizes the state of knowledge on a particular subject for a student who is new to the field. However, the aim is not simply to present views of the literature but also to introduce debates on historiographical or substantive issues, and individual studies may argue for a particular point of view. The aim of the series is to stimulate debate and to challenge students and general readers. The series is not committed to any particular school of thought.

Other Books in the Series

1. *Africa since 1940* by Frederick Cooper
2. *Muslim Societies in African History* by David Robinson
3. *Reversing Sail: A History of the African Diaspora* by Michael Gomez
4. *The African City: A History* by William Freund
5. *Warfare in Independent Africa* by William Reno
6. *Warfare in African History* by Richard J. Reid
7. *Foreign Intervention in Africa* by Elizabeth Schmidt
8. *Slaving and Slavery in African History* by Sean Stilwell
9. *Democracy in Africa* by Nic Cheeseman
10. *Women in Twentieth-Century Africa* by Iris Berger
11. *A History of African Popular Culture* by Karin Barber
12. *Human Rights in Africa* by Bonny Ibawoh
13. *Africa since 1940, Second Edition* by Frederick Cooper

Africa since 1940

The Past of the Present

Second edition

Frederick Cooper
New York University

CAMBRIDGE
UNIVERSITY PRESS

CAMBRIDGE
UNIVERSITY PRESS

University Printing House, Cambridge CB2 8BS, United Kingdom

One Liberty Plaza, 20th Floor, New York, NY 10006, USA

477 Williamstown Road, Port Melbourne, VIC 3207, Australia

314–321, 3rd Floor, Plot 3, Splendor Forum, Jasola District Centre,
New Delhi – 110025, India

103 Penang Road, #05–06/07, Visioncrest Commercial, Singapore 238467

Cambridge University Press is part of the University of Cambridge.

It furthers the University's mission by disseminating knowledge in the pursuit of
education, learning, and research at the highest international levels of excellence.

www.cambridge.org
Information on this title: www.cambridge.org/9781108480680
DOI: 10.1017/9781108672214

First edition © Frederick Cooper 2002
Second edition © Frederick Cooper 2019

First published 2002
13th printing 2016
Second edition 2019
3rd printing 2022

Printed in Great Britain by Ashford Colour Press Ltd.

A catalogue record for this publication is available from the British Library.

Library of Congress Cataloging-in-Publication Data
Names: Cooper, Frederick, 1947- author.
Title: Africa since 1940 : the past of the present / Frederick Cooper.
Other titles: New approaches to African history ; 13.
Description: Second edition. | New York, NY : Cambridge University Press, 2019. |
    Series: New approaches to African history ; 13 | Includes index.
Identifiers: LCCN 2018048289 | ISBN 9781108480680 (hardback) |
    ISBN 9781108727891 (pbk.)
Subjects: LCSH: Decolonization–Africa–History–20th century. |
    Decolonization–Africa–History–21st century. | Africa–Politics and
    government–1945-1960. | Africa–Politics and government–1960- | Africa–Colonial
    influence. | Africa–History–20th century. | Africa–History–21st century.
Classification: LCC DT30 .C595 2019 | DDC 960.3/2–dc23
LC record available at https://lccn.loc.gov/2018048289

ISBN 978-1-108-48068-0 Hardback
ISBN 978-1-108-72789-1 Paperback

Additional resources for this publication at www.cambridge.org/CooperAfrica2ed

Contents

Figures

Maps

Tables

Preface to the Second Edition

The original edition of this book was published in 2002. For a book that begins in 1940, the sixteen years between this edition and its predecessor is a significant portion of the history in question. Much has happened in Africa. New scholarly works with a variety of perspectives have emerged.

We are now at some distance from the millennial expectations that many people around the world held of the year 2000. Some Africanists in 2000 were caught up in those expectations. From one angle came visions of a new era of "millennial" capitalism, a new world of global connections, both linking Africa to economic and cultural trends elsewhere and fragmenting the social fabric. From another angle came the program Millennium 2015, with support from international financial institutions and economists; but despite its name (and the goal of achieving its benchmarks in fifteen years) the call was for a return to concepts of development that had been dominant in the 1950s and 1960s but which had gone into eclipse behind the market fundamentalism of the 1980s. The market model had been imposed on much of Africa under the name of "structural adjustment," with disastrous consequences that were very much on people's minds at the time of the first edition of this book.

For somewhat more than a decade of the new millennium the advocates of a return to vigorous development efforts seemed to be having their way: Africa was now experiencing a "normal" – or even better – pattern of economic growth and attracting attention and investment from people interested both in profits and in improving the welfare of Africans. But by the middle of the second decade of the 2000s it was becoming less and less clear that the nature of economy and society in Africa corresponded to either the model of a new millennial capitalism or the older model of development. More consistent with the evidence is the recent insight of the economic historian Morton Jerven, who identifies a long-term pattern of "growth spurts" in African economies – that is, periods of rapid response to external markets, leading to growth in certain sectors of regional economies that after a time reaches its limits and is followed by relative stagnation. The challenge is to explain both the spurts – which isn't hard – and their limitations, which isn't easy. But what needs to be explained is quite different from a long-term or inherent condition characteristic of "Africa." We may well have just witnessed another of Jerven's growth spurts: rapid growth in primary-product exports largely driven by demand from the booming economies of China and India, followed by a slow-down as demand has stagnated, while the diversification and structural change in domestic economies remains limited.

One can identify "spurts" of other sorts, for example in citizenship initiatives, as in Senegal in 2012 or Burkina Faso in 2014, when ordinary citizens, especially youth, carried out effective demonstrations that forced heads of state who wanted to prolong their time in power to back down. One needs to look as well for examples of relatively durable patterns of democratic governance, as in Ghana since the 1990s, where incumbent parties sometimes lost elections, compared to other places where aging dictators cling to power or warlords vie for control of large regions. This edition of *Africa since 1940* will look at related patterns of openings and closures, at moves toward more democratic politics and assertions of dictatorial control, at violent conflicts erupting and violent conflicts being resolved. It emphasizes the unevenness of historical patterns, that "Africa" is not a single place moving toward a singular destiny. The nature of its connections with the rest of the world are varied and volatile.

A basic objective of the second edition of *Africa since 1940* is much the same as that of the first: to understand the past of the present. To get to the present, however, we cannot proceed as if history must inevitably lead to what we see today. The men and women who made history at any moment in the past did not know how things would turn out, and they acted on the basis of what they could see and what they wanted, in the face of the constraints of their time. The pathways they followed may have turned out to be blind alleys or highways to a promising future, but people at any time were mobilizing resources, forging relationships, and making choices on the basis of continually changing sets of possibilities and constraints. We need to reconstruct those changing worlds if we are to understand how Africa got to be where it is today.

Each chapter is followed by a short list of suggested readings as well as references to scholarly works cited in the text. Some material from my own research also appears in the text, and full references, mainly from French and British archives, can be found in my books *Decolonization and African Society: The Labor Question in French and British Africa* (Cambridge: Cambridge University Press, 1996), and *Citizenship from Empire to Nation: Remaking France and French Africa 1945–1960* (Princeton: Princeton University Press, 2014). A more comprehensive bibliography, keyed to chapters in this book, is available on the web site of Cambridge University Press, at http://www.cambridge .org/CooperAfrica2ed. It will be updated periodically.

Dongil Lee redid the graphs and tables for this edition, using up-to-date data sets. The sources for the updated graphs (figures 9–10 and 13–16), all online, are World Bank, *World Development Indicators*, Food and Agriculture Organization, *FAOSTAT*, United Nations, *Statistical Yearbook*, and UNESCO, *UIS.Stat*. I am grateful for Mr. Lee's careful work. Figure 11 is reproduced from the first edition of this book.

The preface to the first edition is reproduced in this volume, and the help I received from colleagues at that time deserves recognition again. In addition, I would like to thank Eric Allina, Lisa Lindsay, Kate Luongo, and an anonymous reader for the Press for their critical reading of the text of this edition. I am grateful to Maria Marsh and Marty Klein for encouraging me to undertake this new edition.

Preface to the First Edition

It is now forty years since the exciting, hopeful days when most French, British, and Belgian colonies emerged as independent states. Still, much writing on politics, development, or other aspects of contemporary Africa treats this period, or the post-World War II era generally, more as background than as a subject for consideration, while most textbooks and many courses in African history treat this period more as an epilogue than as a full part of the continent's history. The present book attempts to meet the needs of general readers, students, and teachers who would like to do more than that, who want to look at the past of the present in a more coherent way. The dividing line between colonial and independence eras is sometimes thought of so axiomatically that no one asks just what difference acquiring sovereignty made – especially given the continued inequalities of the world order – and just what processes unfolded over a longer time frame. In many ways, the time of World War II (really the late 1930s through the late 1940s) is as important a break point as the moment of independence. More precisely, different aspects of African history present different rhythms and ruptures, different continuities, adaptations, and innovations – a theme developed in the "Interlude".

The book is organized to promote discussion of such issues. *Africa since 1940* is thus intended for readers with an interest in both history and current affairs, to encourage the former to look farther forward – to see that history doesn't come to an end point – and the latter to look farther backward – to see that the unfolding of processes over time is essential to understanding the present. I have written this book both within and against the genre of a textbook. Within, because it is intended for readers, students, and others, who seek an introduction to a subject and who are not presumed to have prior knowledge of it, and against, because I have eschewed both the comprehensiveness and the blandness characteristic of textbooks. In putting themes ahead of coverage, readers may find that a part of Africa that particularly interests them, say Ethiopia, is neglected, but they should find that it is easier to obtain specific information elsewhere than it is to find a framework through which to analyze and debate the post-war period as a whole. The choice of examples is shaped both by what I know – and there is more to know about Africa than any one scholar can assimilate – and by what works well within the thematic structure and space constraints of the book. Such choices should not be taken to mean that one part of Africa is more interesting or important than any other.

Africa since 1940 is as much an interpretive essay as a textbook, and its contents are intended more to provoke discussion than to be learned. It is argumentative and even opinionated, but I know of no other way to write African history than to do so from my own point of view and to acknowledge that it is one among many ways of approaching the subject.

It was Martin Klein's innovative idea for a series of modular texts on different themes of African history that inspired me to write this book, and my attempt to make it accessible to students of political science, development, and perhaps world history as well is, I think, compatible with Marty's goals for the series. I am grateful to Marty and to his advisory committee for several rounds of suggestions on my prospectus and the draft of the book. I would also like to thank Mamadou Diouf, Devra Coren, Nancy Hunt, Andrew Ivaska, David Newbury, Luise White, and Jennifer Widner for their helpful critiques of earlier drafts.

Devra Coren's skills in building and using databases and presenting them graphically deserve the credit for the figures and tables presented in chapter 5. I am grateful to Agence France Presse, Documentation Française, Bettmann/CORBIS, and the Eliot Elisofan Photographic Archive of the National Museum of African Art of the Smithsonian Institution for permission to reproduce photographs. I am also grateful to the staff of the Map Room at the University of Michigan Library, and particularly Karl Longstreth and Chad Weinberg, for working with me on the maps.

MAP 1 Africa: countries and cities, c.2019

CHAPTER 1

Introduction

On April 27, 1994, black South Africans, for the first times in their lives, voted in an election to decide who would govern their country. The lines at polling stations snaked around many blocks. It had been more than thirty years since African political movements had been banned, and the leader of the strongest of them, Nelson Mandela, had spent twenty-seven of those years in prison. Most activists and observers inside and outside South Africa had thought that the apartheid regime, with its explicit policy of promoting white supremacy, had become so deeply entrenched, and its supporters so attached to their privileges, that only a violent revolution would dislodge it. In a world that, some thirty to forty years earlier, had begun to tear down colonial empires and denounce governments that practiced racial segregation, South Africa had become a pariah, subject to boycotts of investment, sports events, travel, and trade. Now it was being redeemed, taking its place among nations that respected civil rights and democratic processes. This was indeed a revolution – whose final act was peaceful.

Three weeks earlier, part of the vast press corps assembled to observe the electoral revolution in South Africa had been called away to report on another sort of event in another part of Africa. On April 6 what the press described as a "tribal bloodbath" began in Kigali, the capital of Rwanda. It started when the plane carrying the country's President, Juvenal Habyarimana, returning from peace discussions in Arusha in Tanzania, was shot down. The government was dominated by people who called themselves "Hutu," which most of the press assumed was a "tribe" that had long been engaged in rivalry, and eventually civil war, with another "tribe," known as "Tutsi." Indeed, a significant number of Tutsi had fled from periodic massacres over the previous decades, and a group of exiles was invading Rwanda from neighboring Uganda to fight for a place for Tutsi in Rwandan government and society. The Tanzanian discussions were an attempt to resolve the conflict. But on the night of the plane crash there began mass killings of Tutsi that within a few days became a systematic slaughter conducted by the Hutu-dominated army, by local militias, and apparently by angry mobs.

The killing spread throughout Rwanda, and it soon became clear that this was more than a spontaneous outburst of hatred; it was a planned attempt to destroy the entire Tutsi population, from babies to elders. When it ended, some months later, around 800,000 Tutsi had died – a large portion of the Tutsi population – as had numerous Hutu who had opposed the genocidal leaders. It only ended because the Hutu-dominated army, deeply involved in the genocide, proved unable to fend off the invading forces, which captured Kigali and moved to take control over the rest of the territory. The "Tutsi" military victory now produced a wave of "Hutu" refugees into neighboring Zaire. By the fall of 1994 many of the soldiers, militiamen, and thugs responsible for the genocide had joined fleeing children, women, and men in the refugee camps. These genocidal militias were intimidating other refugees into participating in raids on Rwanda, and counterattacks by the new Rwandan government were taking a toll among civilians as well as the militias.

It is now quarter of a century since the first fully free elections in South Africa and the genocide in Rwanda. South Africa has had regular elections ever since; presidents have succeeded each other in orderly fashion. The powerful apparatus of racial discrimination has been dismantled; the hated laws that required black South Africans to carry an internal passport and the restrictions on where black South Africans could live are gone. Black South Africans are well represented in the upper and middle classes. More Africans than before have access to running water and electricity, and many Africans in need receive some kind of cash aid from the government. Yet South Africa remains one of the most unequal countries in the world. Although the higher strata of society are now relatively integrated, the lower strata are entirely black and deeply impoverished. Unemployment is estimated at around 30 percent. Although elections are contested, the de facto domination of the party that led the struggle for liberation, the African National Congress, has been so strong that the real contest for power takes place in the process of nominating candidates for legislative and executive office, and these processes are less than transparent. Critics of the current regime fear that patron–client relations, not open competition for office, are the substance of politics.

Rwanda has, since 1994, been a peaceful country, and it has achieved substantial economic growth. International tribunals, national courts, and locally constituted bodies – known as *gacaca* – have attempted to bring those responsible for the genocide to justice, with mixed results. That Rwanda has been as orderly as it has been is remarkable given the fundamental problem of building a post-genocide society: the families of victims and perpetrators often live side by side, and the fact that Tutsi were once a minority oppressed, exiled, or murdered by a government pretending to represent the majority makes it difficult for Tutsi as well as Hutu to feel that a truly democratic regime would protect them. Paul Kagame has ruled Rwanda since 1994. Because of the memory of the genocide, the rest of the world has tended to overlook his clinging to power and his government's marginalization – or worse – of potential opponents.

Rwanda itself has experienced surprisingly little violence in terms of retribution or renewed anti-Tutsi pogroms, but the same cannot be said of the wider regional context. The Rwandan government has intervened repeatedly in neighboring Zaire (later renamed Democratic Republic of the Congo or DRC), claiming to defend itself against raids by exiled Hutu militias, but its military, or militias allied to it, have engaged in violence against Hutu refugees and others in eastern Congo that some observers consider to border on genocide itself. Some see economic motivation in the sponsorship by Rwanda, as well as Uganda, of militia activity in Congo: access to its mineral wealth, channeled through Rwanda and Uganda to ports in Kenya and Tanzania.

In the spring of 1994 South Africa and Rwanda seemed to represent two possible fates of Africa: liberation from a racist regime into a democratic order; and descent into "tribal" violence. The trajectories of both countries since then reveal the ambiguity and uncertainty of Africa's situation. Both states have remained under the control of elites that came to power in 1994; both regimes have been politically stable; neither has been a model democracy. South Africa more than Rwanda has retained the formal structures of a democratic regime:

regular elections, a critical press, multiple political parties. Neither can
be written off as an economic failure, but South Africa – already a
relatively industrialized economy in the 1990s – has not become the
Africa-wide powerhouse that some expected, and it has not lifted its
population out of poverty. Rwanda has benefited from a generous
foreign aid regime and its largely agricultural economy has grown,
but it remains a country of farmers dominated by a small,
government-connected elite.

The Past of the Present

What trajectories have led South Africa and Rwanda to their respective destinies? Looked at as a snapshot, in April 1994, they appear to
represent the alternatives of liberal democracy and ethnic violence.
But if one looks to earlier periods, what happened in South Africa and
Rwanda becomes more complicated. That South Africa has come to
be governed by institutions familiar in the West – an elected parliament and a system of courts – does not mean that those institutions
function in the same way as they do in Western Europe or North
America, or that people do not form other kinds of affiliations, view
their lives through other kinds of lenses, and imagine their society
through categories distinct from those of the West. Nor is it helpful to
think of the Rwandan catastrophe as the result of the age-old division
of Africa into neatly separate cultures, each a distinctive and exclusive
community with a long history of conflict with people who are "different," unable to function within Western-style institutions that do not
fit the reality of Africa.

   History does not inevitably lead all peoples of the world to "rise" to
Western political forms or to "fall" into tribal bloodbaths. This book
explores the period when the rule of European colonial powers over
most of the African continent began to come apart, when Africans
mobilized to claim new futures, when the day-to-day realities of life in
cities and villages changed rapidly, and when new states had to come
to grips with the meaning of sovereignty and the limits of state power
faced with the social realities within their borders and their even less
controllable position in the world economy and global power relations. It is a book about possibilities that people made for themselves
as members of rural communities, as migrants to cities, and as the
builders of social organizations, political movements, and new forms

FIGURE 1 South Africa's first non-racial election, April 1994. A poster of Nelson Mandela, presidential candidate of the African National Congress, behind a military vehicle – of the kind typically used to control "township violence" – in the black township of Rammulotsi, South Africa. Philip Littleton/AFP/Getty Image

FIGURE 2 Genocide and looting, Rwanda, April 11, 1994. A looter removes a bed frame from a house whose murdered inhabitants lie on the ground behind him, Kigali, Rwanda. Pascal Guyot/AFP/Getty Images

of cultural expression. It is also about the ways in which many of those openings closed down.

This book cuts across the conventional dividing point between colonial and post-colonial African history, a division that conceals as much as it reveals. Focusing on such a dividing point either makes the break seem too neat – as if colonialism was turned off like a light switch – or suggests too much continuity, positing continued Western dominance of the world economy and the continued presence in African states of "Western" institutions as a mere change of personnel within a structure of power that remains colonial. We do not have to make a dichotomous choice between continuity and change. Indeed, even while colonial regimes remained in power, their institutions did not operate as their designers intended, but were contested, appropriated, and transformed by colonial subjects. Acquiring formal sovereignty was an important element in the historical dynamics of the last half-century, but not the only one. Family life and religious expression also changed substantially in Africa, but not necessarily in rhythm with changes in political organization.

Most important, one needs to understand how the cracks that appeared in the edifice of colonial power after World War II gave a wide range of people – wage laborers, peasants, students, traders, and educated professionals – a chance to articulate their aspirations, be they the hope of having clean, piped water in a rural village or of taking an honorable place in global political institutions. A distinguished Ghanaian historian, Adu Boahen (1996: 434) says of intellectual life in the 1950s, "It was really great to be alive in those days ..." – a phrase that conveys not only the excitement of being part of a generation that could shape its own future but also hints that "those days" were better than the ones that followed.

The colonial state that came apart in the 1950s represented colonialism at its most intrusively ambitious, and the new rulers who came to govern independent states had to take over the shortcomings of colonial development as well: even if the mineral and agricultural production of Africa had increased in the post-war years, the African farmer and worker had not become the predictable and orderly producer European officials dreamed of. African governments inherited both the narrow, export-oriented infrastructure that development-oriented colonialism had not transcended and the limited markets for producers of raw materials that the post-war boom in the global economy had only temporarily improved. But now they had to pay for the administrative structure that 1950s colonial development had put in place and, more important, to meet the heightened expectations of people who hoped that the state might really be theirs.

The historical sequence outlined in the first chapters of this book brought into being states that had the trappings recognized around the world as "sovereignty." But the particular characteristics of those states were consequences of the sequence, not merely the sovereignty. Colonial states had been gatekeeper states. They had weak instruments for entering into the social and cultural realm over which they presided, but they stood astride the intersection of the colonial territory and the outside world. Their main source of revenue was duties on goods that entered and left its ports; they could decide who could leave for education and what kinds of educational institutions could come in; they established rules and licenses that defined who could engage in internal and external commerce. Africans tried to build networks that not only made use of but also got around the colonial state's control over access to the outside world. They built economic and social networks inside the territory that were beyond the state's reach. In the 1940s and 1950s access to officially recognized economic institutions and networks seemed to be opening wider to Africans. Social, political, and cultural associational life within African territories became richer and links with outside organizations more diverse. The gate was becoming wider, but only so far.

The development effort of late colonial regimes did not provide the basis for strong national economies after independence. African economies remained externally oriented, and the state's economic power remained concentrated at the gate between inside and outside. Meanwhile, African leaders' own experience of mobilization *against* the state gave them an acute sense of how vulnerable the power they had inherited was. The mixed success of colonial and post-colonial development efforts did not give leaders the confidence that economic development would lead to a generalized prosperity for which they could get credit and flourishing domestic activity that would provide government revenue. To differing degrees governments in the years immediately following independence tried to encourage economic development, but they also realized that their own interests would benefit from something like the strategy of gatekeeping that had served the colonial state before World War II: limited channels for advancement that officials controlled were less risky than broad ones that could become a platform for opposition.

The post-colonial state, lacking the external coercive capacity of its predecessor, was a vulnerable state. The stakes of controlling the gate were so high that various groups might try to grab it: officers or non-commissioned officers in the army, regional power brokers. A regime not so dependent on gatekeeping benefits from the fact that its opponents can afford to lose; they have other avenues for wealth and other loci for power. Gatekeeper states are in danger for the same reason that rulers provisionally in control of the gate have strong incentives to stay there. Hence ruling elites tended to use patronage, coercion, scapegoating of opponents, and other resources to reinforce their position, narrowing the channels of access even further.

As long as export prices for African products remained high, states could have things both ways – promoting economic growth while protecting the interests of the ruling elite – but the world recession in the mid-1970s inaugurated a period of some decades in which ruling elites (except in oil-exporting regions) had great difficulty in putting together the resources for either patronage or the services that citizens demanded. By looking at the post-war era as a whole one can begin to explain the succession of crises that colonial and post-colonial states faced, without getting into a sterile debate over whether a colonial "legacy" or the incompetence of African governments is to blame. Africa's present did not emerge from an abrupt proclamation of independence, but from a long, convoluted, and still ongoing process. Understanding the trajectories of different parts of Africa – and the variations within the continent are considerable – also poses challenges.

Some observers were ready in the 1990s to consign Africa to its fate as the world's poorest, least educated, most disease-ridden continent. But in the 2000s journalists and economists adopted the slogan "Africa rising," pointing to high rates of economic growth in some countries. In the late 2010s both narratives are looking short-sighted, simple extrapolations of what might be temporary trends. The ups and downs of economic growth and social progress and above all their uneven distribution within and among African countries form a complex and elusive pattern.

Trajectories

When we look back from a longer time perspective, the two stories of April 1994 illustrate the openings and possibilities and the closures and dangers of politics in Africa during the last half-century. Let us start to look backward at the history behind the more painful of the two, Rwanda. The murderous violence that erupted on April 6 was not a spontaneous outburst of ancient hatreds. It was prepared by a modern institution, a government with its bureaucratic and military apparatus, using modern means of communications and modern forms of propaganda. The hatred in Rwanda was real enough, but it was hatred with a history, not a natural attribute of cultural difference. Indeed, cultural difference in Rwanda was relatively small: Hutu and Tutsi speak the same language; most are Christian. Rwandans and Westerners often think that there are ideal physical features of each group – Tutsi tall and slender, Hutu short and broad. In fact, appearance poorly distinguishes them.

Indeed, one of the horrifying features of the genocide was that militias, unable to tell a Tutsi when they saw one, demanded that people produce identification cards that listed their ethnic group, and then killed people who were labeled Tutsi or who refused to produce a card. In the years before the mass killings, a shadowy organization of elite Hutu, connected to the government leaders, had systematically organized a propaganda campaign – especially over the radio – against Tutsi. Apparently, many Hutu still had to be convinced that there was a Tutsi conspiracy against them, and social pressure had to be carefully organized, village by village, to bring people into line. Thousands of Hutu did not accede to this pressure, and when the genocide began Hutu judged to be overly sympathetic to Tutsi were themselves frequently killed; many Hutu acted with courage to save Tutsi neighbors.

One has to push back further. There was a "Tutsi" threat – to the government, at least. It had its origins in earlier violence. In 1959, and again in the early 1970s, there were pogroms against Tutsi that caused thousands of them to flee to Uganda. The government strove thereafter to consolidate its position at what its leaders considered both a social revolution – against the supposedly feudal order dominated by the people who controlled land and cattle – and a Hutu revolution against Tutsi. Some of the Tutsi refugees became allies of the Ugandan rebel leader Yoweri Museveni, as he worked in the 1980s to take over a state submerged in the chaos left by the dictatorship of Idi Amin Dada and his brutal successors. President Museveni was grateful for their assistance, but eager that they go home. The Rwandan Patriotic Army (RPA), trained in Uganda, attacked Rwanda in 1990, and attacked again more vigorously in 1993. Whether their objective was to take over Rwanda or to be reintegrated into "their" country was in dispute. In 1994 mediators from inside and outside Africa tried to devise a power-sharing arrangement that would provide security to both Hutu and Tutsi. President Habyarimana took his fatal flight in April to attend a conference aimed at resolving the conflict. He may or may not have been killed by "Hutu Power" extremists for fear that he would compromise, and in order to provoke an already-planned slaughter. Some think his plane was shot down by the RPA, but it is not clear that they had the weaponry, the position, or the incentive to do so. Within hours of the crash, in any case, the hunt for Tutsi engulfed the capital, and it soon spread. Whenever local people and local officials weren't enthusiastic enough in their bloody endeavor, the Rwandan army stepped in to run the killing machine.

We need to push back further. The radio campaign did not build up hatred from nothing. Rwanda had originally been colonized by Germany at the end of the nineteenth century, then turned over to Belgium after Germany lost World War I. Belgian officials conceived of Tutsi as natural aristocrats, as less "African" than the Hutu. Only Tutsi were accepted as chiefs under colonial supervision; missionaries were more likely to welcome them into schools and convert them to Catholicism. Belgian officials decided that they needed to know who *was* Tutsi and Hutu, and so they classified people into one or the other and made them carry identification cards. It took work to turn difference and inequality into group boundaries, into ethnicity.

We can push back still further. German and Belgian understanding of Rwandan history was inaccurate, but it was not made up out of whole cloth. Rwanda, like other kingdoms in the Great Lakes of East Africa, was highly differentiated. There was much movement of peoples in Rwanda's fertile hills and a blending of people who lived by hunting and gathering, by keeping cattle, and by agriculture. Some – largely European – versions of Rwandan history have Tutsi pastoralists migrating as a people from the north and conquering agricultural peoples, but there is little evidence to support such a story. More likely, a variety of migratory streams intersected and overlapped, and, as particular kinship groups claimed power, they developed their myths of origin and historical narratives to justify their power.

Rather than a history of conflict following from the fact of distinction, social distinctions were a product of a history. Several kingdoms developed in the area. Most royal families were considered Tutsi, although most Tutsi were not rulers. Royal men married both

Tutsi and Hutu women, so that genetically the categories meant less and less, if they had ever meant much at all. Wealthy people owned cattle, and the wealthiest claimed to be Tutsi, but Hutu could become cattle owners, and some of them began to think of themselves, and to be accepted, as Tutsi. The nearest English word to describe what Tutsi meant in pre-European Rwanda is "aristocracy," but it was an aristocracy linked to ordinary people via marriage, cattle exchange, and a common way of life. This does not mean that it was an egalitarian society; the difference between owning many cattle and owning few was important. Nor was it a peaceful society. Violent conflict, however, rarely pitted Tutsi against Hutu, but took place between rival kingdoms, each of which consisted of both Tutsi and Hutu.

If we look back far enough, then, we see that "difference" is part of the story that led to April 1994, but we do not find a long history of "the Tutsi" in conflict with "the Hutu." Interaction and differentiation are both important. When did polarization become acute? The answer appears to be in the 1950s, as the political structures of the colonial era unraveled. Belgian favoritism toward Tutsi, and particularly Tutsi chiefs, became increasingly problematic when government officials began to be challenged on their own terms by Rwandans who had a Western education, who were Christian, and who were asking why they should be excluded from a voice in their own affairs. Because schools had discriminated in favor of Tutsi, the anti-colonial movement began among people so classified. Belgium, and also the Catholic Church, began to favor Hutu, who were now alleged to represent an "authentic Africa" against the pretentious Tutsi. In 1957 a "Hutu Manifesto" accused Tutsi of monopolizing power, land, and education. One of the principal leaders of Hutu politics, Grégoire Kayabanda, had been editor of a Catholic journal and a critic of social injustice. Riots in 1959 were in part an uprising of peasants with genuine grievances – who were most likely to be Hutu – and in part ethnic pogroms. The ethnically based political party PARMEHUTU decisively won the elections that brought Rwanda to the threshold of independence.

Belgium did little to prepare a peaceful transfer of political institutions into the hands of Africans. But elsewhere in Africa French and British colonies were moving rapidly toward self-government and independence, and Belgium could not escape the trends. The independence of Rwanda in 1962 was for most Rwandans an eagerly sought moment of liberation from colonial rule. But many Tutsi feared that they would now become a minority group, in danger from a resentful Hutu majority, whose representatives had won the first elections. Many Hutu, on the other hand, feared that Tutsi were conspiring to keep by devious methods that which they could not retain through free elections. The pogroms and the elections chased Tutsi leaders from the political scene and created the first wave of Tutsi exiles. Although most Catholic priests were Tutsi, the Church leadership allied itself with the new government and kept quiet about its Hutu chauvinism.

The ensuing Rwandan regime, like many others in Africa, was clientelistic, focused on delivering state-controlled assets to supporters. Like other regimes of that era it was ineffective and insecure, and it was thrown out in 1973 in a military coup led by Juvenal Habyarimana, who would remain in power until his murder twenty-one years later. This regime proved to be as corrupt and ineffectual as its predecessor, but it received considerable support from France and other suppliers of foreign aid. When export-crop prices fell and the International Monetary Fund (IMF) made the government tighten its belt in the 1980s, government supporters felt that they were not getting the spoils they deserved. Some groups tried to organize opposition, but Hutu extremists linked to Habyarimana scapegoated Tutsi and worked harder to exclude them from Rwandan society. Then came the invasion of a Tutsi refugee army in 1990, itself the consequence of past waves of killings and expulsions of Tutsi. The government army (aided by France) grew in response, and Hutu extremists instigated killings, organized local militias, and generated anti-Tutsi propaganda. International organizations tried in 1993 to engineer a peace settlement. Whereas some Hutu leaders, perhaps including Habyarimana himself, entered negotiations hoping that power sharing would ease a desperate situation, others were thinking of another, final, solution.

In the neighboring former Belgian colony of Burundi, with a similar social structure, complex power struggles among elites had emerged in the run-up to independence, and by 1972 the conflicts had become ethnicized and increasingly violent. The ruling clique that consolidated itself was of Tutsi origin, and massacres of Hutu led to waves of refugees fleeing to Rwanda or Tanzania. Internationally brokered peace efforts sought some kind of inter-ethnic power sharing, but the assassination of the Hutu Prime Minister Melchior Ndadye in

1993 reversed that initiative and was seen by Rwandan Hutu leaders as a sign of the threat to their very existence. In both Rwanda and Burundi the decolonization process had brought to power governments that were insecure and anxious: in Rwanda led by a section of Hutu, in Burundi by a section of Tutsi. In both cases, oppressive government action and widespread anxiety were cross-cut by often close relationships across the Tutsi–Hutu divide and by uncertainty over who, exactly, was a Tutsi and who a Hutu. In the months before April 1994, the sowers of hatred in Rwanda still had work to do.

I have begun by looking back, step by step, to see the layers of historical complexity leading up to the events of 1994. We began with what might look simple (and did to most foreign journalists): a tribal bloodbath, old hatreds coming to the surface. We have found something more complicated: a history of interaction as much as of distinction, and a murderous trajectory that was less a burst of ethnic enmity than a genocide organized by a ruling clique anxious about its ability to stay in power and willing to define itself and its supporters against an ethnic "other."

Let us look back into South African history – briefly now, in more detail in Chapter 6. One can trace the peaceful revolution of 1994 back to the founding of the African National Congress (ANC) in 1912 and find a durable thread: the belief that multiracial democracy was the ideal polity for South Africa. However, the negotiated end of white power emerged not just from principled, democratic opposition, but also from a wave of violence that neither the ANC nor other African political groups could control, from the mid-1980s to the very eve of the 1994 election. Not all the political movements challenging white domination fit the liberal-democratic mold. The white regime also turns out to have been more complicated than simply die-hard racists from a bygone era. The apartheid government was pragmatic, and in the era when late colonial and independent governments elsewhere in Africa were striving – with mixed results – to achieve "development," it presided over the most thorough industrialization of any African economy, producing great wealth and a European standard of living for its white population.

In 1940 segregation, denial of political voice to black people, and economic disenfranchisement did not distinguish South Africa from colonial Africa. But by the 1960s South Africa had become a pariah in much of the world. It took a great deal of political and ideological labor to make colonial domination appear abnormal and unacceptable to people who did not live under its yoke, and it was this process that began the isolation of South Africa's white regime. This reconfiguration of what is and is not acceptable in international norms might make us pause to ponder what in today's world that appears normal – if not necessarily virtuous – may one day become as loathsome as apartheid became in the 1960s and 1970s, perhaps including the rampant inequality that characterizes societies such as contemporary South Africa or the United States.

Nothing in South Africa's past determined that it would one day be governed by a non-racialist, democratically elected political party. When the ANC was founded in 1912, its program of peaceful protest, petition, and the evocation of democratic principles was one of several ways in which Africans expressed themselves. Alongside this liberal constitutionalist conception of freedom was a Christian one, profoundly influenced by a century of missionary activity, and part of that tendency, influenced by African-American missionaries, linked Christianity to racial unity and redemption. Others operated within the frameworks of Xhosa, Zulu, and other ethnically based African political units seeking, for example, to mobilize behind a chief who would represent the solidarity of what people perceived to be their community. By the 1920s the back-to-Africa politics of Jamaican-born, US-based Marcus Garvey linked South Africa to a Black Atlantic world via black sailors who stopped in South African ports and influenced political movements in the interior. Other versions of Pan-Africanism came out of educational and cultural linkages to African Americans. A single rural district in the 1920s might witness all these varieties of political mobilization.

Even as the ANC successfully linked its struggle to that of labor unions and militant city-dwellers in the years after World War II migrant workers with less permanent roots in the cities, often dependent on rural brethren and rural chiefs for access to land when they returned, were sometimes attracted to militant ideologies of "tribal identity." By the 1980s the clashes were both between different networks of people and rival organizations and different ways of thinking about solidarity. In Johannesburg "comrades" – youth associated with the ANC – sometimes fought, with bloody consequences, "impis": young men associated with the Zulu cultural/political organization Inkatha. In South Africa, as in Rwanda, "tribal" rivalries were not part of the landscape; they were a product of history, of the realities of ethnic connections, the manipulations of the South African regime, and the quest of ordinary people to forge a world consistent with their values. Much as one might think of racism as forcing all Africans into a single category and producing a united struggle that reached its successful climax in April 1994, the struggle generated rivalries as much as affinities, internecine killings as well as armed struggle against the apartheid regime.

Looking backwards from 1994, the peaceful election appears even more remarkable than it did at first glance. Elections do matter: they channel political action in certain ways, and if participation in the politics of the voting booth in some sense narrows the possibilities of how people act together, it can also discourage some of the more deadly forms of rivalry, which is what the enthusiasm for the election of April 1994 accomplished. Africans flocked to the polls to decide on their future. But the history of how resources – land, gold mines, factories, urban real estate – got into the hands of particular people, and the consequences of such unequal access, is a deep one, and that history did not suddenly turn a new page on April 27.

The Many Africas: Locating a Space

At any one moment, Africa appears as a mixture of diverse languages and diverse cultures; indeed, linguistically alone, it is the most varied continent on earth. It is only by looking over time that "Africa" begins to appear. But what is it that emerges? As a land mass, Africa goes from the Cape of Good Hope to the Nile Delta, embracing Morocco as much as Mozambique. But many people in that continental space, as well as most Americans and Europeans, do not think of it as united, and make a clear distinction between "North Africa" and "sub-Saharan Africa" or "Black Africa." The dividing line is often seen in racial terms: Africa is the place where blacks are from. The Ghanaian philosopher Kwame Anthony Appiah (1992) has posed the question of how one conceives of "Africa" if one doesn't accept the validity of classifying the world's population into racial groups – something biological scientists see as without basis. Africans are as different from each other as they are from anybody else, and it is only by elevating skin color to supreme importance that one can stipulate that Africans are a unique race.

But can all of the individuals who live south of the Sahara Desert be considered a people, if not a race? Or does the fact that about a third of these people are Muslim mean that, after all, they should be classified together with their fellow Muslims of North Africa, whether or not the latter perceive themselves to be Africans? Does the alleged strength of kinship ties among Africans, the widespread respect that people from the Zulu to the Wolof give to elders and to ancestors, and the centrality of face-to-face social relations in village settings define a cultural collectivity that is continent-wide and has influenced peoples of African descent in Brazil, Cuba, and the United States? Or is what all Africans share with each other also shared with most "peasant" communities? Does what people call "culture" in Africa or elsewhere represent durable and shared traits or continually changing patterns of adaptation to new circumstances?

Following Appiah, one can argue that the notion of Africa – specifically sub-Saharan Africa – does in fact have a meaning, and that meaning is historical. From the sixteenth century, European slave-traders began to treat various African ports as places to buy slave labor. The physical features of the slaves served as a marker of who, on one side of the Atlantic, could be bought and who, on the other side, could be kept in slavery.

But if Africa was first defined by the most horrific aspect of its history, the meaning of Africa began to change in the African diaspora itself. Enslaved people and their descendants began to think of themselves as "African," not just other people's property; they were people who came from somewhere. In the United States, some Christians of slave descent began to call themselves "Ethiopians," not because their ancestors originated from that part of Africa, but because it evoked biblical histories of King Solomon and the Queen of Sheba. "Ethiopia" or "Africa" marked their place in a universal history. Later, some African-American intellectuals – and some African scholars as well – began to claim that the ancient Egyptians were black Africans, and that, via Egypt, Africa had contributed centrally to Greece, Rome, and world civilization. Whether the evidence supports such a contention, and the very question of what "heritage" or "descent" actually means, are not what is at stake here. The point is that "Africa" emerged as a diaspora that asserted its place in the world. This book approaches Africa as defined by its history: its focus is on the African continent south of the Sahara Desert, but in the context of the connections, continental and overseas, that shaped that region's history.

Studying networks that crossed the Atlantic Ocean, the Indian Ocean, and the Sahara Desert, or that criss-crossed the African continent itself, gives a different picture of Africa from the stereotypes of

African "tribes." Muslim scholars in Sahelian West Africa crossed the desert to North Africa or went to Egypt and Arabia as students and pilgrims; similar Islamic networks extended down the East African coast and inland to Lake Victoria and Lake Tanganyika. The Sahara itself produced communities that thrived on the exchange of commodities between distinct economic zones north and south of the desert, and these communities were often conscious of their distinctiveness in racial as well as cultural terms. Within Africa, some kingdoms or empires incorporated culturally diverse populations, sometimes assimilating them, sometimes allowing considerable cultural autonomy while demanding obedience and collecting tribute. In some regions, kinship groups recognized affinity with relatives living hundreds of miles away.

That there was cultural diversity is true; that cultural specificity sometimes crystallized into a sense of being a distinct "people" is to an extent also true. But distinctiveness did not mean isolation, and it did not extinguish interconnection, relatedness, and mutual influence. The cultural map of Africa is marked by gradations of difference and lines of connection, not by a series of bounded spaces, each with "its" culture, "its" language, "its" sense of uniqueness. To be sure, a political entrepreneur trying to organize "his" people to fight for their interests had some shared group feeling to draw on, but so too did a political or religious organizer trying to bring together people across short or long distances. Which tendency would prevail was a matter of historical circumstances, not something determined by a supposed African nature of racial unity or cultural distinctiveness.

In the mid-twentieth century the political meaning of Africa could be defined in different ways. To a Pan-Africanist the diaspora was the relevant unit. For Frantz Fanon politics were defined by imperialism, and he deprecated the idea of an African civilization in favor of a conception of the unity of people oppressed by colonization. When President Gamal Abdel Nasser of Egypt challenged British, French, American, and Israeli power in the Middle East, he became a symbol for many Africans of a truly national leader. In the 1950s the shared struggle against colonial powers, for the building up of national economies, and for national dignity, gave rise to a militant conception of the "Third World" – neither capitalist nor communist, uniting Asia, Latin America, and Africa against "the North" or "imperialist" powers. Still others sought a specifically African unity, limited to the continent. Other political leaders divided themselves into ideological blocs and formed alliances with power blocs led by the United States or the Soviet Union.

Long-distance connections were not just a matter for political activists. Africans – seeking education, developing careers in international organizations, or migrating to European economies which now sought their labor – became a presence in Europe, the Soviet Union, the United States, Canada, and China. They sometimes interacted with indigenous inhabitants, sometimes formed relatively self-contained communities of origin, and sometimes interacted more intensely with other migrants of African descent.

It would be a mistake, nonetheless, to substitute for the misleading notion of an Africa of isolated tribes a picture of an Africa immersed in an infinite web of movement and exchange. Internally, Africa's population was spread unevenly over a large space, meaning that movement was possible but transport expensive. It paid to exchange high-value commodities not found in certain regions, but less so to build dense networks of varied forms of exchange and connection. African leaders could find places for their people to prosper, but there were other places with low population density to which people could flee and survive, making it difficult for power to be consolidated and exploitation to be intensified, in contrast to Europe in the seventeenth through nineteenth centuries. Overseas exchange tended to be focused on a narrow range of commodities, most horrifically in the case of the slave trade. Specific centers of production – of gold or palm products, for instance – or specific trade routes – the ivory traders who connected the interior of East Africa with the coast – functioned very well.

What they did was to forge specific, focused linkages from inside Africa to economies outside Africa, rather than developing diverse and dense regional economies. Colonial regimes, after the European conquest, built their railways and roads to bring out copper or cocoa and send in European manufactured goods, and they directed the movement of goods, people, and ideas so as to privilege connections to the metropole. Colonial regimes based much of their power on their ability to control key nodal points, such as deep-water ports, in a relatively narrow system of transportation and communication. They created obstacles to movement too: racial restrictions on mobility, refusal to accept Africans into social or educational institutions. Africans, meanwhile, tried to forge their own kinds of linkages – from trade routes within the continent to political relationships with other colonized peoples – with at least some success; but when the colonial empires fell apart, African leaders also faced the temptation to strengthen their control of narrow channels rather than widen and deepen forms of connections across space. This is a theme to which I will return.

The Many Africas: Marking a Time

African historians often divide the continent's history into "pre-colonial," "colonial," and "post-colonial" eras. The first and the last, in such accounts, are marked by the autonomy of African societies. The first was a period of kingdoms, empires, chiefdoms, village councils, kinship systems, and the last a period of nation-states, each with its own flag, passport, stamps, currency, its seat in the United Nations, and its claims to regulate and to tax production and commerce within its borders. The Nigerian historian J. F. Ade Ajayi (1968) called the middle period the "colonial episode"; others refer to the "colonial parenthesis." Ajayi's argument came directly from a nationalist conception of political life: he wanted to emphasize the direct connection of "modern" African states to an "authentic" African past, allowing the new rulers of Nigeria, Kenya, or Dahomey to assume the legitimacy of the kings and elders of the past. More recently, disillusionment with independent African governments has led some scholars to make the opposite point: that "the state" is a Western imposition, a direct determination of the post-colonial by the colonial, and a complete effacement of the pre-colonial.

In such arguments, history is not a dead past, but a basis for making claims that are very much of the present. All sides, in trying to use a particular version of the past, may miss much of the past's dynamics. It may be that the ballot box is a "European" institution, but that does not mean that the way it is used in Ghana has the same meaning and consequences as the way it is used in Switzerland. Even if one can demonstrate that "kinship" is as important to present-day Tanzanians as it was to people who lived within such a space in the early nineteenth century, that does not mean that kinship groups mobilize similar resources or that their members seek similar ends. To leapfrog backwards across time – to find in the 1780s or the 1930s the cause for something happening in the 2000s – is to risk missing the way change lurches in different directions.

This book bridges one of the classic divisions of African history: between the "colonial" and the "post-colonial." It does so in part so that we can ask just what difference the end of empire meant, as well as what kinds of processes continued even as governments changed hands. Some argue that the end of colonialism meant only that the occupants of government buildings changed, that colonialism gave way to neo-colonialism. It is indeed essential to ask just how much autonomy the governments of new states – many of them small, all of them poor – actually had, and whether states from the North (the United States as well as the former colonial powers) and institutions such as international banks and multinational corporations continued to exercise economic and political power even when formal sovereignty was passed on. But one should not substitute a hasty answer for a good question. One needs to examine as well the extent to which African political leaders, ordinary villagers, and city-dwellers took some of the assertions of colonizing powers and turned them into claims and mobilizing ideologies of their own.

In the 1940s and 1950s colonial governments claimed that their scientific knowledge, experience in running modern states, and financial resources would enable them to "develop" backward countries. Such claims were quickly turned into counterclaims: by African trade unions asserting that if the African worker is to produce according to a European model, he should be paid on a European pay scale and benefit from adequate housing, water supplies, and transportation; and by political movements insisting that if African economies were to be developed in the interest of Africans, it was only Africans who could determine what those interests were. One can thus follow the development idea from colonial project to national project and ask if the national project reproduced certain aspects of the colonial one – such as the belief that "experts" should make decisions for others – and whether it contributed to the building of new kinds of economic possibilities. One should ask as well what development as an *international* project contributed, or took away, from the possibilities for change in Africa.

Static Visions of Dynamic Societies: Colonial Africa in the 1930s

One striking feature of colonial societies on the eve of World War II was the extent to which colonial ideologues and officials imposed a static conception on societies in the midst of change. This static vision was consistent with the way colonial regimes operated. What, after all,

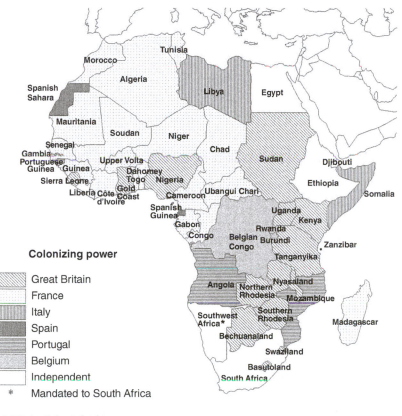

MAP 2 Colonial Africa

is a colony? Rule by conquering outsiders was not unique in either Africa or Europe: African kingdoms often expanded at their neighbors' expense. In Europe the territorial struggles and brutalities of two World Wars, the dictatorial and racist regimes of Hitler and Mussolini, and the survival of dictatorships in Spain and Portugal into the 1970s suggest that each people ruling itself was not something that came with being European. Colonial empires differed from other forms of domination by the extreme nature of their effort to reproduce social and cultural difference. At some level, colonization implied incorporation: the conquered African was the subject of Britain and France, and should not aspire to be anything else. But colonial rule emphasized that the conquered and incorporated subject remained distinct; he or she might try to learn and master the ways of the conqueror, but would never quite get there.

How enthusiastic European publics were for colonies was also not
so clear, despite colonial lobbies that tried to make empire fashion-
able. The weaker French firms lobbied for treating its colonies as a
protected zone for their benefit, whereas some of the strong ones
favored more open markets and sometimes thought of colonization
as risky adventurism. In England, mission lobbies favored a form of
empire that gave space to Christian conversion and to encouraging
Africans to become self-reliant small-scale producers. In France, proponents of the "civilizing mission" helped to reconcile people who
believed in a democratic, secular state to the practice of empire,
although they were often embarrassed by the sordid actions of fellow
imperialists.

In both countries, proponents of conversion and civilization had to
argue with their own countrymen, who looked at Africans as units of
labor to exploit by whatever means possible. Although there were
principled critics of empire from liberal and leftist camps, some people
who saw themselves as progressive favored empire as a means to save
indigenous peoples from their tyrannical rulers and backwardness, or
even to bring revolution and socialism to Africa.

Empire in early twentieth-century France and Britain was politically viable because some influential people wanted colonies very much
and others were not strongly convinced one way or the other. The
powers with the largest colonial empires insisted that each colony
balance its books; they committed little in the way of metropolitan
funds before the 1940s outside of a limited railway and road network.
Private investment was concentrated in mines, commerce, and, in
some cases, plantation agriculture. In the 1920s both powers rejected
"development" plans that would have entailed the use of money from
the metropolitan taxpayer, even though the plans promised more
effective exploitation of colonial resources in the long run. Critics
argued that money was best invested at home, but also that too much
economic change in the colonies risked upsetting the state's unsure
hold over African populations.

By the 1920s the contention that colonial rulers could remake
African societies – by trying to turn peasants or slaves into wage
laborers, for example – no longer held sway. Colonial officials were
convincing themselves that their policy should not be to transform
Africans in a European image, but to conserve African societies in a
colonizers' image of sanitized tradition, slowly and selectively being
led toward evolution, while the empire profited from peasants' crop

FIGURE 3 A French administrator with subordinate personnel and local
notables, around 1920. Colonial administration was heavily reliant on
indigenous personnel and relations – unequal as they were – with local elites.
Place unspecified. Roger Viollet/Getty Images

production or the output of mines and settler farms in the relatively
few areas where they were economically viable.

What Africans were doing was far more complex than "timeless"
African tradition. In the 1920s West African cocoa and peanut farmers
were migrating in order to open up new land, and Hausa and Dyula
traders were covering long distances; central African mineworkers
were moving back and forth between villages and mining centers; near
cities like Nairobi, farmers were linking up to urban food markets as
well as to markets in export crops. Yet European conceptions of Africa
crystallized around the idea of "tribes," bounded and static. The
tenacity of this conviction reflected both the difficulty that colonial
regimes faced in governing, let alone transforming, African societies
and fear of the opposite: that Africans would claim that their meeting of
obligations to the state and their educational and economic achievements
entitled them to a voice in their own affairs. That many Africans served
France and Britain during World War I gave them a special claim: having
paid the "blood tax" should entitle them to the rights of the citizen.

The British concept of "indirect rule" and the French idea of "association," both emphasized in the 1920s, were attempts to put a positive light on the fragility of colonial control. The colonial administrations, in claiming that they were exercising power by working through African "traditional" authorities, were trying to confine politics to tribal cages. Educated Africans and African wage workers became "detribalized natives," identifiable only by what they were not. During this period the expansion of ethnological research, and the increased interest colonial officials took in it, were part of this process of imagining an Africa of tribes and traditions. During the Great Depression following 1929 the idea of tribal Africa carried all the more appeal to colonial administrators, for the social consequences of economic decline could be sloughed off to African communities in the countryside. Men who lost jobs could, supposedly, go back to their villages and subsistence cultivation, while chiefs could extract a little more taxation from "their" people to make up for the government's loss of revenue stemming from lower prices for exports. But with the beginnings of recovery in 1935, the edifice began to crack. That is where the next chapter will take up the story.

This was not the only way of imagining Africa in the 1930s. In Paris, Léopold Sédar Senghor – born and raised in Senegal, educated in France in philosophy and literature, one of the best poets in the French language – met people of African descent from the Caribbean and acquired a new sense of what "Africa" meant within the French empire. Along with the West Indian writer Aimé Césaire, Senghor helped to found the *négritude* movement, which sought to capture and revalue a common cultural heritage across Africa and its diaspora, one which deserved a place in a broad conception of humanity. Senghor and Césaire used the French language for their own purposes, and they fully participated in French institutions – when they saw their democratic potential. They insisted that all French Africans, heretofore treated as French subjects with no civil or political rights, should have all the rights of the French citizen. They rejected the dualist conception of colonial ideology that starkly opposed "civilized" and "primitive" people. Instead of countering the dualism with a rejection of everything "European," they set aside such thinking in favor of a conception of cultural and political engagement that recognized the diverse heritages of humanity. There was not one civilization, but many, each contributing to mankind's heritage. Senghor's *négritude*, as critics within Africa pointed out, simplified, romanticized, and homogenized

African cultural practices, and it only indirectly addressed issues of power and exploitation within colonized spaces. But it was one way of pointing toward a future that built on a painful past.

A full bibliography for this book may be found on the website of Cambridge University Press at www.cambridge.org/CooperAfrica2ed.

Bibliography

General

Ajayi, J. F. Ade. "The Continuity of African Institutions under Colonialism." In T. O. Ranger, ed., *Emerging Themes in African History*. Nairobi: East African Literature Bureau, 1968, 189–200.

Appiah, Kwame Anthony. *In My Father's House: Africa in the Philosophy of Culture*. New York: Oxford University Press, 1992.

Boahen, Adu. *African Perspectives on Colonialism*. Baltimore: Johns Hopkins University Press, 1987.

Boahen, Adu. *Mfantsipim and the Making of Ghana: A Centenary History, 1876–1976*. Accra: Sankofa Educational Publishers, 1996.

Freund, Bill. *The Making of Contemporary Africa: The Development of African Society since 1800*. 3rd edn. Boulder: Lynne Rienner, 2016.

Mazrui, Ali, ed. *General History of Africa: Africa since 1935*. Berkeley: University of California Press for UNESCO, 1993.

Middleton, John, and Joseph Miller, eds. *New Encyclopedia of Africa*. Detroit: Scribners, 2008. 5 vols.

Nugent, Paul. *Africa since Independence*. Basingstoke: Palgrave Macmillan, 2004.

Parker, John, and Richard Reid, eds. *The Oxford Handbook of Modern African History*. Oxford: Oxford University Press, 2013.

Rwanda

Des Forges, Alison. *"Leave None to Tell the Story": Genocide in Rwanda*. New York: Human Rights Watch, 1999.

Longman, Timothy. *Christianity and Genocide in Rwanda*. Cambridge: Cambridge University Press, 2010.

Newbury, Catherine. *The Cohesion of Oppression: Clientship and Ethnicity in Rwanda, 1860–1960*. New York: Columbia University Press, 1988.

Pottier, Johan. *Re-Imagining Rwanda: Conflict, Survival and Disinformation in the Late Twentieth Century*. Cambridge: Cambridge University Press, 2002.

Prunier, Gérard. *The Rwanda Crisis*. New York: Columbia University Press, 1996.

Straus, Scott. *The Order of Genocide: Race, Power, and War in Rwanda*. Ithaca: Cornell University Press, 2008.

Straus, Scott, and Lars Waldorf, eds. *Remaking Rwanda: State Building and Human Rights after Mass Violence*. Madison: University of Wisconsin Press, 2011.

South Africa

Evans, Ivan. *Bureaucracy and Race: Native Administration in South Africa*. Berkeley: University of California Press, 1997.

Habib, Adam. *South Africa's Suspended Revolution: Hopes and Prospects*. Athens: Ohio University Press, 2013.

Lodge, Tom. *Black Politics in South Africa since 1945*. Harlow: Longman, 1983.

Mandela, Nelson. *Long Walk to Freedom: The Autobiography of Nelson Mandela*. Boston: Little, Brown, 1994.

Posel, Deborah. *The Making of Apartheid, 1948–1961: Conflict and Compromise*. Oxford: Clarendon Press, 1991.

Seekings, Jeremy, and Nicoli Nattrass. *Class, Race, and Inequality in South Africa*. New Haven: Yale University Press, 2005.

Seidman, Gay. *Manufacturing Militance: Workers' Movements in Brazil and South Africa, 1970–1985*. Berkeley: University of California Press, 1994.

CHAPTER 2

Workers, Peasants, and the Challenge to Colonial Rule

In the late 1930s and 1940s colonial rule choked on the narrowness of the pathways it had created. Trying to confine Africans to tribal cages, seeking to extract from them what export products and labor it could without treating them as "workers," "farmers," "townsmen," or "citizens," colonial regimes discovered that Africans would not stay in the limited roles assigned to them. Instead, the constrictions created exactly the sort of danger administrators feared. Urban unrest within a very rural continent challenged colonial governments; a small number of wage workers threatened colonial economies; a tiny educated elite undercut the ideological pretenses of colonialism; supposed "pagans" worshiping local gods and ancestors produced Christian and Muslim religious movements of wide scope and uncertain political significance; and commercial farmers in a continent of "subsistence" producers made demands for a political voice for themselves and opportunities for their children that colonial systems could not meet.

These problems came together in the years after World War II, a war which had exposed the hypocrisy of colonizing ideologies and the weakness underlying the apparent power of colonizing regimes. The conjuncture of diverse forms of African mobilization and the loss of imperial self-confidence produced a crisis in colonial policy and colonial thinking, a crisis that would lead the British and French governments, in something of a panic, to swing the pendulum toward an assertively reformist conception of their own role.

From the vantage point of the 1940s it was not clear where all this ferment would end. To assume that diverse grievances, desires, and efforts at individual and collective advancement in the 1940s naturally converged on nationalist politics is to read history backwards from the triumph of African independence in the 1960s. This chapter looks at peasants, workers, and professionals, at husbands and wives, at religious innovators and secular intellectuals during an uncertain, painful, but dynamic period of African history, to convey a sense of different possibilities and constraints and, above all, of different aspirations.

The Politics of the Prosperous Peasant

In parts of Africa, colonization drove rural dwellers into deepening poverty, sometimes as a deliberate policy to create "labor reserves" where people had little alternative to selling their labor cheaply, sometimes as a result of actions that made difficult ecosystems worse. Less familiar, but no less important, are the islands of peasant prosperity that grew up among cocoa producers in southern Ghana and western Nigeria, in the palm-oil regions of coastal West Africa, in the peanut basin of Senegal, or in the coffee-producing highlands near Mount Kilimanjaro in Tanganyika.

Starting in the late nineteenth century in the southern Gold Coast and in the early twentieth century in southwestern Nigeria, cocoa production began among migrant farmers from the edge of the forest zone who negotiated access to good forest land from local land-possessing kinship groups. The colonial state deserved little credit, for the plantings came from missionaries and the initiative from Africans, but colonial governments were glad to have whatever export revenue they could get. Planting cocoa bushes demands labor for years before any income comes in, and the migrant farmers used their kinship networks to survive. As cocoa took off, more distant migrants began to offer their labor, and they were paid a mixture of wages and crop shares, but also established relations of clientage with the first generation of planters, who after a period of loyal service sometimes helped a worker become a planter himself. The cocoa farmers are revealing because they fit so poorly into the categories of agrarian society and agrarian politics deriving from European experience. They were not subsistence cultivators: they participated in markets for labor and for crops. But they weren't exactly capitalist farmers either.

FIGURE 4 Drying cocoa in Côte d'Ivoire, 2001. Cocoa is the smallholder crop par excellence in forest regions of West Africa, planted first in the Gold Coast, then Nigeria, Côte d'Ivoire, and Cameroon, where it brought modest prosperity in certain regions. Tyler Hicks/Getty Images

In its expansive phase, cocoa produced differentials of wealth, but these differences were not a line of class distinction. The wealthy planter cultivated supporters as well as crops, sponsored ceremonies, and otherwise strove to turn wealth into prestige. Rather than push agrarian capitalism to harsh extremes, these planters were more likely to invest excess profits in starting trading or transport companies or insuring their children's access to education and then to positions in the civil service. As good cocoa land became scarcer in the late 1930s in the Gold Coast and in the 1950s in Nigeria, tensions – and frequent litigation – developed. In the Gold Coast, older forms of association among young men sometimes challenged the combination of cocoa wealth and chiefly status. But nothing like a dichotomy of landlord versus landless came into being, and cocoa wealth in fact deepened kinship and community, and the role of the "big man" in both regards.

The big man was, indeed, male. But the gender division of labor was not uniform. In some cash crop areas, men – by virtue of linkages with missionaries, colonial agricultural agents, or traders – had privileged roles in the commercialization of agriculture, even if women were essential to food production and even if men relied on women's labor in export-crop production. But increased economic activity also enhanced some possibilities for women. Among Yoruba cocoa growers, for instance, a complex division of labor within the household insured that women would get some of the earnings of cocoa production, and many used this to invest in marketing of food and household items. The West African "market woman" exercised considerable autonomy in her business and usually in her household; she often contributed to children's education. Men, however, were much better positioned to use wealth to build up networks of clients and to enter the politics of the local chiefdom, and eventually regional and national politics.

Success did not mean acquiescence to a colonial order. African farmers had to do business with the big, monopolistic European import–export firms. In 1937–38 in the Gold Coast, wealthy cocoa planters organized a boycott of cocoa sales, using their considerable prestige and authority to enforce discipline over the smaller producers. They eventually forced the colonial government to intervene in cocoa marketing, replacing the European firms with a government marketing board and networks of African buying agents. The marketing-board system (like a similar one in Nigeria) allowed, for a time, the government to appease concerns about the firms' price gouging, but African political leaders and colonial officials soon came into conflict over how the surplus should be used.

In the coffee-growing zone of northern Tanganyika, relatively well-off lineage heads and chiefs solidified their political control of the region, sometimes clashing with a colonial state that favored middlemen over producers. Among the Kikuyu of central Kenya, peasant agriculture was challenged by land-grabbing by white settlers and extensive labor recruitment. Many lost access to land, but others struggled to find a niche in a structure that left some land in African hands adjacent to zones of white settlement. Young men could work for wages on white-owned farms or in the city of Nairobi and, with resourcefulness and luck, save enough to invest in agricultural improvements as they entered a later phase of the life course. Chiefs used their connections with the colonial state to gain access to land and labor in the African "reserves." Women marketed beans and other crops in nearby Nairobi, where a growing working population needed foodstuffs. But until the late 1940s race-based regulations prevented Africans from growing the most lucrative crop, coffee. When those regulations were eased, the combination of accumulation of land by Africans and by white settlers produced an ever-sharper divide between those who had access to land and those who did not. This complex social system would explode in the early 1950s.

In Senegal, peanut cultivation since the mid-nineteenth century had been dominated by the leaders of Islamic brotherhoods. These leaders, called *marabouts*, pioneered new cultivation zones by establishing settlements of their student followers (*talibé*), who benefited from the protection of a collectivity and the knowledge, seeds, and organizational skill of the *marabouts*. After a period of working for a *marabout, talibé* would go off on their own. The Mouride brotherhood in particular became wealthy and powerful, as a peanut-growing peasantry slowly emerged.

Colonial officials, when they added up their export figures, knew that African farmers – through a wide variety of social arrangements – were innovative and active producers. Yet in policy discussions in Paris or London such knowledge was eclipsed by a prior assumption of backwardness. In the 1930s several governments – in British Central and East Africa for instance – set out to save the soil from bad African practices. Such clumsy interventions would lead to much rural opposition after the war. In a few places, Northern Rhodesia for example, administrators in the 1940s began to think that they should mold "progressive farmers" out of people they had regarded as subsistence cultivators, but they did relatively little to provide the infrastructure that such an ambition required. Most important, official thinking about African agriculture was so wedded to the idea of its backwardness that it was hard for officials to recognize how much African farmers producing cocoa, coffee, peanuts, palm products, cotton, and tobacco as well as a wide range of food for regional markets had already accomplished. After the war, colonial governments asserted the need for an "agricultural revolution" in Africa as if the evolution of the past century had not happened.

The uneven process of agricultural change in colonial Africa on the eve of World War II produced varied political consequences: the anger of the landless against both white land-grabbers and Africans who denied the implications of communal solidarity; the despair of the impoverished, who now needed cash to pay school fees and other "modern" expenses but who had less chance than ever of saving money; the grievances of the successful farmers against the low prices paid by middlemen or the authoritarianism of colonial agricultural agents; the patriarchal politics of chiefs who turned position into wealth and wealth into power; and the widening linkages that successful farmers developed via trade, investment, and the education of their children. Linkages put farmers in a position to act politically, and also brought them into contact with the constricting arms of the colonial state. In the post-war era rural political mobilization would come from several directions, from the moderately wealthy to the extremely poor.

Intellectual Linkages

One of the ironies of African political history is that the moment which seemed to open a new era in Pan-Africanist mobilization proved to be its highest point. Politics would move in other directions. Interwar Pan-Africanism had several elite versions. One was set out by African Americans and Caribbeans, who challenged imperialism for its racism on a world scale and argued that educated African Americans would be a vanguard leading Africa out of its wilderness; another was developed by Léopold Sédar Senghor and Aimé Césaire, whose concept of *négritude* posited a contribution by Africans to world civilization. Pan-Africanism also had its populist version, animated by Marcus Garvey, that spread via African and African-American sailors in African ports. There were London-based organizations, notably the International African Service Bureau, linked to communist or Trotskyite anti-imperialist networks. These movements were appalled and angered when Italy invaded Ethiopia in 1935 and the League of Nations failed to act against Italian aggression. African and African-American political leaders tried to raise public opposition to this new imperialist conquest, but made little headway with European governments.

There were also regional linkages. Sierra Leone, where since the late 1700s the British government had sent "freed" Africans taken from captured slaving vessels and elsewhere, had been a dispersal point for African traders and missionaries, educated and Christian, who helped to build hybrid cultural forms along the West African coast from Gambia to Nigeria. Traders, artisans, lawyers, and doctors of Sierra Leonean origin lived in most port cities under British influence. In western Nigeria many of these "returnees" – who had originally been taken from this region as slaves – pushed the diverse

Yoruba-speaking peoples to see themselves as a "nation," while emphasizing that this nation needed the help of African missionaries to advance. Afro-Brazilians, also with western Nigerian roots, traded between Brazil and Nigeria and also helped to forge a diasporic nation. In Nigeria, Yoruba might be Christian, Muslim, or otherwise, wear English clothing or otherwise. Yoruba could be culturally self-aware, yet look outward, toward Africa as a whole and toward its diaspora, but to certain aspects of British culture as well. Just what practices were to be followed in, say, marriage, was very much in question.

In West African cities such as Lagos this self-conscious, professional, Christian class – linked by school ties, friendships, and business relations with similar people in other cities of British West Africa – was deeply affected by the exclusions of colonial rule. In the interwar years the colonial government proclaimed that Christian Africans were not the "real" Africans. It was out of this milieu, and the frustrations that colonization imposed on it, that early political associations were built, notably the National Congress of British West Africa (NCBWA). The NCBWA was a regional organization of well-educated Africans who came together after World War I to write petitions, to publish journals and pamphlets, and to demand seats on the white-dominated advisory and legislative councils created by the British. The organization insisted that such people – not just the most seemingly "African" of chiefs – should have a voice in articulating affairs. Their political focus was not Nigeria, the Gold Coast, Sierra Leone, or Gambia, but the cosmopolitan space that connected all of them. They were not necessarily opposed to the British empire, but at the very least demanded a role in its governance and substantial local autonomy.

In French West Africa the equivalent population was much smaller; mission education was more limited. But in four towns in Senegal (the Quatre Communes) colonized in the seventeenth century, inhabitants (called *originaires*) had most of the rights of French citizens. In 1914 a black African, Blaise Diagne, was elected to represent these cities in the legislature in Paris, breaking the political monopoly of mulatto and white citizens. During World War I Diagne realized how much France needed his help in recruiting soldiers, and he used his leverage to entrench the citizenship rights of his constituents, to expand the voter rolls, and to build his own political machine. The French administration later tried to contain these gains by emphasizing the "traditional" nature of African society and the authority of chiefs; citizenship was proving to be too compelling an idea.

African political representation thus became an imaginable phenomenon, and even if most "subjects" stood no chance of becoming
citizens, they knew about the concept and could aspire to it. Later,
politicians such as Senghor would operate in a political milieu that
emphasized both citizenship and *négritude*: the rights and obligations
of the citizen of the French empire and the forms of expression and
sensibilities of an African were not, according to Senghor, incompat-
ible. Senghor summed up his vision in 1945 with the expression
"assimilate; do not be assimilated."

These were the politics of connections – regional and imperial. In
the late 1930s the people traveling along these circuits moved in a
more radical direction. It was partly a matter of generation, of
younger men who saw their elders as stodgy. The West African
Student Organization and the various "youth leagues" formed among
African students and young city-dwellers made this point in the
names they chose for themselves. Leaders were coming out of wider
circuits: Kwame Nkrumah and Nnamdi Azikiwe were educated in
historically black colleges in the United States, and they experienced
at first hand America's brand of virulent racism. They were exposed
to a variety of radicalisms in leftist circles in London and among
African Americans in American cities. I. T. A. Wallace Johnson went
from Sierra Leone to Moscow and took back with him an internationalist concept of struggle against imperialism. Meanwhile, the increasing activism of a labor movement in African port cities and mines (see
pp. 40–46) pushed a better-educated stratum in a more militant
direction.

Communications within Africa were also providing possibilities for
connections. Although Africa had long been criss-crossed by trade
routes, pilgrimage circuits, and other connections, railways, roads,
postal services, and radio facilitated the movement of people and
messages. Colonial governments both established post offices and
censored the mail. They used the written word and radio as propaganda as well as a means of coordinating messages and actions by
officials. But communications could be a two-edged sword.
A newspaper that only a few people were able to read could be read
aloud; a radio that one person could afford could be heard by many;
and the content of communications or ways of interpreting them were
not easily controlled. Literate Africans could promote the value of
their own cultures and histories through written texts or reinterpret
the lessons missionaries were teaching into calls for their own

emancipation. Africans working in a post office or telegraph station could acquire information. It is perhaps no coincidence that two of Africa's more radical leaders of the 1950s began their careers as postal clerks: Ahmed Sékou Touré in French West Africa and Patrice Lumumba in the Belgian Congo.

For Africans engaged in regional and global circuits, World War II was experienced in a cruelly contradictory manner. They were hearing constantly about the evils of Nazi racism and Nazi conquests, and the virtues of "self-determination" for which the Allies were fighting. The Italian invasion of Ethiopia had brought fascism to the African continent. British Prime Minister Winston Churchill's contention that the principle of self-determination applied to recent conquests in Europe but not older conquests in Africa was not convincing to many Africans. Some – Wallace Johnson for instance – experienced the war as repression, for they faced detention, censorship, and bans on political activity. All the while, great sacrifices were being made by colonized peoples in the name of the war effort: soldiers from British West Africa in Burma, from French Equatorial Africa in North Africa and Italy, workers throughout the continent who were forced to produce commodities deemed useful for the war effort. So 1945, the moment of victory, took on a special meaning: political debts fell due, and African elites saw in the new-found anti-racist rhetoric of the Allies a language in which to extend their critique of colonial rule.

It was a moment that Pan-Africanist leaders tried to seize, to formulate goals and strategy for confronting the edifice of colonialism across Africa and its diaspora. But it was also a moment in which the issues of wages, housing, education, and crop prices were acute, all the more so because of the economic hardships of the war. The racism of colonial society was felt not only as the denigration of African culture and African life generally, but as hundreds of acts of discrimination felt day by day, and city by city, mining town by mining town, colony by colony. These issues were being pried open, both during the war and in the years immediately after it. The post-war moment presented opportunities to political and social movements to take on imperial administrations uncertain of their continued authority and aware of their need for Africans' contributions to rebuild imperial economies. A turning point had arrived, but whether change would mean the reform of empire, the destruction of empire, or the forging of new kinds of political units was not yet possible to discern.

Religion beyond the "Tribe"

Intellectuals were not the only Africans who crossed frontiers. The image of "one tribe – one religion" that many Westerners have of Africa never fit. Beliefs traveled different routes from people, so that networks of religious leaders or particular belief systems were often quite widespread. The influence of Islam and Christianity dates back long before colonization, but colonial rule opened new spaces to Catholic and Protestant missionaries. Less obvious is the fact that colonization, despite the intentions of the colonizers, also resulted in a large-scale extension of Islam; something like a third of sub-Saharan Africa's population are now Muslims. It is even less clear that the new religions have meant the eclipse of all elements of the old. Old and new concepts of the supernatural and different forms of spirituality are still capable of making sense of the world and articulating moral beliefs, and many of these coexist with the newer faiths.

The wide-ranging social changes that followed increases in communications and trade before colonization, as well as the increased mobility fostered by the colonial peace, labor migration, urban growth, and the commercialization of agriculture, brought people into contact with others whose beliefs were not necessarily the same. Robin Horton (1993) interprets the expansion of Islam and Christianity in the nineteenth and twentieth centuries as a consequence of people leaving the domain where "local" gods held sway. Monotheistic religion, he argues, traveled better and provided shared symbols, beliefs, and moral codes that permitted cooperation across distance. But indigenous religious practices could also extend in scale beyond ethnic borders, and prophets, healers, and spirit mediums were often regional, not local, figures. Religious practices often changed bit by bit, so that the idea of "conversion" to Christianity or Islam can give a misleading impression of how religious ideas and practices were diffused among rural populations, perhaps over decades, before an institutional structure of missions and churches or mosques and madrassas (Koranic schools) was established.

Some scholars argue that adoption of Christianity signified the colonization of the mind, that it went beyond changing a specific dimension of human behavior labeled "religion," to embrace the transformation of many personal practices, from mode of dress to design of houses to initiation rites. Missionary practice focused on

FIGURE 5 Rural mission church in Cameroon, 1949. Such missions not only added Christianity to the religious repertoire in much of Africa, but also provided education and entrée into clerical and professional occupations. ©ECPAD/La Documentation Française.

the individual, shunting aside kinship groups, councils of elders, age groups, and other collectivities basic to African social life. Missionaries often thought that they were tearing down an entire complex of "savage" beliefs. What they accomplished is another question.

From early on, many African Christians refused to follow the missionary script. At times, African clerics took their flocks away from the heavy-handed control of white missionaries to build churches that were much like those they had left. Or else, converts might remain within mission communities, but use their literacy to write the histories of their communities or to work out their own moral discourse that defined themselves as Christians of a distinct sort. Autonomy movements in both senses widened the range of doctrinal possibility by denying that being Christian meant acting like a European.

In the 1930s a "revival" movement swept across parts of East Africa, calling on people to participate in a worldwide vision of the Christian community, rejecting local religions and kinship systems. But some of the places where the revival took place experienced what Derek Peterson (2012) calls "ethnic patriotism," a renewed emphasis on community, on patriarchy, and on kinship. The patriotism being advocated was Kikuyu, Haya, or Toro, not Kenyan or Ugandan. Different moral visions were contesting a space where social relations were changing.

Even beyond the places where revivalists and patriots were contesting each other's beliefs, the relation of Christianity to indigenous social practices could be a sensitive issue. Polygamy was one source of contention, initiation rites another. Leaders who emerged among Kikuyu converts in the late 1920s and 1930s, for example, founded schools and churches to enable them to maintain the Christian faith and educate their children, while rejecting what they saw as missionary efforts to destroy Kikuyu culture. Tensions came to a head over a missionary campaign that attempted to abolish clitoridectomy, part of female initiation rites considered by many Kikuyu to be essential to carrying a girl over the threshold to adulthood and to marking by shared ritual the solidarity of Kikuyu. Missionaries excluded girls who had undergone this process from church and school – and their families as well – to which some Kikuyu responded by founding their own schools. The culture conflict fed into a wider confrontation that would take a violent turn after the war, but in the 1930s it provoked a profound debate over what it meant to be Christian and to be Kikuyu.

For some Africans the "white man's religion" could serve instrumental purposes – acquiring literacy and other marketable skills at mission schools – or it could provide a mode of integration into a cosmopolitan world in a city, a world linked to but not reducible to "colonial society." It could also give rise to movements, such as those in neighborhoods of Salisbury or along labor migration routes in Northern Rhodesia, that emphasized separation from the values and authority of colonizer, chief, and kinsmen.

The diversity of the religious organizations that proliferated in Africa, and which proliferate to this day, suggests the many ways in which one could synthesize and combine different belief systems. Many missionaries reduced African beliefs to "superstition," and while colonial-era anthropologists were often more sympathetic, that field of inquiry tended to emphasize the holistic nature of beliefs and social organization within each "tribe." More recent thinking about religion in Africa emphasizes the flexibility, adaptability, and interactive nature of religious practices. Individuals juggled different belief systems and conflicting moral codes. The successful entrepreneur, for example, might be subject to pressure to distribute his wealth to kinsmen and neighbors, lest he be accused of having used occult forces to "eat" his competitors. Such an individual might in turn use his resources to acquire the services of diviners and other ritual specialists to bring the supernatural to his defense, or he might take up the practice of Islam to indicate his withdrawal from the moral domain of his demanding relatives and his entry into what he might see as a more inclusive moral universe.

Ambiguity about collective norms was thus part of a tension over social relations: what did it mean for an individual to act within a kinship group or a village community, or to become involved in schools, wage labor, or crop markets? What was the relationship between individual achievement and the social body? Accusations of violating community norms could be a leveling mechanism, directed against selfish accumulation, or it could be a distancing mechanism, marking marginal people as outside the protective circle of a community.

These tensions were linked to the uncertainties of life: people tried to understand why some children became sick and died while others survived; why some men had good jobs and bountiful crops while others suffered immiseration; why some women were at the center of strong family relations while others were not.

A doctor might explain that malarial parasites or contaminated water led to a high incidence of disease, or a union organizer might explain the devastating effects of colonial capitalism, but neither could explain why a particular individual suffered and another did not. In the late 1930s in Central Africa, a region facing agricultural degradation and disruptive forms of labor migration, witch-finding cults proliferated, crossing boundaries of language and culture to identify individuals who were transgressing social norms and whose fortune was seen to be based on their use of supernatural forces against others.

In the late 1930s and 1940s, in short, invention and innovation were characteristics of the religious field. The question of whether individuals would forge new sorts of connections across space and culture or seek to solidify the defenses of a perceived community against outside assaults affected much of Africa. But either position forced people to rethink the role of ritual specialists, to consider what they shared and where they differed with neighbors, and to ask what kinds of moral codes could govern their relationships with the familiar and unfamiliar people with whom they came in contact.

Men and Women, Migrancy and Militance

Between 1935 and 1950 numerous strikes enveloped ports, mines, railways, and commercial centers in Africa. The Northern Rhodesian copper-mine strike of 1935 revealed that these were not routine industrial relations conflicts. Copper miners came from cruelly impoverished rural areas – deliberately bypassed by colonial transportation facilities – and they worked for periods of several months to several years. They were paid miserable wages, lived in inadequate housing, were disciplined arbitrarily, and had little chance to advance. Employers did not think that mineworkers were really workers; they were villagers temporarily earning money to meet fixed needs.

Employers also thought of workers as single males. In fact, many women came to mine towns to join husbands, and other women found in town the sort of autonomy their family members would not have allowed. Just as young men could use wage earnings to distance themselves from their fathers' control over the family resources that they needed to marry, young women could find in town a partial escape from rural patriarchy. In the 1930s lineage elders, chiefs, and colonial officials were trying to restrict women's movement to town, and extensive litigation in colonial courts over marriage produced a "customary law" more patriarchal and restrictive than what had been practiced before.

The 1935 strike in Northern Rhodesia spread from mine to mine, and enveloped entire towns. Town workers struck alongside miners, and women were noticeably present at demonstrations. The strike was repressed and several miners were killed. A government investigatory commission – of the kind that would sit numerous times in the next decade – concluded that such events could best be forestalled by more rigorous repatriation of miners whose contracts were up. The genii of African labor unrest had to be put back in the tribal bottle.

This was not an isolated event in the British empire. Between 1935 and 1938 a series of strikes, demonstrations, and riots in the British West Indies profoundly shook the government's sense of control. The strike wave washed ashore in parts of British Africa as well, particularly in the form of general strikes that crossed lines of occupation and sometimes of gender: in Mombasa and Dar es Salaam in 1939; on the railway and mines in the Gold Coast in the late 1930s; on the Copperbelt once again in 1940. During World War II the strike wave continued, with major strikes, strike threats, and other menaces to economic continuity in Kenya, Nigeria, the Gold Coast, the Rhodesias, and South Africa.

The British government saw this for what it was – an empire-wide problem. The Colonial Office slowly came to realize that further disorder could only be prevented if the colonial populations in Africa and the West Indies were provided with decent services and better job prospects. In the wake of the strikes – and only then – the Colonial Office got serious about a concept that had been occasionally debated: that a colonial government should undertake systematic programs of "economic development" aimed at providing infrastructure to allow for greater and more efficient production by a workforce that was no longer living in misery. The Colonial Development and Welfare Act of 1940 was the first enactment by which Great Britain undertook to use metropolitan resources for programs aimed at raising the standard of living of colonized populations. Spending was to be focused on housing, water, schools, and other social projects, mostly geared to wage workers, as well as on infrastructure and directly productive projects. Behind the Act was the idea that better services would produce a healthier and more efficient workforce, and above all a more predictable and less combative one.

The war, especially in British Africa, both increased the demand for African products – and hence the need for African labor – and reduced the availability of European manufactured goods Africans wanted to buy. It also delayed the implementation of the Development Act. Wartime hardships and tensions led to escalating labor conflict, in Kenya, Nigeria, the Gold Coast, and South Africa. Immediately after the war, living conditions did not improve. There was a continued high demand for African labor, continued shortages of consumer goods and hence inflation, urban overcrowding, and poor services, all within a labor system that treated Africans as interchangeable units of labor power, whose desires to build a career or found a family were irrelevant to colonial businesses and the state. There were more general strikes in Mombasa and Dar es Salaam in 1947, more strikes plus a serious urban riot in 1948 in the Gold Coast, a colony-wide strike in the civil service and railway in Nigeria in 1945, a huge gold-mine strike in South Africa in 1946, a railway strike in 1945, and a general strike in 1948 in Southern Rhodesia, plus numerous other actions. These confrontations, as before, tended to spread throughout cities or even regions.

Precisely because workforces were little differentiated, strikes tended to become mass actions. African workers, whether organized in trade unions (as in Nigeria or the Gold Coast) or not (as in Kenya or the Rhodesias), sensed that colonial regimes were economically and politically vulnerable. The strike wave was an embarrassment to the ideological pretensions of colonial governments after the war and a direct threat to the development drive.

In French Africa, with a smaller wage-labor sector than in British Africa, the strike wave came later. The wartime experience was different as well, for the most economically advanced parts of French Africa were blockaded by Britain and its allies after France fell to the Germans in 1940. The strike wave came ashore in French West Africa in December 1945, when a two-month-long strike movement began in Senegal. In 1947–48 the entire railway system of French Africa was shut down by a very well-organized strike, and most of the system stayed out for five months, until a settlement on terms relatively favorable to the African railwaymen was finally reached.

The Belgian government gave no opening to any forms of labor (or political) organization, and with difficulty kept the lid on in urban areas, although it could not control rural ones. The Portuguese government used a great deal of forced labor, so that the reaction of angered workers was more likely to be desertion than strikes, and the Portuguese version of "development" relied heavily on white workers who came from the metropole. Portugal avoided the strike wave that beset French and British Africa in the late 1940s, but set the stage for a long and deadly struggle in the 1960s and 1970s.

South Africa, repressive as its government was, was relatively industrialized, and urban workers were the vanguard of a struggle for better living conditions for Africans that had begun long before the war but escalated as the urban workforce grew in the war years and immediately thereafter. Aware of the increasing need for labor in manufacturing and other urban enterprises, the government for a time contemplated "stabilizing" its urban workforce, encouraging African workers to settle for the long term in cities. But after the victory of the Afrikaner nationalists in 1948 the government opted instead for more rigorous policing of migration and massive expulsions of Africans from cities, except for people properly registered as working. That non-solution to the problem would also come home to roost at a later date.

Across Africa, the overwhelming majority of wage workers at this time were male. Scholars argue over why, in the early colonial period, wage labor was both short term and masculine: men worked for limited periods in mines, railways, or cities, leaving their wives, children, and non-working relatives in villages. Some think of this as an effort on the part of colonial capital to lower labor costs, since a worker with a family in a rural setting could be paid less than the actual costs of keeping a family alive. But whatever the intention of employers, it is not at all clear that many Africans wanted to commit themselves to a life of wage labor, except where the extent of land-grabbing undermined the ability of African agriculture even to produce a partial subsistence, most notably in South Africa. The potential dangers and loss to family economies of letting young women leave the villages was greater than that of young men. Early colonial labor supplies depended on a mixture of pressures and incentives: government pressure on chiefs to supply unwilling workers to public and private colonial enterprises; the inadequacy (deliberate or otherwise) of marketing and transport facilities in rural areas; taxes that had to be paid in cash; and generational tensions within African societies that led young men to seek the autonomy of wage employment.

Most zones of wage employment – the mines of Northern Rhodesia, for example – were surrounded by vast areas where food cultivation and periods of wage labor were both possible and necessary. By the 1930s the migratory labor system was being criticized by officials and missionaries, for it seemed to produce stagnation in both town and countryside by depriving agriculture of labor and initiative and leaving cities with a workforce poorly trained and poorly socialized into industrial labor and little acculturated to city life. In this situation, the chiefs and male elders in the labor recruitment areas of Central Africa tried to assert control over young women to insure that the rural community would not lose the labor and childbearing capacity of females and the money and labor of males.

The migratory system required high levels of coercion to insure that both men and women would be at work when needed and away from town when not wanted. In South Africa, police rigorously enforced control of movement. Men (and women starting in the late 1950s) were required to carry passes, and an African without a pass indicating that he was at or going to a place of employment could be arrested. In Southern Rhodesia women were not legally permitted to be in cities unless they could prove that they were married to a man who was entitled to be there (or, in some cases, were themselves employed and living in a supervised setting). Kenya had a pass law, too. Such restrictions were a focus of outrage and political organization in the post-war years.

Even in the face of such harsh policing, African urban life in South Africa, the Rhodesias, and Kenya proved to be impossible to control. Women asserted their own place within that space, and male migration created occupational niches for women, including cooking, beer-brewing, and prostitution. In West African cities, especially those such as Lagos or Dakar which had older traditions of urban life, established populations were able to defend their rights to urban property. Africans played active roles in trade, artisanal production, and sometimes in professions such as law and journalism. Officials still had to face the presence of "casual" laborers moving in and out of short-term jobs and of certain quarters of town where people could engage in all sorts of activities, legal or otherwise, without government control.

By the 1940s what colonial officials did not want to think about – an urban society, in which men and women, adults and children were trying to put together a life – had become a reality. Colonial policing and colonial neglect only made such a life harder – and potentially more explosive. So when strikes swept from the Copperbelt to Accra and Mombasa, colonial officials wondered whether the migrant-labor system was really in the best interest of colonial economies and whether the presence of a mass African population moving into and out of cities without being fully integrated into an urban social fabric was in the best interest of colonial societies. They could, as in the 1935 Copperbelt strike, pretend that the problem would go away, or they could try to shoehorn the labor question into the "development" question and hope that a little capital investment and a little urban planning would solve it.

A third colonial reaction was more complicated: a realization that how workers and their families lived would affect both how efficiently they produced and how orderly and predictable they were likely to be. The social engineers in French and British Africa coined a new word: stabilization. It was not exactly "proletarianization" as used in Europe, for officials still did not see wage labor enveloping all of Africa. Stabilization meant separation: creating an urban working class capable of living in the city and producing a new generation of workers in the city, independent of the "backward" countryside. It meant paying Africans more: "family wages" or "family allowances."

In the British Copperbelt the mining companies began to proclaim such a policy after the second major strike in 1940, but workers had in fact begun to stabilize themselves even before. In the port of Mombasa officials began to talk about stabilizing the dock labor force, on which the entire import–export economy of Kenya and Uganda depended. Pushed by major dock and general strikes in 1939 and 1947, the Kenyan government actually began to do it. "Casual" workers had previously been hired by the day to load and unload ships, depending on fluctuating needs, but by the mid-1950s many workers were being hired by the month. These policies took colonial regimes into the daily intimacy of what work and urban life were all about: patterns of residence, conflict over work regimes, contentious issues about discipline, delicate relations between unions and managers. I will return later to consider the actual effects of such policies.

The fact that British and French regimes were driven for the first time to take the labor question seriously is itself critical. The urban mass, in official thinking, would become less of a factor, the trade union more. Cities would be crucibles of social, cultural, and political change throughout the post-war era. It was not that they were intrinsically dynamic while rural villages were passively culture-bound. In cities, whatever happens in one street or neighborhood occurs in close proximity to everything else. Density has its consequences – and, for a colonial regime, its dangers. The juxtaposition in cities of respectable mission converts with young male wage laborers, of established merchant families with women seeking autonomy, and of migrant workers with the offspring of urban households was becoming increasingly volatile.

The mix changed not only as urban populations grew in the 1940s, but also as women became a larger part of the urban population. The growing differentiation and interaction among urban Africans took place in proximity to facilities intended for white residents and where the institutions and symbols of power stood, with all of their implications of possibilities and racial exclusions. Associational life was becoming richer and more varied, built around occupational and residential affinities, connections to common regions of origin, churches or mosques or indigenous religious institutions, mutual aid needs of various sorts, the collective interests of traders or workers, and new forms of music and artistic creation. Most important was the mix of urban-born and migrant youth, a category marked, as Rémy Bazenguissa-Ganga (1997: 12) puts it, by its "availability" – a vibrant, volatile force that could be channeled in different directions.

Black Men and Women in a White Man's War

Europe's war lasted from 1939 to 1945. Africa's struggle began earlier and lasted longer. The era of general strikes, starting first in British Africa, lasted from 1935 to about 1948. There was also conflict in rural areas over soil conservation and other heavy-handed interventionist policies. The World War weakened European powers both militarily and economically. It fundamentally shook their self-confidence, and it destroyed the assumptions that had given colonial ideologies their fragile coherence.

At first, warring powers tried to use colonies as they normally did – as a resource. France was already stepping up pressure, above all through forced labor, on Africans before its short-lived participation in the shooting war began. When France fell in June 1940, its African empire split, a clear sign of the tenuousness of metropolitan control. The French administration in West Africa accepted the Vichy regime, which was collaborating with the Nazis, while French Equatorial Africa (not coincidentally administered by a black Governor-General born in French Guyana, Félix Éboué) refused to take orders from

Vichy and insisted that the London-based Free French of General Charles de Gaulle was still France. Both sets of colonies tried to mobilize colonial resources for their respective sides. Neither was able to act very effectively, Equatorial Africa because the French had already stripped it of much of its assets (hardwood and rubber) and done little to develop others, West Africa because the Allies blockaded it. Later, the Allies' reconquest of France began in France's North African territories, and troops from French Equatorial Africa participated in the battles while workers from that region, often working under compulsion, supplied important raw materials to the Allies. Africans thus played a significant role in demonstrating that French efforts, not just those of Britain and the United States, contributed to the victory over the Nazis. French West Africa, once its rulers realized who was winning the war, abandoned Vichy in favor of the Free French. De Gaulle recognized the African colonies' contribution to liberating France and that gratitude and self-interest required a reexamination of French colonial policy – a subject to which I will return.

Great Britain lost many of its Asian colonies – with the enormous exception of India – to Japan and relied more than ever on Africa for tropical products. It used African troops in Asia, and needed African labor power still more. In Kenya and the Rhodesias it revived forced labor for crops that were held to be in the imperial interest, but which also profited settlers and corporations. Even where work was voluntary, Great Britain tried as much as possible to restrict imports into colonies. One result was the accumulation of surpluses: the colonies' budgets were credited with revenue derived from a high level of exports, which they were not allowed to spend. Funds built up in London banks, and would become a source of contention after the war as African political leaders demanded that the surpluses be spent in the interest of the people who had produced them.

The war years offered some opportunities to African agricultural producers; at least they were receiving money for their exports, and they were not dependent on food imports. The war economy was even more profitable for white farmers. But for urban workers these years were hard; imports were scarce, and nearby farmers could make more money producing export items than food for local markets – hence the wartime strike wave described earlier in this chapter. The pattern continued after the war, for Great Britain's factories were so badly damaged by German bombing, its debt to the United States was so large, and its inability to meet the needs of its domestic population –

which, unlike that of its African colonies, voted in elections – was so great that basic consumer goods such as cloth remained in short supply in the colonies. Britain's intention to undertake development projects was constrained by the scarcity of steel and concrete. Inflation continued, as did the strike wave.

Both Great Britain and France thought they would regain control through their new concept of "development." Post-war imperialism would be the imperialism of knowledge, of investment, of planning. The British Colonial Development and Welfare Act of 1940 was authorized at a higher spending level in 1945; the French passed their Investment Fund for Economic and Social Development (under the French acronym FIDES) in 1946. Even Portugal and South Africa would try – however implausibly – to claim the mantle of development for themselves (Chapter 3).

In France and Great Britain, the two powers with the most extensive territories in Africa, new ways of thinking went the furthest. That process entailed a reimagining of African society and culture, and indeed of Western knowledge itself. Up to World War II "scientific" theories of racial inequality, policies to curb the fertility of people whose genes were supposedly inferior or unhealthy, and sharp cultural distinctions between the "primitive" and the "civilized" were controversial but within the norms of acceptable debate. Hitler gave racist ideologies and racist theories a bad name. The widely publicized Atlantic Charter, an Anglo-American agreement that set the Allies' belief in "self-determination" against the Nazi and fascist wars of conquest, left Africans wondering why it did not apply to them.

Once the French and British publics had to think about why democratic states were worth defending, the kinds of questions previously raised by a colonized intelligentsia and some anti-racist intellectuals at home acquired a new pertinence. Developmental colonialism was in part a response to the narrowing grounds on which a convincing case could be made for the exercise of state power over people who were "different." African society was now seen to be malleable, and not just by gradual changes within the framework of African "traditional" frameworks. Some Africans, at least, could be pulled out of those frameworks, turned into "modern" workers or progressive, market-oriented farmers. Developmental ideologies implied that difference would over time be eclipsed. When would the time come to declare that the backward were sufficiently developed to strike out on their own? Who was to judge whether the "tutorial" power was acting in the interest of its charges rather than for its own benefit? Such questions were not new, but they became much more immediate during the war.

European leaders would not get the chance quietly to think through their uncertainties. In this atmosphere of ideological uncertainty they faced an escalation of demands coming out of the African continent itself. The demands were not necessarily focused on taking over the state. But they were focused on what states actually did: on education, taxation, investment in social services and productive resources, judicial systems, and the question of who was to participate in the making of vital decisions.

A full bibliography for this book may be found on the website of Cambridge University Press at www.cambridge.org/CooperAfrica2ed.

Bibliography

Austin, Gareth. *Land, Labor and Capital in Ghana: From Slavery to Free Labor in Asante, 1807–1956*. Rochester, NY: University of Rochester Press, 2005.

Bazenguissa-Ganga, Rémy. *Les voies du politique au Congo*. Paris: Karthala, 1997.

Berry, Sara. *No Condition is Permanent: The Social Dynamics of Agrarian Change in Sub-Saharan Africa*. Madison: University of Wisconsin Press, 1993.

Byfield, Judith, Carolyn Brown, Timothy Parsons, and Ahmad Alawad Sikainga. *Africa and World War II*. Cambridge: Cambridge University Press, 2015.

Comaroff, Jean, and John Comaroff. *Of Revelation and Revolution*, vol. I: *Christianity, Colonialism and Consciousness in South Africa*. Chicago: University of Chicago Press, 1991.

Cooper, Frederick. *Decolonization and African Society: The Labor Question in French and British Africa*. Cambridge: Cambridge University Press, 1996.

Hanretta, Sean. "New Religious Movements." In John Parker and Richard Reid, eds., *The Oxford Handbook of Modern African History*. Oxford: Oxford University Press, 2013.

Higginson, John. *A Working Class in the Making: Belgian Colonial Labor Policy, Private Enterprise, and the African Mineworker, 1907–1951*. Madison: University of Wisconsin Press, 1989.

Horton, Robin. *Patterns of Thought in Africa and the West*. Cambridge: Cambridge University Press, 1993.

Jennings, Eric. *Free French Africa in World War II: The African Resistance.* Cambridge: Cambridge University Press, 2015.

Luongo, Katherine. *Witchcraft and Colonial Rule in Kenya, 1900–1955.* Cambridge: Cambridge University Press, 2011.

Manchuelle, François. *Willing Migrants: Soninke Labor Diasporas, 1848–1960.* Athens: Ohio University Press, 1997.

Mann, Gregory. *Native Sons: West African Veterans and France in the Twentieth Century.* Durham, NC: Duke University Press, 2006.

Matera, Marc. *Black London: The Imperial Metropolis and Decolonization in the Twentieth Century.* Berkeley: University of California Press, 2015.

Moodie, T. Dunbar, and Vivienne Ndatshe. *Going for the Gold: Men, Mines, and Migration.* Berkeley: University of California Press, 1994.

Moore, Henrietta, and Meghan Vaughan. *Cutting Down Trees: Gender, Nutrition, and Agricultural Change in the Northern Province of Zambia, 1890–1990.* Portsmouth, NH: Heinemann, 1993.

Peterson, Brian. *Islamization from Below: The Making of Muslim Communities in Rural French Sudan, 1880–1960.* New Haven: Yale University Press, 2011.

Peterson, Derek. *Creative Writing: Translation, Bookkeeping, and the Work of Imagination in Colonial Kenya.* Portsmouth, NH: Heinemann, 2004.

Ethnic Patriotism and the East African Revival: A History of Dissent, c. 1935 to 1972. Cambridge: Cambridge University Press, 2012.

Ross, Robert, Anne Kelk Mager, and Bill Nasson, eds. *The Cambridge History of South Africa Volume 2: 1885–1994.* Cambridge: Cambridge University Press, 2011.

Tilley, Helen. *Africa as a Living Laboratory: Empire, Development, and the Problem of Scientific Knowledge.* Chicago: University of Chicago Press, 2011.

Van Beusekom, Monica. *Negotiating Development: African Farmers and Colonial Experts at the Office du Niger, 1920–1960.* Portsmouth, NH: Heinemann, 2002.

CHAPTER 3

Citizenship, Self-Government, and Development: The Possibilities of the Post-War Moment

Looking backward from the 1960s, it is easy to see why the story of post-war politics is often told as if everything led to a single, inevitable outcome: national independence. It is more difficult to see what somebody in 1945 or 1947 – say, a young, politically minded African returning from higher education abroad – aspired to and expected to attain. Or a family who had just settled in a mining town after years of periodic separations, missed the familiar sociability of village life but perhaps not the constraints of their elders, and hoped that their children could obtain an education. Or a farmer, selling his cocoa in the booming world market, aware that colonial marketing boards were holding onto much of what his crops earned, and wondering if his children would continue to help with the harvest.

Africans faced the constraints and humiliations of a colonial state, but they were, above all, human beings trying to survive, form relationships, find opportunities, and make sense of the world. They cannot be reduced to stick figures in a drama with two actors, colonizer and colonized, or a story with one plot line: the struggle for the nation. What is striking about the years after the war is how much seemed possible.

This chapter is about political imagination, constraint, and conflict in the post-war decade. It examines colonial imaginations, for the rulers of colonial empires did not think in 1945 that their empires were about to end, but they did realize that they would have to think in new ways about their domains. Their illusion was that they thought they could control political evolution. In fact, the most reformist and flexible empires, those of France and Britain, collapsed the first; the most obdurate, Portugal's, survived the longest. The dynamics of reform and mobilization were crucial. In the late 1940s African political and labor movements saw that they had an opportunity; but what they saw as a goal in 1945 was not where they ended up twenty years later.

This chapter is built around three examples that illustrate the widening and narrowing of possibilities after the war. The first is French Africa. Officials believed that the slow admission of Africans into the category of citizen would preserve the unity of the French empire. In fact, the strategy turned into a trap, as African social and political movements used the language of imperial legitimacy to claim all the social and economic entitlements of metropolitan citizens. The second example is that of the Gold Coast, where Great Britain, after the war, seemed to be pursuing an opposite strategy. British leaders claimed that their policy had long been to bring colonial subjects first into local government and then slowly, as they proved worthy, into territorial "self-government" within the British Commonwealth. But the government was unable to define political change in such terms: urban youth and parts of organized labor joined a radical intelligentsia in quickly pushing for African self-government at the central, not the local, level of each colony, favoring street demonstrations, general strikes, and consumer boycotts over the orderly politics of petition. What in 1945 looked like Britain's model colony, moving toward development and self-government within the empire, became in a remarkably few years the place from which a rapid devolution of power to other colonies would spread.

Finally, there is South Africa. In its whites-only electoral system, a serious debate occurred over issues faced in colonial Africa as well, including whether Africans not actually living in isolated tribes had become a potentially useful component of a partly urban, partly industrial economy. But the decision that emerged was different: the 1948 election brought in a government that policed migration ever more vigorously, expelling millions of Africans from cities, clamping down on union and political activity, and reinforcing urban residential segregation and the removal of Africans from agricultural land. By the 1950s it was turning the watchword of self-consciously progressive colonial rulers – development – into a manifesto for maintaining distinct and grotesquely unequal destinies for South Africa's supposed races: "separate development."

FIGURE 6 Charles de Gaulle giving opening speech to the Brazzaville Conference, January 30, 1944. As World War II neared its end, colonial officials attempted to reaffirm the unity of French territory while promising economic, social, and political progress to its inhabitants. Far from averting dissent, these policies opened the door to escalating demands for equality within the French Union. Historic Images/Alamy Stock Photo

These cases are illustrative; the variations are numerous. Each one, in different ways, shows how social movements pioneered different forms of collective mobilization and affinity, not just "nationalism." African politics did not develop in an autonomous world, but via interaction and conflict, and the struggle itself reshaped the kind of political projects that were or were not imaginable. The turning of the French and British toward a development-minded colonialism – the desire to expand empire resources while legitimizing colonial rule – became the basis for a profound engagement of African and European actors, which in turn changed the meanings of "development," "citizenship," and "self-government." In the final sections I will examine other kinds of political projects that were pushed aside in the conjuncture of the late 1940s and 1950s as African political movements pursued other courses with some success and as colonial states tried to draw the line at the forms of politics they could accept. We begin by asking what African intellectuals, workers, traders, and farmers could imagine at the end of World War II and how they turned imagination into action.

Citizens of Empire: French Africa, 1944–52

As German defeat became inevitable and the liberation of mainland France a matter of time, Free French forces installed their government in newly reconquered Algeria. The colonial establishment proclaimed that the colonies had helped save the metropole and that the significance of "Greater France" would have to be rethought. In February 1944, in the presence of General de Gaulle and in the absence of colonial subjects, leading officials met at Brazzaville in French Equatorial Africa to plan the future. They divided African society into two categories, the *évolués* (Western-educated Africans, literally the "evolved ones") and *paysans* (peasants). Workers, traders, and artisans barely existed in the official mind, and the main labor issue on the agenda was forced labor, whose evils were fully acknowledged but which was seen as so essential, given Africans' supposed work habits, that the officials gave themselves five more years to phase it out. *Évolués* would be incorporated into French institutions; their numbers were too small to pose a threat. Peasants would benefit from lower taxes and the abolition of forced labor, and Africans growing crops within their own communities would make the empire more productive and raise the standard of living of its subjects. A new development initiative would reduce labor needs in transportation. Industrialization would take place slowly and prudently.

These high officials were uncompromising on one point: the French empire would remain unified and permanent. When faced with militant action by colonized people involving even a limited degree of violence, administrators and police forces sometimes reacted with racialized brutality, as in the incidents of Thiaroye in Senegal, in 1944, Sétif in Algeria, in 1945, and later a more threatening rebellion in Madagascar in 1947. In the spirit of Brazzaville, however, France allowed a limited number of Africans to vote in elections in 1945, with separate voting and separate representatives for "subjects" and "citizens." A tiny number of Africans took their seats in the legislature in Paris, but they soon became a significant factor. They would participate in the writing of a constitution for the French Union, as the empire was renamed. They could say things about colonial policy that would otherwise be covered up; their votes could make a difference when metropolitan deputies were evenly divided (as they often were); and these deputies (like their foes representing white settlers) cared passionately about colonial politics, whereas most politicians focused on other issues. Settlers had support on the legislature's right, the African deputies on the left, but also at times from a swing group of "social Catholics," centrists who sought to overcome conflict and combat communism by promoting decent wages, family welfare, and social harmony. There have been endless debates over whether these constitutional reforms represented progress or hypocrisy. Both sides miss the point: the reforms meant no more and no less than how they were used.

In the spring of 1946 Léopold Sédar Senghor (Senegal), Lamine Guèye (Senegal), Félix Houphouët-Boigny (Côte d'Ivoire), Aimé Césaire (Martinique), and other deputies were instrumental in the passage of two crucial measures. The first, known as the Houphouët-Boigny law after the deputy who introduced the law to the National Assembly, definitively ended forced labor in all French colonies, three years ahead of the schedule advanced at Brazzaville. This initiative had its roots in rural Africa: Houphouët-Boigny's support in Côte d'Ivoire came from the people victimized by the forced labor recruitment imposed by government-sponsored chiefs to supply white farmers as well as from the African cocoa farmers denied any such assistance. The second, the Lamine Guèye law (later given constitutional status), turned rightless subjects throughout the overseas territories into rights-bearing citizens of France, without specifying how such a principle would be carried out. Meanwhile, the demeaning judicial regime that gave French district administrators arbitrary power to punish non-citizens was abolished.

The ending of forced labor was barely debated: merely reminding the world that a system akin to enslavement existed in French Africa rendered it indefensible. The citizenship measure was more complex, and its discussion was part of a wider debate on exactly how people in colonies would participate in affairs of the empire. It was a vivid affirmation that France was serious about treating the empire as a unity, while reserving to the Paris legislature – with its large metropolitan majority – the right to determine just what kinds of institutions would actually function at the level of each territory within Greater France. Whereas Great Britain emphasized the specificity of each colonial territory, making it harder to reform the inequities of the colonial system, France insisted on centralized authority, in which Africans would be given a minority voice at the center, while institutions in each territory remained largely under the control of the ministry in Paris.

Citizenship arguments carry particular power because officials hope that citizenship entails obligations as well as rights, that it gives rulers legitimacy at the same time as it gives people a voice. Leading French officials hoped that their propaganda might really be true: that Africans, following French models, would prove to be orderly participants in politics and steady contributors to economic growth. The Lamine Guèye law and the post-war French Constitution extended to overseas citizens a right that citizens in European France did not have: to maintain their personal status under Islamic or "customary" law rather than under the French Civil Code. This provision meant that affairs of marriage and inheritance came under different rules. The most cited difference concerned marriage: Muslim men, for example, could have up to four wives under Islamic law, whereas the French Civil Code enforced monogamy. The implication of the citizenship regime of 1946 was that not everybody had to be a citizen in the same way – a historical point largely forgotten in the way citizenship is discussed in France today.

The dialogue across the colonial divide was not limited to the Paris legislature. Also in 1945 and 1946, in Dakar in Senegal, the labor movement opened up an important space for making claims and reconfiguring politics. Unions suppressed by Vichy came back into operation under the less repressive post-war regime. In December

1945 laborers in the port of Dakar went on strike to improve their miserable wages, and in January the strike spread throughout the city, embracing unskilled laborers, literate clerks in banks and businesses, skilled workers in the metal trade, and civil servants. For twelve days Dakar was shut down by a well-organized general strike, and other cities were engulfed as well. The movement transcended the workplace: women participated and demonstrated; market sellers refused to supply food to whites; and daily mass meetings were held to keep the entire public involved. French officials were unable to regain control. Finally, a new sort of expert came to Dakar from the metropole – a specialist in labor issues – and he set about dealing with this unprecedented strike as if it were an ordinary industrial dispute, negotiating with each group of workers and making major concessions. Laborers got large wage increases, and civil servants won family allowances, a victory of particular symbolic importance, for it implied that the needs of African families were those of any French family. Throughout the strike the slogan of the workers had been "equal pay for equal work." They did not literally achieve equality, but they did much to show that, politically, African workers and their families would have to be considered in the same terms as French workers and families.

The 1946 strike revealed that the distinction between citizen and subject was breaking down even in the months before it was formally abolished by the legislature: both African citizens – from the old colonial cities on which citizenship rights had been bestowed – and African subjects – migrants from the interior – had participated side by side. The long railway strike of 1947–48 over all of French West Africa drove home the lesson that African workers would insist not only on equality, but on having a say about all dimensions and details of their working conditions.

From 1947 labor unions made the passage of a unified labor code, which made no distinction based on the race or origins of the worker, their prime political objective. The stakes of each provision were high, and the debate dragged on for five years. As it reached a climax, a solidly organized one-day general strike across all of French West Africa increased the pressure. African deputies in Paris played key roles in making sure that other deputies understood the dangers of compromising the principles of universal equality of wages and benefits. They had influence beyond their (small) numbers because other deputies realized that a code imposed over the objections of the

African parliamentarians would have no legitimacy and because social Catholics in the legislature wanted to promote their vision of the family and to be sure that communists did not gain exclusive control of the movement for social progress. Whereas unions wanted a code to guarantee workers' rights, officials wanted it as a clear map of what was negotiable, what procedures would be, and what sanctions could be used against violators from labor or employers. Both the government and the labor movement had before their eyes visions of a "modern" system of labor relations, with one party emphasizing stability and predictability and the other workers' entitlements and the dignity of labor, while the social Catholics wanted both. When at long last the code became French law in 1952, it guaranteed all wage workers in the private sector a forty-hour work week, paid vacations, the right to organize and to strike, and other benefits. No sooner was this battle won than unions began fighting for family allowances for private-sector wage workers (African public employees having already won equal benefits), and this goal was achieved in 1956.

Here was an argument conducted by an African labor movement and elected representatives in the language of citizenship, universality, and entitlement – the conceptual apparatus of the modern state – and which put money into workers' pockets. Colonial officials' dream of the African as universal worker never did come to pass – workers on the job and in their homes had their own ideas about how to live and work – but this was, for unionized workers, a very useful fiction.

What the labor code left out is also important: the debate applied only to wage workers. It excluded "customary workers," those whose labor took place within the nuclear or extended family. It was ambiguous about the kind of relations that many agricultural laborers had with landowners, since much of their compensation came not in wages but as rights to land and crops as well as to the patronage of the landowner. It excluded the apprentices of the urban artisan. African politicians, union leaders, and employers were content to leave these categories out of the 1952 code: such forms of work were too pervasive, too steeped in social relations that bureaucrats did not understand, and in some cases too vital to the patron–client relations that African elites had with rural landowners who did not want their labor practices questioned. Few women were in wage employment, whereas many were in unpaid and unregulated domains of the economy. In the debate over the labor code, women's role was, as far as most deputies were concerned, in the family.

The reformed wage-labor sector thus stood in uneasy contrast to an unknown, unregulated, and unreformed social domain, where far more people lived and toiled. Officials wanted to "stabilize" the one, and feared that the other would overwhelm whatever progress they made. This division between a protected wage-labor class and everybody else would come back to disturb the governments and societies of independent Africa.

The development program, using the tax revenues of France, aimed at reaching rural as well as urban Africa and at bringing the range of services characteristic of a modern state, from schools to piped water, to the colonies. Compared to what went on before the war, investment in infrastructure and productive resources shot upward. Complications soon developed. The old infrastructure was so bad that the equipment brought in for roads, buildings, dams, and other projects quickly clogged ports, railways, and storage facilities. Private investment did not come forth as expected, leaving many colonies with high-cost, poorly functioning facilities that were still not providing the expected growth in production.

Even in the midst of a large-scale expansion of agricultural and mineral exports driven by high prices in Western markets, the development initiative was at best a partial success. Most important, colonial regimes had set a largely unattainable standard. Europe had made itself the model for what a developed economy should look like. Hence, one can see in the archival records from the 1950s the disappointment of officials with the development effort even when the results, measured in exports, wages, and farmers' incomes, were relatively good. The problem was with the colonial development concept itself, particularly its detachment from what was happening in the countryside and cities of Africa.

At the same time, development, like labor, was a concept around which demands could and were being formulated. French officials could not simply dismiss such claims, for their own legitimacy depended on the concepts of citizenship and development. Most crucially for politics in the late 1940s and 1950s, the state's key role in access to resources encouraged participation in its institutions. African leaders would become deeply involved in the developmentalist state even before they acquired power.

Issues of labor and development were now being debated in political institutions in which Africans participated. Politics took different forms across French Africa. In Senegal, citizens of the four original colonial settlements had since 1914 been represented by a black African in the Paris legislature. Suppressed during the war, electoral politics reemerged with renewed vigor afterward, and leaders who had seized the initiative from the first legislative elections in 1945 continued to do so. Senegal's two deputies to the French National Assembly differed in an important respect: Lamine Guèye was a distinguished and experienced lawyer from the Quatre Communes, and the brilliant scholar–politician Léopold Sédar Senghor came from an interior village.

After 1946 the old citizenship regime, restricted to the Quatre Communes, burst its bounds. As soon as subjects beyond the Communes became citizens, the voting rolls grew steadily until universal suffrage was achieved in 1956. Senghor realized the potential of the extension of citizenship. Born a French "subject" in 1906, he had received citizenship as a result of his extraordinary achievements in education and the patronage of some members of the administration. Initially an ally of Guèye, he split from his mentor in 1948, founding the Bloc Démocratique Sénégalais (BDS). Although a Christian himself, Senghor slowly worked via the leaders of Islamic brotherhoods to forge a rural political machine.

The *marabouts* were themselves masters of networks, and offered to their disciples both membership in a religious community and access to the resources of the entire network. This web of connections, not the blind obedience of *talibé* (follower) to *marabout*, was crucial. The brotherhoods crossed lines of region and ethnicity, which were in any case blurry in most of Senegal. Senegal has had a relatively stable political life because the relation of leader to follower in both the religious and political fields went along with a broad sense of commonality among a large portion of the population, as Muslims, as Mourides, as citizens, as Senegalese. Senghor captured the imagination of the Muslim countryside. He acted similarly in linking himself to other constituencies, including labor, working through the leadership to obtain the support of the rank and file. In 1951 his party soundly defeated Guèye's, and Senghor was in a position to guide Senegal through the complex politics of the 1950s.

In Côte d'Ivoire, Houphouët-Boigny also built a political machine early and came to be the undisputed father of a nation. He came from a chiefly family, earned a medical degree, and became a successful cocoa farmer. After the Vichy regime, which had been especially coercive in Côte d'Ivoire, fell apart, he put together an organization of African cocoa farmers, the African Agricultural Society. The Society was part lobby, part labor-recruiting network. Beginning in 1944, the African Agricultural Society turned the continued practice of forced labor into a political issue, not only mobilizing rural constituencies but also proving to the government that there were alternative ways to get workers onto farms producing export crops. Its labor-recruitment system, and the tenancy arrangements it used to attract people from the arid and populous north to work for African planters in the cocoa belt in the south, demonstrated that "free" labor was economically practical as well as ethically and politically necessary.

The African Agricultural Society was the vehicle for Houphouët-Boigny's election to the French legislature in 1945, and he repaid his constituents by sponsoring the law that definitively abolished forced labor. Over time the white settlers, no longer benefiting from forced labor, were marginalized, and Ivorian cocoa planters made this territory the wealthiest in French West Africa.

Houphouët-Boigny then brought together political leaders from territories across French Africa in 1946 in Bamako, in the French Sudan, where they decided to found a political party for all of French Africa, the Rassemblement Démocratique Africain (RDA, or the African Democratic Assembly). Houphouët-Boigny became its president. Fledgling political parties within each territory constituted themselves as branches of the RDA; the Ivorian one was called the Parti Démocratique de la Côte d'Ivoire (PDCI). The branches exercised considerable autonomy, but the RDA maintained a degree of common action and publicity, and acted as a unit in the Paris legislature, where it formed a marriage of convenience with the French Communist Party (despite the property-owning credentials of much of its leadership).

In Côte d'Ivoire, Guinea, and some other territories the RDA became the dominant African party; in Senegal it attracted working-class support but could not match the machine put together by Senghor. The RDA, like Senghor's party, set out to demand both equality with all other French citizens and a degree of autonomy for elected African legislatures and executives within French Africa. What it did not demand was independence. As its 1946 manifesto declared: "We have taken care to avoid equivocation and not to confuse PROGRESSIVE BUT RAPID AUTONOMY within the framework of the French Union with separatism, that is immediate, brutal, total independence."

After 1947, when the government in France lurched to the right, officials began to crack down on the Ivorian RDA. The administration, fearing that the RDA was becoming a kind of parallel government in some districts – collecting revenue and dispensing justice – provoked clashes with PDCI militants in rural areas. French security harassed the RDA, but they could not break it. Finally, in 1950 François Mitterrand, Minister for Overseas France, negotiated with Houphouët-Boigny for the RDA to end its legislative cooperation with the Communist Party. In return Mitterrand ordered an end to the repression. Each side in this conflict came to understand the limits of its own power. Houphouët-Boigny later took a seat in the French cabinet.

Ever since his early days campaigning against forced labor, Houphouët-Boigny had made use of French institutions and French rhetoric to make demands. He would continue to do so throughout the 1950s, as would Senghor and most other leaders of French Africa. They were frustrated by the French government's insistence on its own controlling role and by disagreements among themselves over what form of a "Franco-African community" they wanted. But their efforts – as with the labor code of 1952 – were successful enough for French leaders to fear that demands for social and economic, as well as political, equality would only escalate, and would confront France with the high cost of a maintaining a more inclusive and egalitarian version of the French empire.

The RDA in Côte d'Ivoire sprang from strong rural roots; in Senegal the RDA was largely urban, and Senghor's BDS, working via rural power brokers, dominated politics in the countryside. In Guinea, Sékou Touré used the union movement – and his leadership of major strikes in the early 1950s – as a springboard to building a territorial political party linked to the RDA, the Parti Démocratique de la Guinée (PDG). He eventually found that expanding beyond his base meant dropping the trade union's way of seeing the world – its quest for equality with French workers – in favor of a language of politics that could appeal to peasants and pastoralists, for whom French life did not represent a meaningful basis of comparison.

These examples illustrate an important point: party organization did not spring automatically from any one social category or from the generalized grievances of the colonized. Some aspirations, such as those of the labor movement, focused on comparison with a French reference point; trade unions campaigned for equality of wages and

FIGURE 7 Women voting in legislative elections in Dakar, Senegal, 1956. These elections, just before the *loi-cadre* devolved many government functions to legislatures in each territory, were an important step toward expanding suffrage and giving the local people more political voice in the internal affairs of each French territory. Keystone-France/Gamma-Keystone/Getty Images

benefits for all French workers. Others rejected the French reference point and looked toward connections that united Africans. A skillful politician such as Senghor could weave together, in some circumstances, different forms of affiliation into a political machine that articulated the aspirations of people who called themselves "African."

Senghor was careful to avoid too sharp a break with the idea of citizenship in an empire, given his success in using French institutions and the French language to claim rights and resources for his constituents. Politics takes work; it implies persuading people to think of linkages they may not have perceived before. Parties such as Senghor's BDS or Houphouët-Boigny's PDCI represented particular social experiences of living in a specific place, but covered over tensions among the people they were meant to represent. The RDA was actually a coalition of diverse parties, but because it operated all over French Africa (Equatorial as well as West) it kept a focus on the inequities of Africa's relationship with France. Houphouët-Boigny's property-owning, export-producing constituency clashed with some of his RDA comrades' leftist, populist outlook, opposed to accommodation with the French government. All of this meant confusion and conflict, but it also constituted real politics: the effort to bring together people with different interests and conceptions of themselves.

The leadership of political movements was male, but activism was not exclusively masculine. In 1944, when the female citizens of France, at long last, were enfranchised, women in Dakar and Saint Louis – where the original inhabitants were citizens – had successfully protested when the government tried to exclude them from the extension of voting rights.

The engagement of women in politics took several forms, including the development of associations such as the Union des Femmes Camerounaises, which, while not directly hostile to the French government, campaigned for equal rights with men, fairer election legislation, better access to education, and social services helpful to mothers. It sent petitions to the United Nations. The Union at times worked with the most radical of the Cameroonian political organizations, but had to put up with the paternalism of its male leaders. In Côte d'Ivoire women were in the thick of the RDA-led demonstrations during its confrontation with the French administration. One of the female Ivorian activists, Macoucou Coulibaly, traveled in 1949 to Beijing to take part in conference of the Fédération Démocratique Internationale des Femmes, opening a link between women activists in French Africa and a worldwide, communist-connected mobilization for the rights of women. Local linkages were equally important, especially as the RDA got into competition with more conservative political parties. Since markets, streets, and courtyards were the sites of confrontation and were privileged spaces for women, RDA women (and their opponents) were involved in shouting matches and fights. But as the RDA and other parties moved closer to power, women, generally less educated and less prominent in trade unions, student organizations, and farmers' associations, were at a disadvantage in the quest for seats in legislative bodies and party or government offices and were more likely to be seen by top leadership as useful auxiliaries rather than as equal members, their causes marked as secondary relative to the quest for liberation and for power.

The political situation was rather different in French Equatorial Africa, but in that region electoral institutions created their own defining logic. This was (at the time) a thinly populated region, first miserably exploited then miserably neglected, with a tiny wage-earning class, a tiny educated minority, and farming communities more detached, less well off, and less capable of making the leap to acting collectively than those of Senegal or Côte d'Ivoire. But the centralizing tendencies of French politics meant that they were part of the same post-war political institutions as other territories and held the same elections on the same day. Politicians tend to fill a vacuum, and they did in places such as Gabon and French Congo. Florence Bernault (1996) argues that social constituencies grew out of politics rather than the reverse: the few people in a position to be candidates for office – because of education, civil service experience, and missionary connections – created rather than mobilized constituencies.

Urban youth played a particularly important role in this process, for they were available, loosely attached to other urban institutions, and trying to find a way in a situation where following their fathers' model of social relations was not the only option. Youth did the door-to-door work of politics, and at times something more muscular than that. The thin communications of French Equatorial Africa meant that chiefdoms, administrative units, and language-cultural groups were weakly cross-cut by trade union affiliation or by the cosmopolitan experience of people with diverse migration patterns, wider religious affiliations, or long trading networks. Politics created its own logic, which was largely ethnic, as inchoate cultural similarity was hammered into group identification by political organization itself.

That France gave particular play to the citizenship concept and to administrative centralization gave certain social groups an opening to claim equality with an affluent European society. It was precisely the Frenchness of colonial society that was painful to other Africans – the pretense to representing civilization, the reduction of African society to either the "primitive" or the delightfully "exotic." Beginning in the early 1950s, the Fédération des Étudiants d'Afrique Noire en France developed a radical critique of French colonialism, which students returning to their homes brought with them, producing considerable anxiety among government officials and the police. But only in the late 1950s would leaders coming out of this movement put themselves before a wider public and participate in electoral politics (Chapter 4).

During most of this decade France appeared to many Africans, particularly those away from centers of economic activity, as a periodically intrusive and oppressive, but otherwise distant, ruler. More people, however, were experiencing the ambiguous consequences of the regime's new-found interest in economic and social development. French colonial education and the increasing need for wage workers gave some Africans a chance to escape from patriarchal authority in their villages; but the city could be a humiliation as well as a liberation. Many Africans operated and made demands within French institutions and rhetorical norms but felt the alienation of the colonized subject.

From today's vantage point, the danger in looking back on the 1940s is the assumption that people should have known that their future was the nation-state; or that they should have seen through the nation-state and celebrated instead the authenticity of African culture and supposedly African forms of politics. But in 1948 or 1949 the cracks in the colonial edifice were opportunities. French institutions and French ideology could be used against French power. In the early 1950s the Senghors and the Houphouët-Boignys tried to turn French citizenship into something meaningful and useful to their constituents, rather than to claim another sort of sovereignty. It is hard to tell whether they – or the more radical critics of all that was French – knew that this was a logic whose time would be short. The labor code of 1952 marked, in one domain, the partial success of this kind of politics.

Self-Government Unbound: The Gold Coast, 1947–51

British officials did not try to legitimize empire by making their colonial subjects into imperial citizens, although in India and the British West Indies, in particular, they faced demands for political and social rights and the right to settle anywhere in the British empire that were in effect a demand to be treated as full-fledged citizens of the British empire. In British Africa the ruling fiction was "self-government": each territory, according to officials, would follow its own path. Unlike the case of French Africa, there would be no representation of Africans in Parliament in London. Before the war, educated elites from different British colonies had sometimes acted together – in the National Congress of British West Africa, for instance. After the war, Great Britain carefully channeled electoral politics into individual territories. It thus avoided making the equivalence of voting rights or the social and economic benefits of inhabitants with those of British citizens such a salient issue, and it provided no institutional framework in which an organization like the RDA could act.

The British Colonial Office in 1947 thought that the Gold Coast was "the territory where Africans are most advanced politically." It had great plans: new investment, more educational opportunities, agricultural improvement. The government, now in the hands of the Labour Party, moved from the old policy of "indirect rule" toward "local government," in which regional councils and educated people from each region would play a strong role. But the Colonial Office was convinced that "internal self-government is unlikely to be achieved in much less than a generation." If one looks beyond the public pronouncements from the top to the secret correspondence of British officials, one sees that in official eyes farmers were backward subsistence cultivators, political leaders were demagogues manipulating unthinking masses, and African participation in their own affairs was a kind of apprenticeship, practicing leadership rather than exercising it. Britain, in 1948, was a long way from having a plan to devolve power.

By 1951 it had been backed into a situation in the Gold Coast where it did just that. Since the late nineteenth century, Gold Coast Africans had been self-consciously debating what kind of political institutions best suited their unique and complex world at the intersection of European and African cultures. J. E. Casely Hayford, a lawyer and journalist, had, as early as 1903, proposed that a federation of coastal peoples could govern themselves within the British empire. Farmers in the Gold Coast had decades of experience with the cultivation and marketing of export crops such as cocoa. Trade unions were familiar with the task of representing the interests of diverse workers. Between 1939 and 1947 the population of the Gold Coast's major towns – Accra, Kumasi, Sekondi-Takoradi, and Cape Coast, increased by 55 percent. Some 45,000 African soldiers ended their wartime service, having joined other subjects of the British empire in a war for freedom that was not truly theirs; on their return many sought to live in cities, facing difficult urban labor markets, housing shortages, and inflation. All city-dwellers confronted consumer-goods shortages and price gouging by monopolistic European importing firms.

In the second half of 1947 the Gold Coast experienced a wave of strikes, strongest among miners and railwaymen. Farmers, although benefiting from favorable cocoa prices, reacted against heavy-handed government attempts to cut out allegedly diseased cocoa trees. Then came a boycott of urban commerce which focused on the sorest spot of all, the acute commodity shortage and galloping inflation. The boycott was organized by Nii Kwabena Bonne II, an Accra chief, a former worker and businessman, the kind of figure cutting across social categories who turns up in populist movements. Africans in Accra, Kumasi, and other cities boycotted European- and Syrian-owned businesses, arguing that their price gouging was responsible for the misery. After a month of conflict the government engineered an agreement under which the firms in question cut their gross overall profit margins.

The boycott ended in February 1948, just when a group of army veterans in Accra, encouraged by the leading political party, the United Gold Coast Convention (UGCC), was planning a protest march against the government's failure to help them find jobs. The undermanned and poorly led police contingent protecting the government headquarters panicked and fired into the marchers, killing several. As the news spread, a riot developed in downtown Accra, directed above all at European-owned shops. Women and men participated in the violence and looting, which spread to other towns. There were more casualties: a total of 29 deaths and 237 injuries over the period of unrest.

The UGCC was moving gingerly toward a more militant direction, and it seized on the riot and the repression. Its second-in-command was now Kwame Nkrumah, whose education in the United States had exposed him to the racism faced by his African-American fellow students and whose time in London had plunged him into leftist, anti-imperialist, and Pan-Africanist circles. The party head, J. B. Danquah, who came from the traditional coastal elite of West Africa, also saw an opening in the situation. The UGCC offered to provide an "interim government" to the Gold Coast, using the same rhetoric about mass disorder as officials and offering themselves as leaders who could restore order. The offer was not appreciated.

The UGCC leadership was using social tension to make self-government into an immediate issue, not a distant goal. It did not mobilize revolutionary action to effect such an end, nor, despite administration fears, did the hotbeds of trade unionism in the mines and railways capitalize on the aftermath of the Accra riots. But colonial issues were now generating international controversy: anti-imperialist groups issued statements, and Africans and West Indians organized a protest meeting in London. British officials took the threat seriously: an Emergency was declared; troops were called in from other colonies; warships were sent to the area; and troops in nearby Nigeria patrolled the streets in case the movement spread.

Officials blamed the riots on disorderly masses and unscrupulous demagogues; they alleged "communist influence." Six leaders of the UGCC, including Danquah and Nkrumah, were detained without charges. In a radio broadcast Governor Creasy insisted that the arrests "are like the quarantine which is imposed on people who have caught a dangerous infectious disease." In London the Colonial Secretary also worried about the dangers of "detribalised urban people." The government would seek "the sympathy and goodwill of responsible and educated elements."

Such dualisms would be heard again and again: the unruly, detribalized Africans, led by demagogues, versus the responsible leader and the respectable population. Officials did not yet realize that their brittle conception of Africa was providing a chance to leaders who could prove that they were popular and claimed to be moderate. Instead of a single mass threat, there was a differentiated society producing a range of political mobilizations. Unions were hesitant and divided on the issue of striking for "political" objectives; unemployed youth were angry; elite professionals were maneuvering for advantage.

The quest for the responsible African politician led colonial officials to appoint a committee to recommend new policies. The Coussey Committee, as it was called, represented as wide a spectrum of moderate, educated African opinion as officials could tolerate. It included five of the UGCC Six, with the conspicuous exception of Nkrumah. The strategy insured two results: the Colonial Office would not be in a position to reject a consensus recommendation of the Coussey Committee; and a recommendation coming from the professional and modernizing Africans on the Committee would focus on constitutional reform and elections as the source of legitimacy. It also gave Nkrumah a position from which to criticize the incomplete nature of proposed reforms. He used the opportunity brilliantly to forge his own support base among urban workers, young men with only a limited education, and other popular (and largely urban) elements. He and his followers eventually broke away from the UGCC to form the Convention People's Party (CPP).

In official eyes, the UGCC turned from the demagogues of 1948 into the moderates of 1949, while the CPP took on the mantle of irresponsibility. Another wave of strikes in 1949 was attributed to Nkrumah's effort to turn labor into "the spear-head of his attack on ordered government." Officials thought the colony was "on the edge of revolution." At the end of 1949 the unions were contemplating a general strike, and Nkrumah was building up support for a campaign of "Positive Action," civil disobedience intended to make it impossible for government to function.

In fact, officials underestimated the extent to which their policy of encouraging trade unions as autonomous bodies devoted to raising wages and other "industrial" issues had succeeded. The union movement was divided over Positive Action. Nkrumah himself vacillated on the subject of a general strike, and the strike, when it came, proved less than general. Seeing its chance, the government arrested Nkrumah for fomenting an illegal strike.

Isolating the demagogues meant accepting the new steps toward devolving legislative and executive power recommended by the Coussey Committee. Otherwise, the British government concluded, "moderate opinion will be alienated and the extremists given an opportunity of gaining further and weightier support and of making serious trouble." But London could not convince the people of the Gold Coast that its moderates were what they wanted. With Nkrumah in jail, the CPP won the legislative election of February 1951. It garnered the overwhelming majority of votes in the cities, where the enthusiasm of workers and of youth was high, but voter registration and turnout were still low. Nkrumah's majority translates into about 30 percent of the voting-age population – not quite the mass mobilization of nationalist myth, but enough to make him the only viable political option.

Nkrumah went almost directly from jail to state house, as Leader of Government Business, a sort of junior prime minister. The next ideological task for the British bureaucracy was to reconstruct Nkrumah, the Apostle of Disorder, as the Man of Moderation and Modernity. By June the Colonial Office was writing about the need "to keep on good terms with the more responsible political leaders such as Mr. Nkrumah." If Great Britain had wanted to keep Nkrumah in jail, ban the CPP, and suppress all trade union activity, it could have. It had put down larger rebellions in Malaya in the late 1940s, and was doing so in Kenya in the early 1950s. But in those situations it had been drawing limits, in the first case against an explicitly communist movement, in the second against an uprising of "primitives" – a misleading perception discussed in Chapter 4. In the Gold Coast the question was, what could it do after the agitation had been put down? Great Britain's legitimacy in the global political climate of the 1950s depended on at least the illusion of orderly political progress. Betting on the moderates seemed more hopeful than shutting down all political activity, but officials could not impose their definition of moderate.

Meanwhile, plans to increase exports and build infrastructure were vulnerable to the actions of organized workers and farmers. The British government thus felt constrained to accept Nkrumah as the most responsible and plausible politician available. He became the head of an African-majority cabinet serving under a British Governor. Officials had become trapped in their own theory of political change as a series of necessary steps and in their need to legitimize their role as teaching democracy. By 1951 the people of the Gold Coast had made it clear whom they wanted to lead them, and British officials had to adjust their political imaginations to the reality before them.

South Africa: Nationalism for Whites and Struggle for Blacks

South Africa was not quite in a colonial situation – so much the worse for its black population. White South Africans were citizens of their own country, not people living "somewhere else." Many traced their ancestry to Dutch immigrants from the seventeenth century. Once farmers, cattle owners, or rural traders, many now worked in gold mines or industry; they called themselves Afrikaners. Other immigrants came from Great Britain or continental Europe, and new waves were attracted by the mineral revolution after the 1880s. In colonies, the state was something of an abstraction; the people who represented it came and went. The state in South Africa existed in a very human – and very inhumane – form. Most importantly, white South Africans voted.

South African capitalism also had a more down-to-earth existence than elsewhere on the continent. The bulk of South African land – some 87 percent – was designated for ownership by whites, and very few Africans had access to commercially viable land. From the 1890s a proletariat was born, albeit a racially constructed one, still linked to "reserves," where families stayed and eked out a below-subsistence living while young men ventured to gold mines and urban areas under the watchful eyes of white employers and white policemen, who enforced a strict control over migration.

Africans fought hard to find niches in the system, and they forged a more viable urban culture than most whites knew about. But the simultaneous presence of a strong state, powerful mining companies with draconian control over the "compounds" where single men lived, white bosses on farms, in shops, and in households who directly supervised black labor, and a system of ethnically structured "reserves" where government-backed chiefs exercised arbitrary authority constituted an apparatus of control over African populations that went beyond anything found elsewhere on the continent. By the 1940s this system, far from being a throwback to bygone notions of white supremacy, was fostering industrialization and urbanization.

But it was not without contradictions and conflict. In some urban neighborhoods, such as Sophiatown in Johannesburg, Africans became permanent residents, with access to property. Lively urban cultures developed, and because of back-and-forth migration urban culture increasingly influenced rural Africans. Meanwhile, relatively extensive mission education and the economy's need for literate African workers produced a segment of the population as aware as their West African counterparts of worldwide trends in political thought. The Garvey movement had been influential in South Africa, as were African-American missionaries. This social complexity contributed to different political currents: a liberal view of politics oriented toward constitutional reform, a Christian vision of social justice, urban labor militance, and different forms of African nationalism.

The spurt in industrialization during World War II augmented the demand for urban labor. Industrial capitalists generally supported expanding – selectively – the rights of Africans to live in cities, hoping for a more flexible labor market and less turnover. Gold-mining magnates were content to preserve a migratory system of labor, including the balancing of recruitment within South Africa and controlled immigration from outside. White farmers opposed the loosening of control over migration, fearing that their workers would rather take their chances in cities than face the predictable misery of agricultural labor. White workers feared competition.

Meanwhile, there was cultural and intellectual conflict among white South Africans. Afrikaner ideologues, anchored in a fraternal order, the Broederbond, as well as the Dutch Reformed Church, observed their group's increasing success in an industrial society, but feared that Afrikaners were losing their moral vision. The National Party (NP), which garnered most Afrikaners' votes, was unequivocal in its defense of white political domination but pragmatic in its thinking about implementing it. The party was doing its best to reconcile the various demands of its constituents, and it was not inhibited by the agonized reflection about self-determination and egalitarian values that beset certain wartime and post-war empires. Some leading Afrikaners had, on the contrary, been sympathetic to Nazi racial thinking. South Africans of British origin, or descendants of immigrants from elsewhere in Europe, were more likely to value their connection to the British empire and see themselves as more cosmopolitan, without necessarily opposing the existing racial order.

All of this came to a head in the 1948 election. The United Party (UP), although close to big capital and English speakers, was led by an Afrikaner, Jan Smuts. The UP was aware of political ferment elsewhere in the continent, and it favored a flexible policy of urban migration and residence and a "native" policy that was paternalist, pragmatic, and no real compromise from principles of white supremacy. The NP articulated a strong defense of Afrikaner culture and a restrictive vision of African participation in the economy; it was favorable to the interests of farmers and small businessmen, less so to big business. The Nationalists and their allies narrowly won the 1948 election and over the ensuing years tightened their grip on an African population that was increasingly restive politically.

The basic tools of what the Nationalists called apartheid ("separateness") had long ago been put in place, and not particularly by Afrikaners. But these measures were now used more rigorously. Massive expulsions from urban areas occurred, although a divide-and-rule strategy implied important distinctions between those Africans entitled to live in cities and those officially consigned to miserable rural reserves. Many Africans moved illegally between reserve and urban jobs, with frequent stops in prison.

Until the mid-1950s women were not covered by the pass laws, and their ability to establish themselves in cities constituted a weak spot in the mechanisms of apartheid. Their presence helped make urban life and family formation possible for men as well. Controlling women was thus one of the central preoccupations of government planners, and the attempts to impose pass laws on women led in turn to widespread mobilizations, boycotts, and marches by women, including a dramatic march on Parliament in 1956 in which women came from far afield to present petitions to the government. The state eventually got its way, and the "endorsing out" of many women from cities separated families and rendered women in impoverished rural areas increasingly vulnerable. But many women persisted in finding niches within the illegal urban economy, and others remained activists in the townships, both trying to bring a measure of stability to township life and fighting apartheid.

The state's repressive action criminalized much of urban family life; being jailed for violation of pass and residency laws was an ordinary experience. The state inadvertently contributed to the emergence within cities of an alienated and often violent youth culture, as well as organized gangs that both preyed upon and drew support from young men caught between the vitality of urban life and the increasing impossibility of providing for a family.

Social and political mobilization among black South Africans reveals important parallel developments to the rest of the continent as well as an awareness of events elsewhere in Africa. The wave of strikes that hit much of Africa in the 1940s was particularly powerful in South Africa, notably with numerous strikes in the city of Durban and a giant gold-mine strike in 1946. In the Johannesburg area "squatter invasions" were frequent, and between 1944 and 1950 somewhere between 60,000 and 90,000 South Africans organized themselves into bands, seized a piece of vacant land somewhere in the peri-urban sprawl, built their shacks as quickly as possible, and defended themselves against police raids. Their actions went against the efforts of the state to build planned, segregated cities and gave rise to a combative political culture within certain encampments. The state's efforts to build fenced-in African townships at some distance from cities – the most notorious being Soweto (for South Western Townships) outside Johannesburg – reflected as much a response to African collective action as a grand design of apartheid.

In other South African cities, relatively settled working-class communities expanded in the 1940s, and in some of them the Communist Party of South Africa (CPSA) made headway by concentrating on immediate issues: residential rights, transportation, and housing. The CPSA was banned in 1950, and many of its activists committed themselves to the African National Congress (ANC), but in a certain moment the party brought together African trade unionists, white radicals, and activists in the African locations, helping to push the ANC into greater concern with the plight of working-class Africans. The ANC remained committed, as it had been since its founding in 1912, to building a multiracial South Africa in which no category of people would be discriminated against.

But politics moved beyond the petitions and constitutional claims characteristic of the pre-war ANC and toward strikes, boycotts, "stay-aways," and other forms of collective action that ultimately depended on getting a large number of people to act together at considerable risk to themselves. Political coherence was affected by tensions between Africans strongly rooted in urban culture and those more closely connected to rural areas. Yet migration brought the effects of urban radicalism to rural districts too, catalyzing, for example, the Sekhukhuneland revolt of 1958 against oppressive government land and agricultural schemes and chiefs who cooperated with them.

The trend toward urban and industrial life remained strong in the 1950s, and the long-term effect of apartheid regulations restricting migration was to degrade rural conditions and encourage new waves of urban migration. The state was constantly trying to disrupt community building among Africans, and from the 1950s to the 1980s ruthlessly "removed" people from some places, especially city locations, and put them in others, especially state-run townships or barren settlements in rural "homelands."

The long presence of mission schools in rural South Africa meant that a significant number of Africans acquired a decent education. Fort Hare University in the Transkei developed out of mission schools, and through its doors around the 1940s passed future leaders of the struggle against apartheid, notably Nelson Mandela (who was expelled) and Oliver Tambo, as well as people who served the apartheid regime's system of homeland administration, such as Kaiser Matanzima (first President of the Transkei).

A new tendency, typical of the generational transitions in Africa in these years, emerged from the 1940s among better-educated South Africans. This became known as "Africanism," associated with leaders such as Anton Lembede. It emphasized the integrity and value of African culture, and above all the militance that lay within it – if only it could be mobilized. Africans were not just victims of injustice; they were agents of a national future. This Africanist tendency influenced the ANC's Youth League. Nelson Mandela himself came out of the

Youth League into the main part of the ANC. In the late 1940s Africanism did more to give a shot in the arm to the ANC than to create a separate movement.

Both the communist and Africanist tendencies drew on and contributed to an increasingly politicized urban culture. The ANC's "programme of action" in 1949 emphasized demonstrations and civil disobedience. This strategy was pushed further in the "defiance campaign" of 1950–52, in which ANC supporters massively violated segregation laws and courted arrest. Boycotts and stay-aways were organized. Women's groups also became active. At the national level this pattern included the ANC's Women's League, but it ran up against a tendency of the male leadership to treat gender issues as secondary to the struggle for national liberation. Women's organizations, however, were forceful within townships, where women's roles in daily life led their associations to take the lead in actions concerning housing, bus fares, beer halls, and pass laws.

Militance invigorated the ANC, whose membership jumped from 4,000 to 100,000 in the early 1950s. The ANC's increasing forcefulness went along with its continued emphasis on democratic participation, the rule of law, and mulitiracialism, while socialist ideals of economic and social justice and equality were becoming more visible. The 1955 Freedom Charter embodied these principles. The South African government counterattacked in 1956 by indicting 156 ANC members and their allies for treason, a prosecution that tied up the movement for years before ultimately failing. In 1958 the Africanist tendency that had influenced the ANC in the 1940s split off to form the Pan-Africanist Congress (PAC), with Robert Sobukwe and other leaders criticizing the ANC for cooperating with non-Africans. It found in the success of African nationalism elsewhere on the continent a model for a movement for a South Africa that would be truly African.

The most striking difference between South Africa and the colonial empires to its north was the ruling fiction of each power. By the late 1940s Britain and France – and the other empires to a notably lesser degree – were pretending that Africans could be made into "modern" men and women, that they should no longer be kept in their tribal cages. The post-1948 South African government, however, carried to an extreme the idea that Africans existed in their peculiar cultures, that these differences were essential and unbreachable, and that a political system could be organized to keep them that way. South

Africa excluded blacks from citizenship and pretended that their lives should remain centered on tribal homelands, not in the national space that their labor was enriching.

South African industry and its white population prospered as did no other industry or population group in Africa. Whether this was because of or in spite of apartheid has been much debated. The devastating effects of apartheid on African family life are without question, as is the vehemence with which individuals and collective organizations struggled both against the system and to find ways to survive within it. For a long time the apartheid state was strong enough to contain opposition. But the seeds of apartheid's unraveling were already present in the 1950s, in an African urban culture that could not be tamed and a political leadership and organization able to demonstrate to the rest of the continent and the world that they – not the white rulers – represented the values of democracy and the rule of law that the "West" thought it stood for.

Militance in Different Keys: Pan-Africanists and Prophets

Let us stand back from these tales of specific territories to look at a possibility that was shunted aside in the immediate post-war years. One might have thought, at this moment, that Pan-Africanism's time had come: the war against Nazi racism gave plausibility to a critique of imperialism based on the principles of imperial governments them- selves. Pan-Africanist leaders did not fail to seek public attention. That Pan-Africanism did not become the primary organizing principle of post-war politics has much to do with the processes described previously in the cases of the Gold Coast and French West Africa. The political imagination of leaders in each colonial territory was captured by a process that seemed to be going somewhere, which bit by bit conceded to Africans the possibility of entering institutions capable of exercising real authority over the territories in which they lived. Pan-Africanism had opened a much wider dialogue about the meaning of race and oppression and of liberation and solidarity, but it had not developed a clear vision of what sort of institutions would supplant the colonial state.

At the end of the war George Padmore took the lead in organizing a new Pan-African Congress in 1945, with the involvement of past and future leaders such as W. E. B. Du Bois and Nkrumah and an

impressive array of activists from Africa, the Caribbean, and North
America. The congress, held in Manchester in England, aimed to
make the elimination of imperialism and the reconstruction of Africa
part of the post-war agenda. The Manchester resolutions condemned
the oppressiveness of colonial institutions, the "regression" induced
by economic and social policies, the inadequacy of the "pretentious
constitutional reforms" of Britain and France, and indirect rule's
"encroachment on the right of the West African natural rulers." They
affirmed the principles of the Four Freedoms and the Atlantic Charter
articulated by American and British leaders, calling for an end to racial
discrimination, educational and economic reforms, and elections with
universal suffrage. But they were not specific about what sort of
political units would govern themselves, what the role of "natural"
leaders would be in an electoral process, and least of all how Africans
could get from here to there.

Nonetheless, this was a basis on which to build. The trouble was
that other edifices were being built more rapidly – less visionary, more
compromised, but offering African politicians concrete benefits.
To win an election to a territorial or imperial legislative body was to
obtain a platform from which to speak, and possibly dispense patronage, hence the opportunity of enlisting supporters.

Pan-Africanism was one of several ways in which African organizations looked beyond individual territories. African unions, meanwhile,
worked within international trade union organizations, notably the
leftist World Federation of Trade Unions, to link their demands for
equal wages, for the end of oppressive colonialist legislation, and for
fuller recognition of collective bargaining to a worldwide movement.
Anti-communist trade unionists in the United States and Great Britain felt obliged to counter this form of labor internationalism by
promoting their own trade union organizations in Africa and elsewhere, the International Confederation of Free Trade Unions, and
African activists found that this organization, too, would support them
in clashes with colonial administrations.

In rural areas a variety of mobilizations were being made, from
attempts to solidify the power of chiefs who could represent people in
large regional groupings to efforts by farmers to demand fairer prices
for their crops. Often, the first or second generation of Western-
educated people attempted to weave together – in local publications,
mission journals, and other forums – their knowledge of "traditional"
myths and local histories with their command of written language to

foster coherence and self-consciousness within a given area, strengthening ethnic solidarities, which in turn could be used by political parties to mobilize.

Developmentalist colonialism was confronted with a variety of forms of rural mobilization. When colonial agricultural agents in the 1940s cajoled and coerced African farmers into following what officials regarded as proper techniques for cultivating the soil – disregarding the social and spiritual implications of entering a domain of land, rain, and people – tensions mounted. In a hilly region of Tanganyika, Steven Feierman's research (1990) has revealed, the post-war agricultural development regime clumsily intruded into the way people conceived of their relationship to the environment. The Shambaa people linked the idea of spiritual health to the well-being of the land. Religious figures were concerned with rainmaking and above all else with balance and harmony: good relations among people were indicative of good relations with nature, and vice versa.

The peasant movement that countered the agricultural agents stressed the harm that was being done to the land, meaning that social relations as well as food production were being damaged. Chiefs who collaborated with the British were criticized for failing as rainmakers, for their inability to intervene with the supernatural to assure the welfare of the community. Feierman argues that the movement was led by "peasant intellectuals," men with some primary education but who remained farmers and were firmly entrenched in their local communities.

This is an instance of a discourse focused within an ethnic group and using a local idiom. But not entirely. Some peasant leaders constituted themselves as the Ushambaa Citizens Union after comparing notes with a citizens' union formed in another locality, and some years later the movement began to work with the Tanganyika African National Union (TANU), the leading nationalist formation that had begun among city-dwellers and teachers. TANU, like other parties, expanded by convincing people in many localities, rural as well as urban, that the colonial state was the common denominator of their grievances. This pattern of political mobilization that drew upon both "African" and "European" idioms and local and regional connections was found in many other parts of rural Africa. But the two idioms could also be in tension with one another. Values of democracy, openness to individual ambition and initiative, and equality in all its dimensions did not necessarily resonate in societies where respect for elders, patriarchy, and hierarchical relationships had been the basis of a world in which people were at peace with the land and with the ancestors. Whether the tensions would clash or be creatively bridged depended both on the initiative of particular leaders and whether they could produce something to show for their efforts.

Religious affinity, whether Christian, Muslim, or otherwise, often crossed lines of ethnicity (Chapter 2). It is tempting to see religious movements in rural and urban Africa in the late 1940s and early 1950s through the lens of nationalist hindsight, and conclude that religious autonomy, assertion, and organization created both networks that had political implications and a feeling of solidarity that was a precedent for political assertiveness. But does such a conception do justice to the history of religious movements in the 1940s and 1950s?

In the Belgian Congo a Christian messianic movement, partly repressed since the 1920s, took on a new vigor after 1947. Simon Kimbangu, educated by Protestant missionaries, had proclaimed himself a healer and acquired a large following among Bakongo around 1920. Arrested in 1921, he spent the next thirty years in prison, until his death behind bars in 1951. One of his sons and some of his followers, literate and educated, acquired positions close to important officials in the civil service. Secretly, they helped to keep Kimbanguism alive, especially after the leader himself died. Kimbanguism, with its stress on healing, its melding of Christianity with a sense of Bakongo uniqueness, and its sense that the importance of the cult exceeded that of the state or the officially sanctioned Catholic Church, was perceived by officials as a threat.

Elsewhere in the Congo, especially in the copper-mining area that overlapped with British Northern Rhodesia, a movement called Kitawala flourished. This, too, had earlier roots, and it spread throughout this zone of intense labor migration and back-and-forth, cross-ethnic, cross-border movement in Central Africa. It was an offshoot of the Jehovah's Witnesses, carrying with it a Christian messianic vision while adapting to varied religious practices in the area, including the identification of evil with the workings of witches. Adherents believed that the triumph of good over evil would come from the outside, sometimes in the form of African Americans sweeping into Africa in airplanes and driving out whites, a belief no doubt reflecting the influence of the Garvey movement. Belgian authorities, like the British, detested the Witnesses and Kitawala not because they espoused rebellion against the state, but because they proclaimed the irrelevance of both the authority of chiefdom and tradition on which colonial power had long depended and the state's newer developmentalist vision. Such religious movements, despite the repression, appealed to many Africans in the cities and the countryside, and, as movement back and forth accelerated after the war, they kept open, for people living between different cultural and moral orders, an inclusive form of belief and a fervid vision of a future devoid of the tensions of the present.

In the post-war years, Luise White (2000) discovered, rumors of vampirism spread across wide stretches of East and Central Africa. Firemen, ambulance drivers, forest rangers, and other Africans – usually skilled men working with Europeans and with vehicles or other kinds of technologies – were accused of kidnapping people, hiding them in vehicles, taking their blood, and leaving them dead. Unlike witchcraft accusations, usually found within the tense intimacy of kin and villagers, vampire stories were boundary crossing. More complex than a metaphor for capitalist extraction, vampirism appears as a marker of tensions over Africans' participation in non-localized economic processes, over new forms of knowledge not accessible to most people, and over new kinds of objects whose power was difficult to understand in local terms.

Other religious leaders focused on healing. Just outside Salisbury in Rhodesia, a woman named Mai Chaza built a community of believers in her healing powers and in a mixture of indigenous and Christian conceptions of morality and collectivity. In rural Rhodesia shrines and cults spread widely in the countryside. The networks of spirit mediums would one day help guerrilla leaders mobilize support, but in the 1950s they provided people subject to a harshly oppressive regime with a means of expressing a social and spiritual affinity among themselves. Independent Christian churches flourished in rural central Kenya, while certain Kikuyu prophets were revered as pointing the way to a new order, combining messianic visions with a specifically Kikuyu sensibility.

In West African cities, where migrants from northern parts of West Africa became increasingly numerous in the post-war era, spirit-possession cults became increasingly important. By seeing themselves as possessed by spirits specific to the modern city, rural migrants with limited experience of urban life (unlike their well-established neighbors) created spaces to imagine new forms of participation in social life. In other parts of Africa women could make demands in the name of a spirit which possessed them, thus gaining influence within the household without overtly challenging patriarchal assumptions.

This interplay of religious organization and secular politics could take a radical form, as it eventually did in central Kenya, or a quite moderate one, as did the Islamic brotherhoods in Senegal. It could focus on particular municipalities (Salisbury) or entire regions (the Copperbelt). It could provide solace or channel anger. Religious movements deserve to be analyzed in their own terms, as spiritual communities, as attempts to give moral anchorage to people crossing cultural and moral boundaries, and as innovative syntheses of a range of doctrinal and ritual practices. The older interpretations that see autonomous religious organizations as a substitute for or precursor of political parties have a point, but they miss the multiple dynamics that play out over time. What is above all important to grasp is the ferment and sense of possibility of the post-war decade.

The Limits of Modernizing Imperialism

The multiple forms of political and social mobilization in post-war Africa were not confronting a static colonialism but a moving target. France and Great Britain were trying to relegitimize colonial rule, to increase African political participation in a controlled way, and to give Africans a stake in expanding production within the imperial economy.

South Africa, expanding economically as it escalated repression in the 1950s, marked another – overtly exclusionary – vision of development in the post-war era. Economically weak Portugal built its own repressive version of the developmentalist colonial state in Mozambique, Angola, and Guinea-Bissau. Portugal had depended on foreign capital, especially British, to develop plantations and factories in its territories, and much of the post-war effort depended on bringing in whites from Portugal to make up the middle and lower middle levels of enterprises. Africans were largely excluded from whatever benefits economic growth bestowed. Portugal's white citizens, let alone its African subjects, had little political voice – it was ruled by the dictators Salazar and Caetano from 1926 until 1974 – and its leaders did not worry about how to justify ruling over others. That Africans should organize themselves, in trade unions or political parties, was unthinkable.

In Belgium's vast colony, the Congo, a mining corporation forged what seemed the epitome of capitalist order and progress. The copper-mining complex was huge and tightly run, and from the 1920s the company managers accepted that Africans were coming to the mine towns to stay. Its version of stabilization pre-dated the British and French ones, although it flagged during the depression of the 1930s. After the war the Belgian Congo experienced economic growth and urbanization, and its government actively sought to control urban space, improving health and other social services. But it would not tolerate trade unions or political organization.

The Belgian government had never had the resources to develop its vast domain, and it had granted "concessions" to corporations to exercise governmental as well as economic functions in large areas. The Congo was a hodgepodge of zones of mineral and agricultural exploitation and zones of neglect, except for labor recruitment. Even by colonial standards it was highly disarticulated. In some domains Belgium was the most socially interventionist of colonizers: it established childbirth centers, midwife training, and orphanages, and tried to shape how Congolese women took care of their children. But there was little effort to provide post-primary education or to give Africans entrée into professional activities, the civil service, or local politics.

France and Great Britain, for all their interest in economic and political change, made clear the limits of their reformative effort. Even when the African standard of living became the stated goal of development policy, European commercial and mining enterprises remained an important, and privileged, part of the picture. If, as in Côte d'Ivoire, white farmers sometimes faded from view behind the success of African counterparts, in other instances, as in Kenya or especially the Rhodesias, white settlers tried to place their own role at the center of regional economic development. They also invoked the concepts of citizenship and self-determination to claim for themselves a role, even a dominant one, in the political process, and used their position to keep African claims to citizenship and self-determination at bay. In British Rhodesia and, most notoriously, in French Algeria, colonial governments lacked the will to counter such moves, with disastrous results (see Chapter 6 on the Rhodesian case).

French leaders thought that the citizenship law of 1946 epitomized their enlightened outlook, but when the unfairness of having each colonial deputy represent vastly more citizens than each metropolitan deputy was pointed out in the Paris legislature, a deputy replied that it had to be this way, or else France would become the "colony of its former colonies." Senghor, also a deputy, replied that such an argument was racist. It was important that an African deputy could be in a position to say this and that an accusation of racism in an imperial institution carried weight. But there never really was a question of equal representation, for exactly the reason the white deputy had advanced.

British leaders, from near the end of the war, talked a great deal about bringing responsible politicians into positions where they would learn their craft. Yet in the Gold Coast, Nigeria, Kenya, and elsewhere it seemed to them as if all the political activists were irresponsible demagogues. Trade unionism was, from the 1940s, officially encouraged; trade unionists were almost invariably found to be flawed. Officials most often expressed their view of African progress in the language of tutelage: Africans were all young men who needed to be taken under the wing of kindly but firm schoolmasters.

Such limits of citizenship, self-government, and development were, however, not the prerogative of French or British rulers to set. No one exposed this more clearly than Nkrumah, the epitome in British eyes of the dangerous demagogue, who put together a movement sufficiently strong that there was no viable alternative to its claim to govern. The British reinvention of Nkrumah as a responsible leader reveals the importance of political imagination in the decolonization process. It had to be imaginable to the British that a Nkrumah could preside over a self-governing colony, just as it had to be imaginable to the people of the Gold Coast that the colonial territory was the unit on which they could focus their political efforts and get something in return.

The other side of the limit-setting process was the way in which certain groups, individuals, and political tendencies were excluded from the politically imaginable. Even if colonial governments were constrained, they could in the end draw lines, and in some cases make them stick. In Madagascar in 1947 – a year after the French citizenship law, and the year in which a vast railway strike in West Africa was handled cautiously by French authorities – a rebellion broke out. The government insisted that demagogues, including some who sat in the French legislature, had stirred up the primitive masses. Settler farms were burned and settlers killed; officials lost control of parts of the island. It was true that political activists were trying to dynamize the – now legal – electoral politics. To the government, it was not a question of overlapping forms of collective action, but of irresponsible politicians conspiring to set off an insurrection. The self-consciously reformist Colonial Minister and Governor-General orchestrated a brutal repression of the rebellion. Estimates of fatalities vary, but upward of 20,000 now seems the most reliable figure: agriculture was disrupted; and the trauma of 1947 is still in the minds of Malagasy today.

Some years later the French government would also draw the line against a political movement in Cameroon that was too leftist and spoke too early about independence, while in Kenya the British government would banish from the political scene a movement that rejected the modernizing framework of post-colonialism, dragging along with that movement other radical and moderate political forces – but only for a time (Chapter 4). As with Nkrumah, the image of Kenyan leader Jomo Kenyatta would have to be transformed from a force of "darkness" into a spokesman for moderation and British–African economic cooperation. These are themes to which I will return. A Senghor, a Houphouët-Boigny, or a Nkrumah could make use of the very terms in which colonial regimes defined danger – African primitiveness, the specter of communism – to widen a space of "moderation." Colonial rulers, in the post-war decade, knew that they needed to associate themselves with Africans' own aspirations for progress if they were to make their exercise of power in Africa legitimate and effective. In the end, leaders such as Nkrumah and others showed that they were indispensable to help France and Great Britain find a way out of their imperial engagements.

A full bibliography for this book may be found on the website of Cambridge University Press at www.cambridge.org/CooperAfrica2ed.

Bibliography

Austin, Dennis. *Politics in Ghana, 1946–1960*. London: Oxford University Press, 1964.

Bernault, Florence. *Démocraties ambiguës en Afrique Centrale: Congo-Brazzaville, Gabon: 1940–1965*. Paris: Karthala, 1996.

Bonner, Philip, Peter Delius, and Deborah Posel, eds. *Apartheid's Genesis, 1935–1962*. Johannesburg: Ravan, 1993.

Bouilly, Emmanuelle, and Ophélie Rillon, eds. "Femmes africaines et mobilisations collectives (années 1940–1970)," special issue of *Le Mouvement Social* 255 (2016).

Cooper, Frederick. *Citizenship between Empire and Nation: Remaking France and French Africa, 1945–1960*. Princeton: Princeton University Press, 2014.

Decolonization and African Society: The Labor Question in French and British Africa. Cambridge: Cambridge University Press, 1996.

Feierman, Steven. *Peasant Intellectuals: Anthropology and History in Tanzania.* Madison: University of Wisconsin Press, 1990.

Posel, Deborah. *The Making of Apartheid, 1948–1961: Conflict and Compromise.* Oxford: Clarendon Press, 1991.

Ross, Robert, Anne Kelk Mager, and Bill Nasson, eds. *The Cambridge History of South Africa Volume 2: 1885–1994.* Cambridge: Cambridge University Press, 2011.

Vaillant, Janet. *Black, French, and African: A Life of Léopold Sédar Senghor.* Cambridge, MA: Harvard University Press, 1990.

van Onselen, Charles. *The Seed Is Mine: The Life of Kas Maine, a South African Sharecropper, 1894–1985.* New York: Hill & Wang, 1996.

White, Luise. *Speaking with Vampires: Rumor and History in Colonial Africa.* Berkeley: University of California Press, 2000.

CHAPTER 4

Ending Empire and Imagining the Future

French and British rule in Africa collapsed not because of an all-out assault from a clearly defined colonized people, but because African political and social movements opened wider internal cracks in the imperial system. Those movements were demanding not just a political voice, but decent conditions of life, whether within a reformed French or British structure or through the creation of new, independent states. Africans turned the measures intended to reconcile them to colonial rule into escalating demands that made the colonial system untenable. Portuguese and Belgian rulers, and the whites who dominated South Africa, were in the mid-1950s and early 1960s holding onto political power and appropriating economic gains for a tiny fraction of the population. However, they were slowly moving from being ordinary members of an international club where colonialism was the norm to being outliers in a new world where legitimacy was measured in terms of progress toward self-government and economic development (Chapter 6). In the long run, while neither Portugal, Belgium, nor South Africa could contain the pressures coming from neighboring territories or from the transformation of international norms, it was the colonialism that identified itself with political reform and economic development that first came apart.

What was not clear in the decade after World War II was how much either Britain and France or African political movements could define the extent and limits of change. Nor was it clear what African leaders who were gaining a measure of power would do with the opportunities they had. French and British governments on the one hand and

African movements and leaders on the other struggled with and
occasionally fought each other, and ended up defining a certain kind
of decolonization, one which opened up some political possibilities
and shut down others. Supra-national possibilities – federations and
Pan-Africanist imaginings – were in the end excluded from the
political map.

Redefining Political Space

By the early 1950s citizenship was proving to be a powerful construct
in French Africa, seized by African social and political movements to
claim all of the equivalence that being French implied. Self-
government in British West Africa was exploding out of the confines
in which the Colonial Office had hoped to keep it. How wide was the
opening, and how did Nkrumah's and Senghor's generation wish to
fill and expand it?

The agenda for the new political class owed something to the post-
war agenda of British and French colonial rule, but it was taken in a
new direction. The development project, to colonial administrators,
implied that the possessors of knowledge and capital would slowly but
generously disperse these critical resources to those less well endowed.
But to African political parties, development meant resources to build
constituencies and opportunities to make a state they controlled into a
meaningful part of people's lives. In the Gold Coast and Nigeria the
politics of development began with marketing boards, particularly in
cocoa. As noted earlier, British governments in West Africa had put
these institutions in place as the sole purchasers of export crops from
African farmers, first to placate African opposition to the European
businesses that had monopolized such trade, then to use as a source of
development funds, to be doled out (or accumulated) as British officials thought wise. The CPP in the Gold Coast and the Action Group
in Western Nigeria (the cocoa-producing region) quite accurately saw
the surpluses held by these boards by the late 1940s as a source of
development funding, and British arguments that too-rapid spending
of the surpluses would cause inflation were seen, with reason, as self-
serving.

As Leader of Government Business from 1951, Nkrumah was in a
position to manage development in a new way. But he did not choose
to change a crucial element of British policy: maintaining government

control of marketing-board surpluses. The farmer continued to get only a fraction of the world price; the government now used it more actively than had the British to promote government development initiatives. These took the forms of schools and roads – highly visible to a voting constituency – and industrialization, increasingly seen in the 1950s as the answer to economic dependence. The biggest industrial project backed by Nkrumah was originally a British one: building a dam on the Volta River to supply electricity to a hopefully industrializing economy and to power the smelting of the territory's bauxite into aluminum, making it a more valuable export and reducing dependence on cocoa.

Kwame Nkrumah told his followers, "Seek ye first the political kingdom." He captured the imagination of a wide range of followers, who now saw in the building of an African nation a means to combine their personal ambition and idealistic goals, free of the constraints of colonial authority and an inward-looking traditional elite.

Nkrumah's national focus quickly led to serious political conflict with Gold Coast Africans who advocated regional autonomy and a less centralized, federal state. People in the Asante region were not only conscious of the former power of the Asante kingdom, but were among the leading cocoa growers and hence the most affected by the state's confiscatory policies toward cocoa wealth. Such revenue was vital to Nkrumah's national ambitions and, equally important, wealth in Asante hands constituted a danger to those ambitions, for such people were not dependent on the state for resources and were capable of financing political movements.

Asante nationalism, organized into a political party, the National Liberation Movement (NLM), was itself torn between a conservative elite – close to the leading chiefs who had exercised administrative power under the British system of indirect rule – and younger men who saw themselves as nationalists and modernizers and identified "the nation" with the Asante people. Some NLM leaders, such as Joseph Appiah, had been early supporters of Nkrumah but had come to fear that his centralizing thrust was the harbinger of a dictatorial one and that Asante were likely to be its victims. The movement oscillated between a focus on parliamentary action and constitutional change on the one hand and violence on the other.

The British government pretended to referee the contest, but protecting minority rights was not its priority. The NLM, for its part, was both divided and unable to convince people from other regions that it represented something other than Asante privilege. The CPP won elections in 1954 and 1956.

Nkrumah's effort to preclude alternatives to his power went beyond Asante. Chiefs throughout the country were stripped of effective power, replaced by CPP loyalists or co-opted into the CPP fold. Labor leaders, who had been critical of Nkrumah's rise to power, were brought into a CPP-controlled union federation or else marginalized; the militant railway and mining unions were kept in check. Cocoa farmers, outside as well as inside the Asante region, were given little alternative but to market crops through state agencies and participate in CPP-dominated farmers' associations.

But Nkrumah captured the imagination of a wide range of Africans; he understood their dislike of colonial rule, their sense that Africa's time had come, and their belief that a new, African state could improve the lives of its citizens. In 1957 the Gold Coast became independent, and Nkrumah renamed it Ghana, after an old African empire that had been located to the north of the present territory – claiming the legitimacy of African power of another age without privileging any community within the territory. The festivities were exuberant; the joy palpable. One of Nkrumah's first acts as the head of an independent state was to ban all political parties organized on a regional basis – including the NLM.

In Nigeria, Africa's most populous country, the quest for state resources had important consequences for regional conflict from the early 1950s. The British government had divided Nigeria into three regions, Eastern, Western, and Northern, and its vision of the future was of a Nigerian federation presiding over three regional governments that would retain substantial legislative power. This structure had the effect of encouraging first a winner-takes-all quest for electoral power within each of the three regions, and then competition among the regions for power at the federal level. The civil service was regionalized in 1953: each region would control its bureaucracy and hence its patronage resources. But the three regions were not equivalent. The north was the most populous, but had the weakest educational system and was firmly ruled by a traditionalist, Muslim elite. The west, thanks to cocoa, was the wealthiest, and the capital city, Lagos, was within its borders. The east and west had the best-educated population. Easterners were particularly prominent in clerical or skilled labor jobs in Lagos and in northern cities.

In each region a party dominated by members of the majority ethnic group obtained office and used it to provide services and

FIGURE 8 Campaign rally of Nnamdi Azikiwe, Nigeria, 1959. Azikiwe was president of the National Council of Nigeria and the Cameroons, the leading political party in the Eastern Region of Nigeria, and he was premier of the region. When Nigeria became independent in 1960 the NCNC would be in a relatively weak position in the federal government, although Azikiwe became the country's President, a relatively ceremonial role. Eliot Elisofon. EEPA EECL 1666. Eliot Elisofon Photographic Archives, National Museum of African Art, Smithsonian Institution

patronage within its bailiwick: the National Council of Nigeria and the Cameroons (NCNC), with its largely Igbo leadership, in the east; the largely Yoruba Action Group (AG) in the west; and the Hausa–Fulani-led Northern People's Congress (NPC) in the north. The regional governments soon competed with each other to show who could deliver the most to constituents, and what voters, at least outside of the north, wanted above all was schools. Universal primary education became the goal in the eastern and western regions.

In each region, opposition developed, to some extent (notably in the north) as populist challenges to governing elites, but most importantly among communities that came to be classified as "minorities." Each majority party had its patronage system and occasionally used thuggery to maintain its control. The instability was greatest in the west, partly because of the ambiguous position of the federal capital Lagos, in and not of its region, and partly because of intense rivalries among Yoruba factions. Leaders of ethnic groups living near the border between eastern and western regions struggled with the label "minority" attached to them on both sides of the border and sought without success to have a new region carved out. The system encouraged corruption in each region, but Nigeria's agricultural exports in the 1950s were sufficient to allow politicians to play their patronage games while real progress was made in building educational institutions within each region. The NCNC was the most nationally focused of the parties, in part because easterners lived in all of the regions. The NPC was the most conservative, because of its domination by a hierarchy descended from the Muslim rulers of the nineteenth century.

Instead of allowing a wide variety of interest-groups to make claims on the Nigerian state, the federal system focused power on the three regions, each governed by a party dominated by members of a single ethnic group and with the budgetary means to solidify its regional constituency. This structure fostered an unhealthy mix of ethnicity and regional patronage. The center remained important, for in an economy dependent on exporting primary materials and importing manufactured goods, ports, customs, and transportation – all "federal" jurisdictions – were lucrative, and the regions depended on the distribution of the revenue stream. Easterners and westerners wanted to use an active federal government to accomplish their developmental goals – including the provision of education to the entire population – but they feared that the NPC would ally with one or the other to dominate the minority region. Many northerners feared that southerners would use their educational advantage to control administration throughout the federation or would ally with minorities – especially non-Muslims – in the northern region against the NPC. The inter-regional conflict that was to envelop Nigeria was brewing by the mid-1950s.

In French Africa, leaders such as Houphouët-Boigny and Senghor built solid political machines in Côte d'Ivoire and Senegal, through which they were making effective demands on the government of France. More radical tendencies emerged in the early 1950s out of student movements originating in Paris and extending back to Africa, especially the Fédération des Étudiants d'Afrique Noire en France, out of which came outstanding intellectual-activists such as Abdoulaye Ly and Cheikh Anta Diop. But it was only in 1957 that Ly and his colleagues turned this strongly anti-colonial movement into a political party claiming independence, the Parti Africain de l'Indépendance. Its contribution was less notable for electoral success than for the acuteness of its critique of the colonial situation and of African elites deemed to be too conciliatory toward France.

Labor unions constituted a potential node of opposition, but Senghor was able to co-opt a considerable range of opinions into his fold, and his relationship with the Islamic brotherhoods gave him a base that was hard for anyone to crack. Houphouët-Boigny's control was even tighter, and his status within the RDA had a dampening effect on anti-imperialist radicalism in other territories as well. As an inter-territorial organization, however, the RDA contained different tendencies, including one critical of its president's accommodations with the French government, a position eloquently defended for example by Gabriel d'Arboussier.

The boundaries of contestation within the framework of the postwar French Constitution had been challenged in 1947 by the revolt in Madagascar, and the government had made it clear that violence would be met by severe repression that would extend well beyond actual rebels. The conflict with the RDA in Côte d'Ivoire had been more contained and resolved when both sides compromised (Chapter 3). The most prolonged challenge to the rules of the game occurred in Cameroon, where the French government tried from the late 1940s to exclude a political party deemed too radical. The Union des Populations du Cameroun (UPC) had started out much like any other party in this colony, once a German possession, which France ran under a mandate from the United Nations. Cameroon had given less space to *évolué* politics, to trade unions, or to the development of an associative life than had Senegal, and when the same electoral law was applied to it after 1946, politicians had less to draw on. As in French Equatorial Africa (Chapter 3), electoral politics created its own logic: politicians used what cultural capital they had – ethnic associations, ties to the Catholic Church, and above all positions within the colonial bureaucracy – and successful ones immediately turned political office into a basis for mobilizing supporters.

In the late 1940s one party tried to move beyond this form of politics: the UPC. It had a regional base near the southern coast, but tried to make itself national. It was close to the left-wing trade union movement, and it tried to articulate a clear program of social reform and assertiveness at the national level, although it had difficulty breaking out of its regional position within Cameroon. At first it hesitated to take a clear position against the French Union and for independence. The UPC did poorly in the elections of the late 1940s, and without anything concrete to offer its supporters it moved toward increasingly radical positions on social and political questions. The French government disliked the UPC from the start and intrigued against it. What officials could not abide was its call for independence for Cameroon; they did not know that within a decade French policy itself would be moving in that direction.

The government did what it could to disrupt campaigns and rig elections to be sure that the UPC would not be successful, although it is not clear that the party had a broad enough regional base to win an election. The UPC was pushed further into marking its distinctiveness. At home it set itself apart by its increasingly radical positions, and overseas it embarrassed France by taking its criticisms before the UN, the supervisor of France's mandate. In 1955 the UPC's public meetings became increasingly militant, its trade union allies launched a series of strikes, and police repression escalated too, culminating in urban riots. The French government then banned the UPC. After trying to regain legal status, the UPC under Ruben Um Nyobé went underground and began a guerrilla struggle in southern Cameroon. The movement was harshly repressed over several years and Um Nyobé was killed. That left the field to the more ordinary political parties, each balancing its ethnic base, its access to government resources, and its efforts to find just the right degree of militance and collaboration with the government to keep its supporters engaged and anticipating results. The party of Ahmadu Ahidjo prevailed; its conservative policy of cooperation with the French complemented the conservativism of Ahidjo's regional base in the hierarchical Islamic societies of North Cameroon.

The boundaries of Franco-African politics were also tested by Sékou Touré of Guinea. He got his start in the trade union movement, first as a government clerk and organizer within the civil service, then as leader of the Guinean branch of the Confédération Générale du Travail (CGT), the communist-affiliated trade union federation. He became a hero for leading a general strike in Guinea in 1950, for playing a crucial role in the CGT's campaign throughout French West Africa for the enactment of the labor code in 1952 (Chapter 3), and in 1953 for leading a long strike in Guinea over the implementation of the labor code. He made astute use of the language of citizenship to insist that African workers deserved the same pay and benefits as workers born in France, and he looked to allies throughout the internationalist labor left.

Sékou Touré used his union base and his militant reputation to enter politics, running first for the territorial assembly, then for the French legislature, and eventually for the leadership of the Guinean legislature. In order to succeed he had to broaden his appeal beyond the wage workers who could directly compare themselves to French workers, and to do so he invoked his own illustrious ancestry while fashioning a rhetoric that increasingly contrasted French colonialism with African unity. Within the trade union movement, he had by 1956 repudiated the alliance with the French left and insisted that African unions should be strictly African. He and his collaborators wanted to drop "class struggle" from the language of African union- ism, insisting that African workers should set aside their particular grievances and strive alongside peasants and others for the good of Africa as a whole. Within Guinea he assembled a populist coalition of considerable breadth, drawing on tensions between commoners and chiefs in the more hierarchical of Guinea's societies and on the sup- port of women shaking loose from patriarchal control. He did not want at this time to make a sharp break with France, calling for a "Franco-African community" in which all would be equals.

Trade unionists, political leaders, and others had seized the open- ings of the post-war moment and made a variety of claims: for access to material resources, for their voices to be heard, for the exercise of power. The pioneer in the move to independence, Ghana, had shown that elites moving toward sovereignty could exclude alternatives to their exercise of power from the realm of possibility. Others would follow Ghana's lead. Amidst one of the great political openings of the twentieth century, the closures of a particular form of decolonization were emerging.

The Reinvention of Savagery and the Boundaries of Decolonization

At the very time when the British government was accepting that it had to slowly devolve power in territorial governments in West Africa – even, in the case of Ghana, to a leader it had once considered a demagogue – it was refusing to do so in Kenya. British officials attempted to draw the line against a movement they called "Mau

Mau," which they saw as a primitive, violent rebellion against order and progress, and in the process they excluded a wider range of activists from politics.

Before the war, officials had tended to think of Africans as quaintly backward, but with the developmentalist ideology of the post-war era, any militant rejection of the "modern" world became an affront. The story of Mau Mau does not fit the British view – expressed by officials and the British press – of a backward-looking rebellion, but neither was it just another modern mass nationalist movement. The ideology of the forest fighters, who eventually called themselves the Land and Freedom Army, was indeed anti-modern, rejecting more about developmentalist colonialism than the fact that it was colonial.

Many Kikuyu had eagerly entered mission schools in the 1920s and 1930s, but the missionaries' efforts to get their converts to abandon a range of Kikuyu social practices (clitoridectomy as part of female initiation rites most notorious among them) led to vigorous defense on the part of Kikuyu male elders of Kikuyu culture and a quieter defense of their own role in cultural reproduction by female elders. Since the 1930s activist Kikuyu, by founding independent schools and independent churches, had insisted that it was possible to be Christian, Western educated, and Kikuyu at the same time. The cultural conflict overlapped an economic one festering in the 1930s: the take-over by white farmers of land once used by Kikuyu; the exploitation of Kikuyu labor; the pressure that drove many Kikuyu to move from the crowded highlands of central Kenya to become squatters on land owned by whites, especially in the Rift Valley. The squatters were allowed to grow some crops and keep some animals in exchange for providing family labor to settler farms. Their way of life, and not just their immediate economic interests, was vulnerable. Jomo Kenyatta emerged as a defender of both Kikuyu land rights and cultural integrity.

After World War II Kenyatta led a political party whose calls for a political voice for and defense of African interests fell within the norms of party politics elsewhere in British Africa. But the conflict in Kenya was escalating, and a portion of the Kikuyu population embraced a radical rejection of colonial rule, colonial development, and cultural practices associated with colonization. The root causes of rising anger were, above all, the entrapment of Kikuyu in the development initiatives of the post-war colonial state. In some districts the issue was heavy-handed conservation policies that forced Africans, especially women, to do anti-erosion work that did not increase yields. Most starkly affected were the squatters. After the war the booming world market for agricultural goods encouraged settlers to farm more intensively, to mechanize, and to bring more land under export crops. The settlers increasingly expelled squatters and employed wage laborers as needed.

The Labour government of Great Britain in the late 1940s was not pro-settler, but it was pro-development. Officials convinced themselves that settler agriculture provided much-needed revenues and an example of modernizing agriculture. The government also eased restrictions on Africans growing some of the most lucrative export crops, notably coffee. But this opening to African rural capitalism compounded the problem: expelled squatters, returning to Kikuyu settlements where they thought they had ancestral rights, were not welcomed by the Kikuyu elite, who were intent on using the land themselves. Meanwhile, the Nairobi labor market – reflecting British labor stabilization policy – was providing some Africans with more secure and better-paying jobs, but leaving less place for those on the margins. Ex-squatters were caught between different forms of exclusion and marginality, whether in country or city. Development, for them, was catastrophic.

The post-war crisis cut to the heart of social life. To ex-squatters, their inability to gain access to resources – including land in villages they saw as theirs – was a denial of a chance to marry – in other words, to attain full adulthood. But the older, better-off Kikuyu, especially Christians, who opposed the rebellion, also had their moral ideas, a point emphasized by the Kenyan historian B. A. Ogot (1972). They were profoundly offended by the young men who went against their elders. They thought that their long effort to build African churches and schools gave them legitimacy as defenders of Kikuyu integrity, and they resented being told that they were stooges. Kenyatta's political party, the Kenya African Union (KAU), was dismissive of the aspirations of the marginal working class of Nairobi and the increasingly radical labor leaders who were speaking for it. Different visions of moral behavior were at stake.

It was among the excluded that a wave of agitation began in the popular districts of Nairobi, spearheaded by an organization of Kikuyu who had (or should have) passed the rituals of male initiation in 1940 but who lacked the resources to start families and hence faced being denied masculine adulthood. They called themselves the 40 Age

Group. They invigorated an earlier pattern of oath-taking: to swear loyalty to the Kikuyu ancestors, a classic tactic in ambiguous situations to push people to commit to one side. After the failure of a general strike in Nairobi in 1950, urban disorders, including assassinations of moderate African politicians, began. The violence spread to rural areas, and when an important Kikuyu chief was assassinated in 1952, in the midst of escalating raids on settler farms and government posts by guerrillas based in the forests of central Kenya, the government declared an emergency. The government, despite a lack of evidence, assumed that Kenyatta had to be behind the violence, and he was sent off to detention in a remote part of northern Kenya. Political activities were all but suppressed.

The victims of post-war development confronted a moral and ideological edifice that defined them as primitive and their exploiters as progressive. The rebels were increasingly attracted to an ideology which harked back to a mystic sense of Kikuyu integrity, unsullied by the ambiguities of the past hundred years, evoked in the oath and in the songs and rituals of the forest fighters.

Mau Mau cost the lives of 95 Europeans and nearly 2,000 "loyal" Africans, plus 11,503 rebels, according to official figures at the time – many thousands more in the estimates of some scholars. Tens of thousands of Kikuyu were arrested or captured, with many placed in detention camps and put through psychologized rituals to cleanse them of their collective "insanity," accustom them to healthy labor, and reinsert them into a purified Kikuyu society. Many were executed without proper legal procedure, often on the basis of evidence by informants who had grudges to settle.

It is hard to understand the excess of government repression without appreciating the seriousness with which the post-war British governments took their self-definition as progressive, set off against African backwardness, reactionary settlers, and even the past record of the Colonial Office. In 1945 Phillip Mitchell, the Governor of Kenya, had defined the issue in these terms: "the African has the choice of remaining a savage or of adopting our civilization, culture, religion and language, and is doing the latter as fast as he can."

White settlers saw the rebellion as proof that the African could only be kept down by the sustained use of force – a position that offered London no hope for the future. The emergency hardened the conviction of top officials that the crisis of transition could only be solved if the Kikuyu were pushed through the dangerous middle ground between the primitive and modern worlds and out the other side.

By the mid-1950s the colonial government in Kenya was seeking in earnest to work with politicians whom they regarded as both modern and moderate. The violence and repression among Kikuyu provided an opening for politicians from other areas, who were able to position themselves as non-violent critics of the colonial regime, distant from – if not strongly opposed to – the Kikuyu militants, and simultaneously as defenders of the integrity of their respective ethnic groups and proponents of a Kenya in which diverse peoples would have a place. Tom Mboya, a young man from the Luo of western Kenya who started out as a labor leader and became party leader while Kenyatta was in detention and Kikuyu politicians excluded from politics, skillfully wove the specter of disorder before officials to make claims for more active social and economic policies and an increased African share of power.

Colonial officials, as Mau Mau was finally contained by brutal military action, fantasized about property-owning Africans sharing cities with stable, respectable workers, and sturdy farmers in rural areas giving employment to reliable agricultural workers. Class would replace race as the organizing principle of society. As late as 1959 officials could not predict when they could allow Kenya to become independent. The answer turned out to be 1963, and the man who became essential for negotiating independence was Jomo Kenyatta, whom officials had once – falsely – accused of directing the insurrection and labeled the "leader unto darkness and death."

The costs of managing a developmentalist empire had become clear. In the Gold Coast and Nigeria, a combined fear of disorder and hope that "modern" Africans could contain the conflicts of their rapidly changing societies led officials to allow the move toward self-government to accelerate. In Kenya, protecting developmental colonialism eventually meant abandoning white settlers and then colonialism in favor of transferring power to an African elite that, hopefully, would share in the value of development and the importance of protecting property.

In Central Africa another version of developmentalist imperial policy came unstuck. In 1953 the British government had proclaimed the Central African Federation, uniting its three colonies of Southern Rhodesia, Northern Rhodesia, and Nyasaland, hoping that this larger unit would foster economic planning and stave off South African ambitions to bring the region's white settlers into its white-supremacist orbit. African political leaders recognized the danger that the British policy of self-government would be captured by white settlers, most of whom lived in Southern Rhodesia, and used to dominate the entire region. The British promised "safeguards" for the indigenous majority which predictably proved inadequate. The regional economic strategy mainly benefited Southern Rhodesia, where most industry was located, and agricultural expansion there meant encroachment on African lands and restrictions on cattle kept by Africans. In Nyasaland and Northern Rhodesia, educated Africans saw their opportunities constricted by white dominance of federal institutions. In the Northern Rhodesian copper mines the African Mineworkers Union had to fight not only for better pay, but also to get Africans into the supervisory and skilled positions zealously guarded by the union of white mineworkers.

Meanwhile, white settler politics swung in an increasingly racist direction. The region seethed with tension. African political parties in all three territories became more militant and focused on breaking up the federation. There were violent disturbances. In 1959 a state of emergency was declared. African political parties were banned and leaders arrested.

Once again, repression only made clear the untenable nature of the situation. Regional development for all races was an illusion, and maintaining the federation by force would make it a very expensive one. Britain accepted the end of its Central African dream and allowed Nyasaland and Northern Rhodesia to move toward independence as distinct countries (Malawi and Zambia) in 1964. The British government temporized with the white leaders of Southern Rhodesia until the latter, unable any longer to defend racial privilege within the tenets of British colonialism, defended it by declaring their own version of independence in 1965, dragging out the story of this ugly decolonization for another fifteen years at the cost of much human life (Chapter 6).

Colonial officials could not often draw the line where they wished, but in Cameroon and Kenya they showed that movements that were too radical or too anti-modern could be destroyed. Still, Kenyatta had once been identified with the forces of darkness and Nkrumah dismissed as a demagogue. Both forced colonial regimes to move the boundaries of the permissible; they, too, helped to define a certain kind of decolonization.

The End of Empire and the Refusal of Responsibility

In Western and Eastern Nigeria the regional governments, led by the Action Group of Obafemi Awolowo in the west and the NCNC of Nnamdi Azikiwe in the east, had made social development the cornerstone of their programs, and by the mid-1950s they were trying to implement Universal Primary Education – government-provided education for all children. By that time, however, British officials were convinced not only that the ministers of regional governments were corrupt, but that Universal Primary Education exceeded the regions' ability to pay. Given its policy of devolving power to self-governing regions, it could neither kick out the politicians nor alter their policies – unless it suspended the painfully negotiated Constitution. The Governor told London: "Inevitably the people are going to be disillusioned, but it is better that they should be disillusioned as a result of the failure of their own people than that they should be disillusioned as a result of our actions." Here we have a frank, even cynical, statement of British thinking on the eve of decolonization: defining the structures in which the move toward self-government would take place, while preparing to place the blame for the failures of the process squarely on African shoulders.

In 1957 Prime Minister Harold Macmillan asked his officials to give him "something like a profit and loss account for each of our Colonial possessions." The Colonial Office had not dared to ask such questions before. The answers that came back revealed a cold calculation that the benefits and costs of continuing colonial rule had to be set against the economic and political advantages of good relations with ex-colonial states. If defending colonial rule would be prohibitively expensive, the key to policy was managing the transition: "during the period when we can still exercise control in any territory, it is most important to take every step open to us to ensure, as far as we can, that British standards and methods of business and administration permeate the whole life of the territory." The government's best hope was thus that ex-colonies would become Western-style nations. But country-by-country analyses were not optimistic. In Nigeria, "Barbarism and cruelty are still near the surface ... we are unlikely to have long enough to complete our civilising and unifying mission." The Colonial Office did not see "any prospect in the foreseeable future of ... relinquishing control" in all three East African territories.

In France, similar issues were debated more openly. In 1956 a popular magazine published an article on French Africa which insisted that one must ask about each colony, "What is it worth? What does it cost? What does it bring in? What hopes does it allow? What sacrifices does it merit?" Aware that France had just lost a colonial war in Indochina and was fighting another in Algeria, the author Raymond Cartier argued that African demands for self-government were growing and could not be blocked: "It is necessary to transfer as fast as possible as much responsibility to Africans. At their risk and peril." In private, officials were assessing their decade-long development drive and finding that labor costs had shot upward, inadequate port facilities and railroads had choked on the new material coming in, and the private sector had failed to invest where the public sector had pioneered. In the post-war context, colonialism on the cheap was no longer possible: the investments of the development years were not rapidly paying off, and social costs were escalating. The Africa that colonial officials had fantasized about creating was not to be. They faced the difficulties of ruling Africa as it was.

For British officials, self-government presented a way out: each colony would be led step by step along a path that increased the power of the elected legislature and eventually resulted in the appointment of elected members to cabinet positions, including at the end of the process a prime minister. Meanwhile, officials realized how little had been done to Africanize the bureaucracy, and programs were hastily put in place.

It was not so apparent how France could devolve power without abandoning the centralizing structure of the French Union. Even after it granted its African subjects the status of citizen, it kept ultimate legislative authority in the National Assembly in Paris, in which Africans were a small minority. France's African colonies were grouped in two administrative federations – French West Africa and French Equatorial Africa – and the government hesitated about giving any political role to these units. Central control of development policy and uniform legislation regarding labor and other social matters were fundamental tenets of French policy, but the government preferred to see African citizens have a minority – if at times effective – voice in Paris rather than a decisive voice closer to home, especially in the large federations. So devolution would imply repudiating an established centralizing policy. In 1956 the French government did precisely that.

Confidential government files make clear how much officials felt trapped by the ever-escalating demands made within the framework of French citizenship. Discussion of education, health, wages, and urban services invoked metropolitan France as a reference point. By 1956, confronted with the war in Algeria and the dangers of social equivalence with the metropole, French officials came up with a new concept: "territorialization." Each territory – Dahomey, Chad, Senegal, Côte d'Ivoire, etc. – would be given the power to set its budget, under French overview, and to administer much of its domestic affairs and its own civil service. France would maintain responsibility for defense and foreign affairs. If African leaders still wanted to push the logic of equivalence regarding civil service salaries or health facilities, the costs would fall not on "France," but on the taxpayers of each territory, to whom the politicians looked for votes. Pierre-Henri Teitgen, who had helped to draft the new law, asserted that Africans had taken French policy to mean "well, give us immediately equality in wages, equality in labor legislation, in social security benefits, equality in family allowances, in brief, equality in standard of living." And that, Teitgen said, demanded a sacrifice that French people would not accept.

The *loi-cadre* – framework law – of 1956 was in part a victory for African political movements. It provided universal suffrage instead of elections restricted to certain categories of citizens; it abolished rules that guaranteed settlers from the metropole seats in national and territorial legislatures; and, most important, it gave elected legislatures in each territory substantial authority for internal government. Léopold Sédar Senghor, who had campaigned for ten years for these reforms, recognized their importance but saw the fatal flaw in the law: it devolved power to individual territories. Senghor had argued instead for turning the administrative units of French West Africa and French Equatorial Africa into a federation of African territories, with legislative and executive authority. A single African federation, he insisted, would carry more political weight than twelve territories, each with its own structure in which its leaders would establish a political base and be able to control the distribution of government jobs and other resources within the territory.

His argument was made within a larger conception of how politics might work. Senghor called for two kinds of solidarity: "horizontal solidarity," Africans with each other, would express Africans' common heritage and provide political strength, while "vertical solidarity," of African France with European France, would reflect the reality of economic and social inequality and give Africans a claim on the technical and financial resources of France and on its heritage of democratic institutions and educational advantages. Horizontal solidarity by itself meant unity in poverty; vertical solidarity by itself meant a colonial relationship. The two together created the possibility of claiming from a position of strength the resources needed for advancement.

The combination of vertical and horizontal solidarity had enabled the labor movement to lay claim to the wages and benefits that French workers had won for themselves. But by the mid-1950s the efforts of politicians to mobilize an expanding voting population was putting more emphasis on the horizontal dimension – on African solidarity. Even the trade union movement was falling into this pattern. The shift in emphasis did not come from the rank and file; it was the union leadership that spoke in the name of "autonomy," of finding means of expressing African cultural distinctiveness, of speaking with solidarity in the name of an African nation.

Intellectuals, Senghor foremost among them, had long spoken of African cultural integrity, but had argued that this contributed to the larger entity that was the French Union and to the cultural richness of all of humanity. Senghor carefully conjugated African cultural assertiveness with the language of rights and equality within the French Union. But the language of equivalence among citizens meant less and less to an expanding electorate; in 1956, for the first time, elections were conducted with universal suffrage. A railway worker on the Dakar–Niger line might compare his benefits to those of someone working the Paris–Marseille line. But such a comparison would make little sense to a peasant living five miles from the track. As political leaders – even those whose springboard came from the labor movement – looked toward stitching together broad constituencies, they had to look beyond the language of equivalence within imperial citizenship.

Elected African leaders welcomed their newfound power within their territories, and the parties that won the elections of 1957 moved quickly to establish their authority. Like Senghor, some leaders realized the costs. The French government was devolving power to individual territories and weakening the federations of French West Africa and French Equatorial Africa. Dahomey, Niger, Senegal, Gabon, and so on were becoming the units in which decisions were made, in which politicians built constituencies, and on which demands were focused.

Whereas in 1946 the RDA had looked beyond individual territories toward a wider confrontation and engagement with France, juxtaposing a language of equality with a critique of imperialism, now politics was focusing on the territory. A language of "African unity" was becoming abstract at the very moment it seemed to be triumphant. Senghor warned in 1956 against the "balkanization" of Africa, a division of the French African federations into units too small to be economically viable, too weak politically to challenge former imperial powers.

The *loi-cadre* imparted a territorial focus on politics at a time when alternatives for widening the scope of politics were in the air. Since the late 1940s the French government had been involved in negotiations with other European states about some sort of political union. For France, the possibility posed a dilemma, for if only "European" France participated, the French Union would be cut in half, leaving out the African territories that the government was trying to attach more closely. This realization gave rise to a decade-long discussion of creating "Eurafrica," including France's and Belgium's overseas territories within whatever form of union was implemented. For France, that posed the possibility of spreading the costs of development finance at the expense of diluting its control. For Africans, it opened the possibility of duty-free access to larger markets for its exports and more possibilities for investment and aid. It also posed the risk of Europeanizing colonialism. Senghor warned that Africa refused to serve as the wedding china on the occasion of France's marriage to Germany. He insisted that African territories be represented in any institution involved in the governance of Eurafrica.

In fact, ambitions for a European union were delayed – only coming to fruition in the 1990s – and negotiations focused on economic cooperation, eventually resulting in the creation of the European Common Market under the Treaty of Rome of 1957. For a time the French government made the inclusion of its overseas territories in Africa a condition for its participation, but, faced with the opposition of European partners who feared the burdens of ex-empire, it backed off. France's African territories could have the status of "associates" of the European Economic Community. They would be conceded certain benefits in trade and aid, but they would not have a voice in the Community's governing structures. Africa would have a relationship with the innovative new economic community, but it would not be an equal one.

Other possibilities were wider still. The Soviet Union and later the People's Republic of China posed the possibility of a worldwide anti-capitalist revolution. They – before and after their split – backed revolutionary movements in Vietnam, and they gave development assistance to Egypt (for the Aswan Dam) when "Western" institutions didn't come through. The Communist Party of South Africa was one of the most steadfast opponents of the racist government (it was banned in the 1950s but persisted under the radar), and a number of African political leaders had communist connections and occasional trips to Moscow in their trajectories. Marxist ideas influenced a much wider range of African political actors.

What did not develop in the 1950s was a full-scale revolutionary movement across Africa, and communism remained an influence but not a defining goal or strategy for African political movements. Those movements were finding traction elsewhere. Later, as African states became independent, the alternative of cooperation with the Soviet bloc came into play as an alternative to cooperation with the United States and western European states. The Cold War rivals would operate at the level of states, not of larger popular movements, until the struggles in Portuguese Africa and southern Africa more generally sharpened in the late 1960s and 1970s.

The other perspective on liberation that appeared in 1955 was the formation of an anti-colonial front that was neither pro-Soviet nor pro-American. It became known as the Third World. The meeting at Bandung of heads of ex-colonial states entered into the political imagination of political elites in Africa and elsewhere. There is a lot of myth-making surrounding Bandung. It was not a founding moment for a "global" movement, but a conference of state leaders. More than a few later commentators placed Kwame Nkrumah at the conference, linking his Pan-Africanism to global anti-colonialism, except that he wasn't there. The African presence (Ethiopia, Sudan, plus a larger number of sympathizers for African causes) was minimal, since most colonies had not yet attained statehood. There were strong tensions during and after the conference among rivals for the anti-colonial mantle (Nkrumah vs. Nasser vs. Nehru). But the myth if not the substance of Bandung was important as a step toward eliminating the legitimacy of colonialism and toward raising the possibility of future cooperation among ex-colonial states. The United Nations resolution definitively condemning colonialism came later (December 1960), as did the founding of the Non-Aligned Movement (1961). In the 1970s came the attempt by leaders of Africa, Asia, and Latin America to reform international economic institutions and aid regimes in favor of the poorer countries through what they termed the New International Economic Order.

But as African countries became self-governing, they faced a problem of balancing their cooperation with each other against their need for the resources of the wealthy countries, in the context of Cold War rivalries and the efforts of different countries to find a place in global economic and political systems after the collapse of colonial empires. To use Senghor's imagery, vertical connections provided specific benefits, while horizontal connections among the states of the Third World were an aspiration.

Meanwhile, political movements in French Africa, and elsewhere, were operating with the possibilities and constraints in a changing configuration of power. The French government had calculated that it could maintain something of a French-dominated bloc of states while shedding some of the burdens of inclusive citizenship. At one level, its calculations were working: the semi-autonomous African governments installed after the 1956 elections took a harder line against the demands of labor than had the French government, stepping away from the escalating demands for social and economic parity with other French citizens that had been the hallmark of politics since 1946. But with Sékou Touré, officials badly miscalculated. He meant what he said about African unity and independence.

The French government thought it could make its system of semi-self-government endure. In 1958 Charles de Gaulle, newly installed as the French President, preoccupied with the war in Algeria and eager to insure stability in sub-Saharan Africa, tried to firm up this position as his government adopted a new Constitution for what would become the Fifth Republic. He offered each African territory a choice in a referendum between autonomy within the French system or immediate and absolute independence. Overseas territories that so chose would become "Member States" of "the Community." African political leaders pressured de Gaulle into accepting that the new Constitution would give Member States the right to independence if they decided to exercise it and to allow, but not require, Member States to group themselves into a federation. The name "Community" – after disagreements over whether the French Union should be renamed a federation or a confederation – was itself suggested by the leader of Madagascar.

Especially with these concessions, de Gaulle expected that the political leaders were deeply enough entrenched in the current system – with citizenship rights throughout the Community, possibilities of French aid to Member States, privileged entry of export commodities into French markets, and access to French systems of higher education – that continued participation in a Franco-African community would be attractive. For the most part he was right. But the debate was serious. The strongest voice for voting no on the referendum was that of Sékou Touré, a position taken only at the last minute and after a confrontation with de Gaulle, who refused to make any further changes to the Constitution. In the end, only Guinea voted for immediate independence by a huge majority, while most of the other territories – following their leaders' choices – voted for de Gaulle's Constitution by similar majorities.

The French government responded vindictively; Guinea was cut off from aid, and departing French officials reputedly removed equipment needed for a functioning bureaucracy. Guinea was left to its fate. Yet only two years later France would itself decide that the cord needed to be cut to all of its sub-Saharan territories.

Once in power, Sékou Touré's insistence that all Africans, from the peasant to the skilled worker, should unite turned from an appeal into something like compulsion. As he told his former allies in the labor movement in 1958, a strike against colonial employers was progressive, but against an African government it was "historically unthinkable ... The trade union movement is obligated to reconvert itself to remain in the same line of emancipation." Strike movements in newly independent Guinea were suppressed, the trade union movement was subordinated to the political party, and union leaders who advocated different positions were arrested. He also took the initiative against conservative chiefs, especially in parts of his country dominated by Fulani, and while those moves had some appeal to the exploited underclasses of those communities, it also resulted in an exodus of considerable importance of people from the ethnic groups in question to neighboring Senegal.

In the rest of French Africa, leaders disagreed over what to do next. Senghor stuck to his position that Africans should unite in a federation. Each territory, he argued, should govern its own internal affairs, but a "primary federation" with a legislature and executive would bring France's former African colonies together. It would be this federation, not the individual territories, that would constitute, together with European France and any other French or formerly French territory that wished to join, a confederation. Confederation differs from federation in that it recognizes the national integrity of its component parts, in this case of the African federation.

This three-layer approach to political organization was opposed by Houphouët-Boigny, who favored a two-layer approach, in which each territory would associate individually with France to create not a confederation but a federation. He presided over a rich territory and could use its resources for the people whose votes he depended on; he saw an intermediate layer as wasteful and a direct connection to France as more useful; and he did not want to see Dakar, in Senghor's Senegal, turned from being the headquarters of an administrative unit into the seat of a largely autonomous African government. This dispute had begun even before the debates over the Constitution of 1958 and it continued afterward – until the final breakdown of the French colonial system.

Even Senghor was trapped in the "balkanization" against which he warned. Each African government had come to power through the mobilization of its own set of followers. Senghor had worked through the leadership of Islamic brotherhoods in Senegal even as he had appealed to intellectuals, trade unionists, and other constituencies. He tried in 1959 to negotiate a federation of those states that might support it, and for a time he seemed to have lined up Niger, Upper Volta, Dahomey, and the French Sudan. All but the last reneged, in large part because of the influence of Houphouët-Boigny. The Sudan's Modibo Keita, head of the RDA branch in that state, and Senghor, with his own political party, led their constituents into writing a constitution for an African federation. They named the federation Mali, like Nkrumah in the case of Ghana invoking the memory of an African empire of the past. Both Senghor and Keita then had to face the fact that they had built their constituencies in their own ways.

With Guinea independent and only two Member States of the Community willing to federate, it was clear that French Africans were divided among themselves. The reality of the situation was that each territory was engaged in a bilateral relationship with France, rather than forming part of a Franco-African collectivity. In such a situation, independence became a more attractive option than it had been, particularly as other countries around the world were receiving recognition as sovereign states and taking their seats in the United Nations and other international bodies.

The Mali Federation was the first political unit that began to negotiate with France over the terms of independence, and France was so eager to hold together something greater than its national territory in Europe that Mali was in a strong negotiating position. The separation of citizenships between France and countries becoming independent was softened by treaties that allowed both sets of citizens to reside in and own property in the other's territory. The treaties also made it possible for people of the ex-colonies born before independence to have their former French nationality "recognized" – avoiding a naturalization procedure – if they came to reside in the present boundaries of France. The break was softened as well by the continued provision of aid – but this was now foreign aid, a gift rather than an imperial obligation. Subsequent relations would be affected by French political intrigue and military support for Africans it deemed friendly against those it believed to be acting contrary to its interests.

The French government was not only devolving power, it was also disavowing the central tenets of its post-war policy and imperial ideology. It was pulling back from the implicit offer that incorporation into the French Union or Community would mean that all imperial citizens could aspire to French standards of living, French levels of social services, and French education. It was conceding something to claims for forms of cultural expression distinct from those of France, but most important, it was abdicating responsibility for the continued effects of its past policies.

Within two months of independence the Mali Federation became a casualty of the territorial basis of politicians' constituencies, even though Senghor had anticipated such pressures. Keita and Senghor feared that, in a single unit, each would make inroads against the other in his own base, Keita using a unified party structure and Marxist social policies to undercut Senghor from the left, and Senghor using his affiliations with Islamic networks and his good relations with France to offer pragmatic policies to Mali's citizens. The brief attempt at a new federation failed, and Senegal and Sudan (now calling itself the Republic of Mali) went their separate ways, leaving bitterness and non-cooperation that persisted for several years. It was at this point that Senghor and Keita turned to forging national cultures that were Senegalese and Malian respectively.

MAP 3 Decolonizing Africa

In British Africa, meanwhile, the imperial flag had come down first in Ghana in 1957. Nkrumah's coming to power marked for colonized peoples all over an event of great symbolic importance, and this had been one of the reasons why France had to look beyond its regime of semi-autonomy. In 1958 Nkrumah held his All-African Peoples' Conference in Accra, and this became the occasion for proclaiming a universal right to self-government and sovereignty for all African nations. Even South Africa's oppressed political organizations were present, and the occasion allowed them to associate their struggle with the successes of African nationalism.

At the Congress, Nkrumah called upon states that were in the process of becoming independent to come together as a United States of Africa. He was trying to revive Pan-Africanism, set aside for a time in the preoccupation of political leaders with institutions that were giving them a measure of power. But the elites coming to power were not interested in giving some of it up, even to an entity that was truly African. What was left of Nkrumah's ideal was a Pan-Africanism of cooperating independent states rather than a Pan-Africanism of people. Even this would prove to be an elusive goal. For the time being, Ghana's independence marked the fact that the devolution of imperial power was ongoing and irreversible. No matter what alternatives to the national territory Africans might contemplate, and no matter what concerns officials had about the "readiness" of particular territories for independence, territorial independence was becoming Africa's future.

The exceptions to this pattern were found in Portuguese Africa, Rhodesia (former Southern Rhodesia), and South Africa. They too would be caught in the fact that the end of colonial rule was happening all around them. I will return to the long struggles against colonialism and white domination in these parts of Africa in Chapter 6.

The wave of independence came ashore in the Belgian Congo, but it arrived via a stunning reversal of Belgian colonial practices, and it was so ill-prepared that its failure was predictable, immediate, and tragic.

Belgian scholars proclaimed in 1955 that independence was at least thirty years away. Only in the 1950s did Belgium begin to send Congolese to higher education; only a tiny number of Congolese, mainly in cities, were given more than primary-school education. Only after 1954 did it allow parties to act openly. Up to then, the most important associations permitted were those formed along ethnic lines, so that when the stakes of politics suddenly rose, ethnic difference was accentuated. The Bakongo party, ABAKO, centered in the capital of Leopoldville, emerged in 1954. It represented above all the urban *évolué* outlook of the Bakongo population of the city. In the copper-mining province of Katanga a new party, Conakat, focused on regional autonomy and on the ethnic tensions in a region where labor immigration seemed about to swamp long-term inhabitants. ABAKO and Conakat would provide the platforms for two important political actors of the early 1960s debacle, Joseph Kasavubu and Moïse Tshombe.

It was Patrice Lumumba, from the eastern side of the country, who attempted to put together a party that was truly national, and the others regarded him as dangerous to their power bases for just that reason. His Mouvement National Congolais articulated a radical critique of Belgian colonialism and looked toward the forging of a Congolese nation.

The Belgian government saw Lumumba as the most threatening of Congolese politicians. But it realized how difficult it was to control the situation when the rest of Africa was rapidly moving toward decolonization. When riots broke out in Leopoldville in 1959 the government panicked. Perhaps it cynically calculated that an ill-prepared independence would result in continued dependence on Belgium; but if that were the case, officials misread the complexities of conflict on the ground and the eagerness of international actors to meddle. The ensuing "Congo crisis" that began in 1960 at virtually the moment of independence (discussed in Chapter 7) would reveal that decolonization was more complicated than tearing down the flag of an oppressor and raising the flag of a new nation.

Alongside the extreme irresponsibility of Belgium for its brutal colonization and inept decolonization, ending empire French and British style mixed a certain political cynicism with a different kind of political imagination. At the end of World War II the idea that independent nation-states would rule in Africa was to European officials conceivable only in a hazily defined future, detached from their views of actual African leaders as apprentices in need of training or demagogues who had to be restrained. Ordinary Africans needed to learn how to behave in cities or how to run simple organizations and local governments, or else they could participate in small numbers in institutions where they would represent but not decide. By the early or mid-1950s in both British and French Africa, the "modern African" – in a workplace, an urban neighborhood, an export-oriented farm, or a government office – had become an imaginable being. Officials might ignore the connectedness of such individuals to the rest of Africa. The very idea of "stabilization" in labor policy, for example, emphasized that the urban worker must be separated from village life. But the repeated emphasis on the modern quality of city life, on the imperatives of the modern bureaucracy, on the need for modern enterprises and modern forms of labor administration, opened up to Africans a set of possibilities which many were able to seize. Colonial officials now defined those Africans who followed the script as if they were a-cultural, a-social beings, embodiments of modernization, and they now saw Africans who refused to enter such roles as dangerously recalcitrant, as stubbornly primitive. The place in the late colonial vision of the vast majority of people who did not fall into such a dichotomy was not so clear.

This imaginative leap, with the enormous reality that it obscured, allowed French and British officials to think of an Africa they did not rule. They could still think that the modern Africans that they had created would willingly and even eagerly embrace the institutions opened to them. Africans, their former rulers calculated, would continue relations with the Europe that had taught them so much about science, technology, literature, and statecraft, and they would maintain their integration into world markets. France and Britain transformed their colonial development apparatus into a foreign aid system, with the crucial difference that it reaffirmed generous superiority while denying responsibility for the social and political consequences of economic change. Other figures on the world scene, including the USA and the USSR, began to look at the disintegrating colonial empires as spaces that were being internationalized, still at the bottom of a developmental hierarchy but now the object of concern of all "advanced" nations. Africa would become the world's project for uplift, and also a magnet for power politics and exploitative interest.

A full bibliography for this book may be found on the website of Cambridge University Press at www.cambridge.org/CooperAfrica2ed.

Bibliography

Allman, Jean Marie. *The Quills of the Porcupine: Asante Nationalism in an Emergent Ghana*. Madison: University of Wisconsin Press, 1993.

Anderson, David. *Histories of the Hanged: Britain's Dirty War and the End of Empire*. New York: Norton, 2005.

Beckman, Bjorn. *Organizing the Farmers: Cocoa Politics and National Development in Ghana*. Uppsala: Scandinavian Institute of African Studies, 1976.

Berman, Bruce, and John Lonsdale. *Unhappy Valley: Conflict in Kenya and Africa. Book Two: Violence and Ethnicity*. London: James Currey, 1992. 2 vols.

Branch, Daniel. *Defeating Mau Mau, Creating Kenya: Counterinsurgency, Civil War, and Decolonization*. Cambridge: Cambridge University Press, 2009.

Chafer, Tony. *The End of Empire in French West Africa*. Oxford: Berg, 2002.

Coleman, James S. *Nigeria: Background to Nationalism*. Berkeley: University of California Press, 1958.

Cooper, Frederick. *Decolonization and African Society: The Labor Question in French and British Africa*. Cambridge: Cambridge University Press, 1996.

Hodgkin, Thomas. *Nationalism in Colonial Africa*. New York: New York University Press, 1957.

Iliffe, John. *A Modern History of Tanganyika*. Cambridge: Cambridge University Press, 1979.

Kanogo, Tabitha. *Squatters and the Roots of Mau Mau, 1905–63*. London: James Currey, 1987.

Lee, Christopher, ed. *Making a World after Empire: The Bandung Moment and its Aftermaths*. Athens: Ohio University Press, 2010.

MacArthur, Julie. *Cartography and the Political Imagination: Mapping Community in Colonial Kenya*. Athens: Ohio University Press, 2016.

Ogot, B. A. "Revolt of the Elders: An Anatomy of the Loyalist Crowd in the Mau Mau Uprising, 1952–1956." In B. A. Ogot, ed., *Politics and Nationalism in Colonial Kenya: Proceedings of the 1971 Conference of the Historical Association of Kenya (Hadith 4)*. Nairobi: East Africa Publishing House, 1972, 134–48.

Rathbone, Richard. *Nkrumah and the Chiefs: The Politics of Chieftaincy in Ghana, 1951–1960*. Athens: Ohio University Press, 1999.

Schmidt, Elizabeth. *Mobilizing the Masses: Gender, Ethnicity, and Class in the Nationalist Movement in Guinea, 1939–1958*. Portsmouth, NH: Heinemann, 2005.

Terretta, Meredith. *Nation of Outlaws, State of Violence: Nationalism, Grassfields Tradition, and State Building in Cameroon*. Athens: Ohio University Press, 2014.

Tignor, Robert. *Capitalism and Nationalism at the End of Empire: State and Business in Decolonizing Egypt, Nigeria, and Kenya, 1945–1963*. Princeton: Princeton University Press, 1998.

Vitalis, Robert. "The Midnight Ride of Kwame Nkrumah and Other Fables of Bandung (Ban-doong)." *Humanity* (summer 2013): 261–88.

Westad, Odd Arne. *The Global Cold War: Third World Interventions and the Making of our Times*. Cambridge: Cambridge University Press, 2007.

Zolberg, Aristide. *One-Party Government in the Ivory Coast*. Rev. ed. Princeton: Princeton University Press, 1969.

Interlude: Rhythms of Change in the Post-War World

Let us pause for a moment to think about ways to grasp the timing of change during the decades after World War II. A narrative of "triumph and failure," of "hope and disillusionment," captures something of the time. It calls attention to the struggle for independence, the joy of seeing colonial rule end, and the subsequent despair at the inability of independent African states to sustain peace, democracy, and economic and social progress. The crisis that hit the Congo within weeks of independence in 1960, the coup that overthrew the pioneer of nationalism, Kwame Nkrumah, in 1966, and the Biafran war of 1967–70 mark political turning points. By the late 1960s Africa's leading intellectuals were calling attention to moral corruption and political passivity in the wake of earlier hopes. Some scholars began to argue that independence was an illusion: the new states of Africa were "neo-colonial," politically sovereign, but economically dependent and lacking in cultural self-confidence.

If the neo-colonial interpretation located power and blame in the West, others argued that the years after 1960 revealed a weakness in Africa itself, habits rooted in either African culture or the still-powerful mental grip of colonialism. The delayed freedom of Portuguese Africa in 1975 or Zimbabwe in 1979 created new hopes followed again by disillusionment: even intense mobilization for protracted armed struggle in these regions offered no better preparation for independence than the largely peaceful decolonizations of the 1950s and 1960s. Some saw a similar pattern of hope and disillusion following the end of white domination in South Africa in 1994.

116

This rise-and-fall story is too simple. Let's look first at economic change, a process subject not only to rhythms generated in the African continent itself, but to the shifting tendencies of the world economy. The patterns do not fit a break point coinciding with political independence. What can be called the development era began under colonial auspices around the time of World War II and lasted until the mid-1970s, when a recession in the world economy and the abandonment by international financial institutions of development as a worldwide project brought it to an end. Both economic growth and development initiatives reemerged in in the early 2000s, a change whose duration and impact is as yet unclear.

In the last decades of colonization government expenditure in French and British colonies in West Africa was multiplied by approximately four. Part of the funds came from metropolitan taxpayers, part from increased revenue collected in Africa (with modest deficit spending as well). The escalation in government expenditures went first of all to infrastructure development (some 30 percent), followed by administration (including justice and financial services) and education. These development projects contributed – how much is debated – to the boom in exports in the 1950s, which in turn added to tax revenues. The question of growth and its effects on education, health, and other aspects of social welfare will be discussed in the next chapter.

The initiative, as explained in earlier chapters, began with colonial regimes, first Britain and then France, trying to make conflict-ridden colonies both productive and legitimate. Portugal, Belgium, South Africa, and Rhodesia gave little thought to the standard of living of most Africans, but in their own ways used state authority to foster production. Colonial development, in the end, produced more conflict than it resolved, but the development idea had immense appeal to many Africans. Colonial and nationalist versions of development shared a belief that government planning and government investment – not just the "natural" operations of the market – would help African economies emerge from backwardness.

A nationalist vision of development shaped the policies of African governments and received outside support. Its results were mixed and, to many, disappointing. But they should not be slighted. As shown in Chapter 5, growth rates were uneven but for the most part positive in the early post-independence years. Exports grew, often dramatically, in the 1950s and 1960s. In Kenya or Côte d'Ivoire, where a small group of white settlers had once received most of the attention and most of the wealth, small and medium-sized African-owned farms became the leading edge of growing economies, and these farmers took a larger share of the wealth. The labor mobilizations of the 1940s often paid off in the 1950s, with better wages although not necessarily with the growth in employment that planners anticipated. Most important (Chapter 5), literacy rates improved greatly in the 1950s through the 1970s, life expectancies grew, and infant mortality fell. Africa's population surged upward in the post-war decades. These are all strong indicators that life was improving for many ordinary people in Africa. In a social and economic as well as a political sense, one could assert, along with political scientist Nicolas van de Walle (2001: 17), that the 1960s were the "golden years of this postcolonial system."

Sovereignty changed social and economic circumstances: African politicians in the 1950s could make demands on colonial powers who were by then desperately trying to hold an imperial system together. After independence African governments were on their own; they could only ask for aid, including from countries and international institutions beyond the former colonizer–colonized relationship: the USSR, West and East Germany, the Scandinavian countries, the United States. They faced the heightened expectations of their citizens that their struggles would improve their lives, but they had fewer means than the former colonial power to meet those expectations. They faced a problem that former powers had only begun to realize: the perception (not very accurate) of an underpopulated continent was giving way to fears of growing populations, high birth rates, pressure on land resources, and influx of people to cities seeking jobs that did not exist.

Economic growth became increasingly problematic during the 1970s. This can be interpreted as the result of failure to make deep changes in the structure of African economies. Whatever the record of growth, the goal of leaders to achieve economic independence had not been met. Many economists argue that unwise economic policies were catching up with African countries. But the immediate shift in Africa's fortunes came from outside. In 1973 oil prices skyrocketed, as war in the Middle East had widespread consequences, including efforts by oil producers to restrict supplies and raise prices, and later by wealthy countries to manipulate interest and exchange rates to solve the problems they faced. This had a double effect on the externally oriented

African economies: it increased (except for African oil exporters) their bills for fuel at a time when transport, agricultural machinery, and fledgling industries were becoming more energy intensive, and it fostered a recession in the industrialized countries of Europe and North America, lowering demand for and prices of African agricultural and mineral products. It was at this point that a modestly positive economic picture in much of the continent turned negative.

African governments were ill-prepared to cope with the shocks, which continued throughout the 1970s, and their indebtedness shot upward, fostered by unwise lending from financial institutions in the Middle East and Europe and by the rising interest rates through which the United States tried to solve its own economic problems. When the world economy remained sour for years, many countries were trapped, and paying off the debt consumed the capital needed to make economic improvements. Social as well as economic development began to be reversed: school systems declined, and there was a growing lack of medical facilities and supplies. Many African governments turned to international financial institutions for help when they could not meet debt payments or find the foreign exchange they needed for even the most vital imports.

Those institutions imposed conditions – "structural adjustment" – on any country that received their help. Whether the continued economic malaise, including declining per capita income in the worst affected states, was the result of the disease (bad market conditions or bad government policies) or the medicine (imposed austerity, lowered wages, dismantling of educational and medical services) has been much debated.

In the early 2000s there were signs of recovery, notably in the export of raw materials, and influential development economists, the World Bank, and other international financial institutions reverted to their earlier embrace of the goal of improving the standard of living of the world's poor. In some cases, notably exporters of oil or other minerals, gains in per capita GDP (gross domestic product) were high by world standards. The graphs in Chapter 5 show remarkable overall growth rates. Observers attributed the improvement to China, whose export boom fueled escalating demand for raw materials. China was also willing to invest heavily in infrastructures, including rail lines and roads, in some cases with immediate goals of extracting minerals but in others with the more general aim of facilitating import–export trade. Some economists celebrated Africa's boom; others questioned whether it entailed structural change or just another cycle of increased exports of raw materials.

By 2015 China's growth rate was slowing, although still high by comparison with other industrial countries. Africa's boom seemed to be fading, and the claims of some Western (as well as African) journalists to see "Africa rising" began to look like a linear extrapolation of a trend that might be a short one. If this turns out to be the case, what we need to understand is not why African economies don't grow so much or so fast, but why patterns of growth are cyclical. The economic historian Morton Jerven (2010) sees a long-term pattern of what he calls "growth spurts." Africans, he argues, were quick to respond to external demands for specific commodities – slaves in the fifteenth to eighteenth centuries, palm oil, cocoa, and similar products in the late nineteenth and early twentieth centuries, and a wider range of minerals and other raw materials in the period 1945–75. Perhaps the period 2000–15, with a bit of hindsight, will look like another one of these spurts, this one driven by escalating demand from China. Perhaps the explanation for the origins of the growth spurt and for its termination will turn out to be related – a point I will take up in Chapter 5.

For now, the point is to pin down the chronology. In economic terms, the break points occur in relation not so much to political independence as to the rise of the developmentalist state, 1940–75; the reversal of growth and the repudiation in influential circles of development, 1975–2000; a revival of both growth and development projects after 2000; and the present uncertainties about future patterns. The social effects of this sequence have been powerful, drawing men and women into towns and export production, giving them access to new ways to earn an income and new forms of social relations, and then pulling the rug out from under many of them as unemployment rose, social services and pension funds collapsed, and modern health facilities and schools deteriorated. If the expansive phases gave men new resources through wage labor and civil service positions, it accentuated female dependence on husbands' wages and benefits. But as the contracting phase undercut men's jobs and wages and jeopardized the security of families, it made the "informal" income earned by women ever more important to the survival of urban households. In both phases gender roles were rendered uncertain and often conflictual.

The negative turn shows up in life-expectancy statistics (Chapter 5), although there are other causes than the decline in health services.

These reflect to a large extent the HIV–AIDS epidemic that deeply affected parts of Africa. The genocide in Rwanda reveals some of its horror in life-expectancy statistics.

The return to growth after 2000, however, has not led to a return to the social effects seen in the post-war decades, for two related reasons. First, international discourse has changed, and the idea that state intervention to provide the conditions to produce a healthy, educated, and stable labor force – shared by British and French colonial regimes in their final years as well as by the first generation of independent African states and by important international actors in the 1950s and 1960s – has lost at least some of its influence. African states are expected to sink or swim in world markets, and most – with the notable exception of South Africa – have neither the means nor the will to renew the social programs of earlier years.

Second, African populations grew at a high rate in the second half of the twentieth century. The rural population of Africa, according to the World Bank, more than tripled between 1960 and 2015, from under 200 million to over 600 million. Urban growth was even more rapid. That meant more pressure on access to land and tensions over its allocation. It meant that more people, lacking sufficient land to live off, sought wage labor, putting downward pressure on wages and benefits, encouraging forms of employment that entail minimal employer responsibility for the welfare of the worker. Much of the gains some African workers obtained were overshadowed by the poverty and precarity of others. In the 1940s and into the 1950s colonial policy-makers worried about the scarcity of manpower. Now, many worry that there is little likelihood of finding productive employment for millions of people. Many Africans are risking their lives to migrate clandestinely to Europe, in search of jobs that will themselves be precarious owing to the workers' illicit immigration status.

The chronology of political change also poses difficulties. In the Africa of the 1950s many varieties of politics appeared to be open: claims to citizenship, imperial or otherwise; nationalism; reviving African forms of governance and chiefly authority; Pan-Africanism; federalism; healing the earth; ethnic mobilization; political party formation; student movements; labor organization at local, territorial, continental, and global levels; religious movements; Third World solidarity; Soviet- or Maoist-style communism. By the early 1960s the political repertoire had become focused on governing a territorial state.

There is no question that the decolonizations of the 1950s and 1960s mattered. It is unwise to see the post-colonial state as a mere reproduction of the colonial state with African personnel – if only because the Africanization of personnel tied leadership into social networks within the African continent itself, whereas colonial personnel were more rooted in England or France than in Africa. The extent of democracy in African states, however, is very much in question.

We need a broader context. The colonial state of the 1950s, especially in French and British Africa, was already much transformed. This was the era of the activist state, eager to obtain knowledge about all dimensions of life within its territory and to intervene in many of them, from labor policy to health. In the 1920s the model colonial official was a man who "knew his natives" – that is, who understood the politics of the many little communities into which Africa was thought to be divided. In the 1950s the model colonial official was a technical expert, who knew how to eradicate malaria, organize a school system, teach new cultivation techniques, or manage labor disputes. The 1960s African state sought to take over the interventionist aspect of the colonial state, and indeed to intensify it, in the name of the national interest and (for a time) to demonstrate to voters that the state was improving their lives.

But could the new, independent state be simultaneously developmentalist–interventionist and populist–clientelist, insuring support by providing services with general appeal and rewarding personal followers with state resources? By the early 1970s the answer appeared to be negative. In some places and in some ways the activist state ceased to be so – in any interest except the venal ones of its leading agents – even before international agencies began to talk of the alleged need to "shrink" the state. By the early 1980s, some years after the economic steam had been taken out of the development drive, international financial organizations and some African governments were claiming that the activist state should be banished from the realm of the possible. Had the African state gone full circle, presiding by the 1990s over a feeble infrastructure and a country divided into regional and ethnic bastions of power, rather like the politics of indirect rule in the 1930s?

Just as important as the capabilities of states is the question of how much voice people within them had in selecting their leaders. Taking the case of French- and English-speaking Africa, one can note distinct phases in the degree and form of popular political participation. The period 1945–60 featured externally sanctioned and limited electoral competition. In their final years French and British regimes expanded eligibility to vote and the power of elected legislators. They also tried to keep certain political movements, such as the UPC in Cameroon, out of the realm of the permissible, but they learned to live with others, including the CPP in the Gold Coast, the PDCI in Côte d'Ivoire, and the Kenya African National Union (KANU) in Kenya. After independence there was no external power insisting that elections be held. Once on the receiving end of the demands of citizens and independent organizations, African regimes rapidly became distrustful of the kind of political process that they had ridden to power. This closing down of political space was a general trend in Africa, but the degree of closure varied greatly, from dictatorship to guided democracy.

The 1960s thus constitute the period of developmentalist authoritarianism. By the late 1970s and 1980s in much of the continent only the authoritarianism was left, for rarely was the state actually delivering on its developmental promises. With the export and debt crises, state leaders began to lack the resources to pass out to clients – jobs, a share of bribes, privileged access to markets – so that even the patron–client system was tenuous. This was a highly unstable situation, giving rise to numerous coups and regional conflicts.

By the 1990s many African leaders were unable to resist demands from below or outside to democratize, so that the 1990s represent a tentative – very tentative – move toward a kind of guided democracy rather different from that of the 1950s, as this time internal leaders tried to manage democratic openings and to keep them from opening too far. By the early 2000s these initiatives were going in quite different directions: in Ghana, for example, the particular brand of authoritarianism developed by Flight Lieutenant Jerry Rawlings moved through gestures toward democracy toward its substance, and Ghana has since held seriously contested and reasonably fair elections. Likewise in Senegal, incumbents lost elections in 2000 and 2012, the latter following vigorous demonstrations by youth that preserved the rules for proper elections in the face of attempts at manipulation from the president then in power. In Burkina Faso the twenty-seven-year reign of a dictator came to an end in 2014 after demonstrations in the name of citizenship.

Also in the 1990s, in Sierra Leone and Liberia, regimes that were undemocratic and corrupt faced challenges from rivals to power who could recruit violent followers from among the disenchanted, a situation that led to civil war among rival warlords (some claiming to constitute the state) that, after much bloodshed and outside intervention, eventually ended up in an uneasy peace and governments barely able to function. Civil wars in Mozambique (1977–92, with flareups since) and Angola (1975–2002) were long lasting and destructive. The elites who attempted to rule what has variously been called the Congo, Zaire, and the Democratic Republic of the Congo have enriched themselves and impoverished the majority of the population and fostered violence over more than a half century. The range of political possibilities in twenty-first-century Africa includes, in different countries, reasonably open democracy, facade democracy, dictatorship, personal rule, and warlordism.

The chronology of politics in southern Africa was not the same as elsewhere on the continent, but the variations in recent decades are not entirely distinct. Portugal's empire in Africa was much older than that of France or Britain, and it was harder to give up – except that it was difficult to sustain an empire when the normality of the structure was no longer recognized and when national liberation movements found material as well as ideological sustenance from their independent neighbors. When the British empire no longer supported white settlers in Rhodesia, they declared independence (1965) and tried to defend as a *national* mission a racist regime that could no longer be defended as an *imperial* project.

Supporters of the liberation movements in southern Africa thought that the struggles they went through would produce a post-colonial state quite different from those that exited empires peacefully. But after the victories of these movements (1975–79) the histories of Mozambique, Angola, and Zimbabwe do not lend much support to expectations that armed struggle would produce regimes that were truly governed by the poor and the downtrodden. South Africa held out the longest to deny black Africans a voice in their affairs, but the regime of white dominance couldn't sustain itself when it became a pariah both within and beyond the Africa continent. Here too questions remained about the social and economic justice that political liberation would bring about. I will return to this subject.

Finally, culture and religion fit the economic and political chronologies to an extent, but not neatly. The mood of the 1950s and 1960s, directed by the last colonial rulers and the first African ones, shifted toward opening a European conception of social order to people of all races. The first rulers of independent Africa had often been educated in Europe; they had come of age at a time when missionaries and other teachers presented a clear cultural blueprint for the ambitious to follow. This pathway had never been uncontested or unmediated; cultural forms in Africa have long been adaptive and creative. But the political elite of the 1950s was particularly affected by the possibility of using the state to direct the "modernization" of a society it perceived as backward. To varying degrees, socialist and market models influenced African states, but the lack of resources of most states made it hard for any elite to pursue a "pure" version of either model.

By the 1960s national elites were trying to blend their own modernizing tendencies with a political move seemingly in the opposite direction: to give culture a distinctly national character, to make it "Senegalese" or "Kenyan." This entailed a blending of symbols that were not national at all, and separating them from their local logic, to dilute the power embodied in forms of dress or music or art that were "Igbo" or "Kongo" into something that could be considered "Nigerian" or "Zairois." This project, too, came undone in the 1980s, in the face of diverse and unruly forms of particularistic expression, not necessarily the "tribes" of old, but forms of symbolic affinity that left the state and the nation out. There had all along been forces for cultural autonomy among African writers, musicians, and visual artists, who sought their own syntheses of local and global cultural forms and kept a distance from dominant regimes, colonial and post-colonial. In the early years of independence, writers such as Ngugi wa Thiong'o (1986) in Kenya put pressure on writers and the media to "decolonize" themselves more fully than they had been willing to do.

Over time, and in the face of both state authoritarianism and weakness, alternative networks and institutions became more visible. Some were religious, as in the Islamic brotherhoods, or even more strikingly in the mushrooming of evangelical Protestant churches in Africa after the 1980s, with their focus on individual salvation. They could take the form of a volatile popular culture, especially among young men and women in cities, often with a sharp hostility to the powers that be, sometimes shaping their own world of musical, artistic, and religious expression. Young people often took snatches of cultural elements from the rest of the world, from music to fashion, to incorporate into a projected self-image or cultural style. Occasionally – as with the Senegalese rappers who in 2012 successfully defended citizens' rights to a fair electoral system – the exuberance of youthful expression had political effects. The diversification of media in the age, first of video and audio cassettes, more recently of the internet, made expression less easily controllable.

African artists, meanwhile, have acquired a public beyond the continent, and not just in its diaspora. African music, above all, has had a great influence in Europe and the United States – it is at the core of "world music" – and visual artists such as Chéri Samba have been shown in prestigious museums in Europe and North America. Whereas in the 1960s it was the creation of new nations and the development of an articulate cultural expression of politically independent peoples that captured the world's imagination, in the 2000s it is fragments of oppositional culture that are most readily transmitted abroad.

Bibliography

Enwezor, Okwui, ed. *The Short Century: Independence and Liberation Movements in Africa 1945–1994.* New York: Prestel, 2001.

Jerven, Morten. "African Economic Growth Recurring: An Economic History Perspective on African Growth Episodes, 1690–2010." *Economic History of Developing Regions* 25 (2010): 127–54.

Ngugi wa Thiong'o. *Decolonising the Mind: The Politics of Language in African Literature.* Portsmouth, NH: Heinemann, 1986.

Van de Walle, Nicolas. *African Economies and the Politics of Permanent Crisis, 1979–1999.* Cambridge: Cambridge University Press, 2001.

CHAPTER 5

Development and Disappointment: Economic and Social Change in an Unequal World, 1945–2018

No word captures the hopes and ambitions of Africa's leaders, its educated populations, and many of its farmers and workers in the post-war decades better than "development." Yet it is a protean word, subject to conflicting interpretations. Its simplest meaning conveys a down-to-earth aspiration: to have clean water, decent schools and health facilities; to produce larger harvests and more manufactured goods; to have access to the consumer goods that people elsewhere consider a normal part of life. To colonial elites after the war, bringing European capital and knowledge to Africa reconciled continued rule with calls for universal progress. To nationalists, a development that would serve African interests required African rule. After independence, new rulers could claim a place for themselves as intermediaries between external resources and national aspirations. But African rulers were in turn subject to criticism for sacrificing development for the people to personal greed.

The development concept, some have argued, allowed for an internationalization of colonialism, as the one-to-one relationship of metropole to colony was transformed into a generalized economic subordination of South to North, of Africa to Europe and North America. New actors entered into trade relationships and provided capital and foreign aid: the USA, the USSR, China, East and West Germany, and Scandinavian countries, as well as international agencies such as the United Nations, the International Monetary Fund, and the World Bank. Even a country like Côte d'Ivoire, whose apparently cozy post-colonial relationship to France has been much criticized, was able to play off American assistance, investment, and development models against French ones, so as to obtain a certain room for maneuver. Once the sovereignty of African states was established, development became international in the most literal sense, as a process negotiated between sovereign nation-states, legally equal but in fact distinguished into those who gave and those who received.

The idea that human populations could evolve and progress is an old one; that states should intervene to shape such a process much less so. Colonizers' assertions of the benefits of "opening" Africa to commerce through railway construction and health campaigns were precedents for the state project of development. The colonial initiative of the 1940s (Chapter 2) was new, particularly in its stated goal of improving the standard of living of Africans and its insistence that states should do what markets could not. At home in Europe, governments after the war were expanding and consolidating their own institutions of the welfare state, and they were no longer so sure that they could make a sharp distinction between a metropolitan population entitled to social protections and a colonial population – whose allegiance was also important to the state – who could legitimately be excluded from them. As welfare and development were increasingly accepted as preoccupations of a modern state, the boundaries of such a state, and particularly the tension between its "national" and "imperial" dimensions, became a focus of debate.

In academic circles from the late 1940s onward, the field of economics was becoming more activist – advising governments how to stimulate as well as regulate economic growth – and it spawned the subdiscipline of "development economics." Early theorists argued that poor economies needed a "big push" to give them the infrastructure, the quality of workforce, and concentration of capital to compete in world markets. Such theories gave intellectual sustenance to the hope of elites in western Europe and North America that poor regions could improve their prospects without overthrowing the international order. But even before the development economists had consolidated their place in the establishment, they were challenged by economists who used similar scholarly tools to make the opposite argument: that the world economy, far from being a source of progress for all who participated in it, made the rich richer and the poor poorer. This argument emerged first among Latin American economists, and by the 1970s had moved to Africa.

Following this reasoning, some activists called for poor countries to distance themselves from world markets. A different line was taken by a group of Latin American, African, and Asian governments in the 1970s: a demand for a New International Economic Order (NIEO) that would tilt the balance of global economic structures to favor the poorer states. Radical and orthodox versions overlapped to the extent that both agreed on the importance of using resources to build *national* economies. Many agreed that new industries needed protection from outside competition so that each national economy would develop mutually supporting sectors, avoiding a situation where foreign companies picked off the best niches and left everything else to stagnate. The NIEO called for reform of the very institutions and treaties that governed world trade to make the world economy more favorable to developing economies. This initiative led to a reaction from policymakers in the rich nations, not only to reject the specific demands of the NIEO but to articulate a coherent defense of market economies and foster an institutional apparatus to enforce "free trade."

That position would gather more support in the 1980s. But until then, development economics provided an effective language that overlapped the quest of African governments for more prosperous national economies and of the interest of Western governments for the orderly integration of poor countries into a world economic order based on relatively open markets for goods and capital. African governments could appeal to rich nations and international organizations for aid in the form of grants and low-interest loans. During the Cold War, openness to multinational corporations was in effect a condition for aid from the United States and institutions under its influence, but there was room for individual corporations to negotiate deals to protect themselves against competition in particular countries. Those African governments that sought a more radical break with the orthodoxies of the capitalist world economy could seek aid from communist states, notably the USSR, East Germany, and China. In the case of Guinea and Tanzania, and later the liberated former colonies of Portugal, technical assistance and training programs organized by communist states supported socialist experiments (discussed in Chapter 7), but the capacity of these states to provide capital was limited by their own economic difficulties, which became increasingly severe in the 1980s, just when there might have been an opening as Western institutions imposed austerity plans on indebted African countries.

Even states allying themselves with the capitalist world were attracted to elements of planning and central control. They wanted a vigorous program for development whether or not markets would encourage the necessary investments, and they feared that a strong business community might be a basis for opposition. The developmentalist state, in its post-colonial as much as its colonial manifestation, was thus a particular entity: it exercised initiative, yet it suppressed initiative too, and it above all encouraged citizens to think of the state as the prime mover for raising the standard of living.

Still other variants on the theme of development were on the table in the 1950s and 1960s, including a Catholic version that was less concerned with growth than either the more orthodox capitalist or socialist pathways, more focused on building communities, on the well-being of neighbors, on families, and on the environment. Senegal's first President, the Catholic Léopold Sédar Senghor, and his Muslim Prime Minister, Mamadou Dia, commissioned a Catholic priest, Father Lebret, associated with the Economics and Humanism school in France, to develop an approach to economic development based not on preset formulas but on the experiences and wishes of actual Senegalese communities, beginning with a survey of the resources and possibilities each community possessed. This approach ran into vested interests as much as did more orthodox variants. A Protestant variant of developmental humanism was put forward by President Kenneth Kaunda upon Zambia's independence in 1964. Julius Nyerere advocated yet another approach based on notions – mythical perhaps – of the solidarity of the African family (Chapter 7). African leaders domesticated the development concept by using African words to convey the notions of community and progress that they envisioned: *maendeleo* in Kiswahili, *olaju* in Yoruba.

The irony of the period 1960–75 is that most post-colonial regimes, intent on establishing the autonomy of the nation, reinforced the externally dependent economy of the colonial era and did not necessarily aid the most dynamic elements within their own territories. Africa's small-scale farmers of the 1940s and 1950s were a model of modest expansion, adapting kinship and clientage and other forms of social relations within indigenous societies to channel labor and other resources into export agriculture. In the best-endowed regions a class of moderately wealthy farmers became a force for further investment in transport, marketing, and banking, and they used their political influence to get states to spend more money on education and other services for their regions. Like Nkrumah, many rulers of the 1960s feared that such farmers would be the nucleus of conservative opposition to their state-centered visions of the future, and they wondered if small-scale agriculture would really get the country over the economic hump that decades of colonialism had created. They had a point, both because of the limitations of agricultural systems, national infrastructure, and because of global economic structures, but not necessarily a solution to the problem.

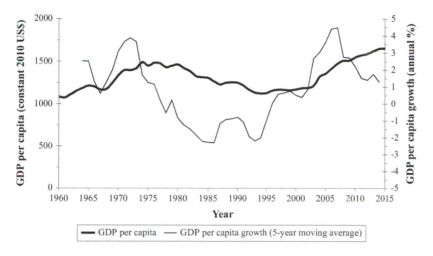

FIGURE 9A GDP per capita and GDP per capita growth in sub-Saharan Africa, 1960–2015

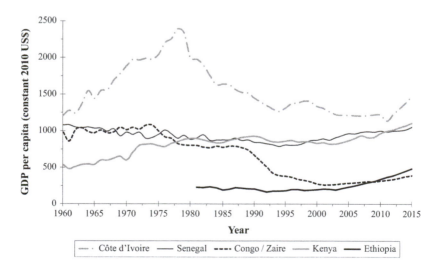

FIGURE 9B GDP per capita in selected African countries, 1960–2015

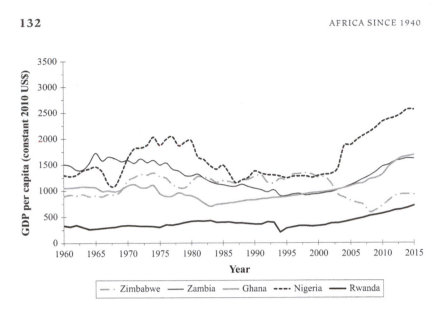

FIGURE 9C GDP per capita in selected African countries, 1960–2015

Growth? Development?

Africa, in the minds of people around the world, went during the 1960s from being a continent of colonies to a continent of "developing countries." Producing more goods and services, as measured by growing gross domestic product per capita (GDP), was both a sign and the substance of economic change: of more productive agriculture and industry, better integration into world markets, and the resources needed to bring the large majority of the population out of poverty. Skeptics soon began to question the linkage of "growth," in terms of GDP, with the deeper goal of "development." Growth did not necessarily mean structural change, and its fruits might not be going to the majority of the population.

These questions returned in the 2000s as high growth rates – among the highest in the world – seemed to some observers to announce that Africa had recovered from the severe economic downturn of the 1980s and 1990s and was back on the path to economic success (Figure 9a). The skeptics returned too, arguing that most of the gains were in the export of minerals – oil, copper, gold – and did not imply that economies were becoming more diversified or more capable of improving the lives of poor people. Indeed, some feared a "lock-in" phenomenon, that high export growth led to a concentration of capital and labor in sectors producing a narrow range of goods that had little use domestically, and that Africa was becoming all the more dependent on markets over which Africans had no control.

It was demand generated by China's extraordinary economic boom, the argument went, that drove the improved statistics for African economies. Three-quarters of China's imports from Africa were in oil and minerals. Chinese investments in Africa were similarly focused on energy, minerals, and transportation, as was foreign direct investment from other countries. With some signs in the mid-2010s that the Chinese miracle was becoming less miraculous – although growth was still high by world standards – prices of some of Africa's raw materials began to fall, and the future of growth became less sure. In the case of oil, whose place in the Chinese-led boom was particularly large, tiny elites in countries such as Nigeria, Angola, Gabon, and Equatorial Guinea were pocketing most of the proceeds, doing little to bring about sustainable economic structures or alleviate the grinding poverty of the majority of the population, and putting their countries' budgets in jeopardy when the price of oil fell. While the percentage of Africans living in poverty has declined significantly in the last twenty years, the absolute number of impoverished Africans – considering population growth – has risen. In its *Africa Competitiveness Report 2015*, the World Economic Forum concluded: "More than a decade of consistently high growth rates have not yet trickled down to significant parts of the population: nearly one out of two Africans continue to live in extreme poverty, and income inequality in the region remains among the highest in the world."

Given that Africa's population has been increasing rapidly, the absolute growth in GDP had to be quite high for per capita GDP even to keep pace, let alone rise. Not only is interpretation of the figures controversial, but some scholars have questioned the accuracy of statistics themselves, including both GDP and population. Statistical bureaus in some countries are barely functional, censuses rare and sometimes politically inflected, so that much of what appears as comprehensive data actually consists of extrapolations from samples. Better statistical services can themselves produce misleading data, as they did in the case of Ghana, which in 2010 revised its GDP estimate upward by 60 percent. Not only do country-wide figures miss the concentration of wealth in the hands of national elites and foreign corporations, but they also tell us little about how the poor manage to survive. Much of what people consume is grown and exchanged outside of visible and readily measurable market transactions. Indeed, if the official figures for production in a country such as the Democratic Republic of the Congo were valid, much of its population could not have remained alive.

So what appear to be hard data may actually be rather soft; but they still allow us to sketch patterns, if not to draw them precisely. The years 1960–75 and 2005–15 were, for the most part, periods of unevenly distributed growth, with stagnation and even contraction in between. It is too early to tell whether the most recent slide in China's demand for African raw materials will continue. Overall, the data are consistent with Morten Jerven's notion (2010) – which he sees going back centuries – of "growth spurts" followed by periods of stagnation or decline. Such a pattern should not be surprising given the extraverted nature of African economies, hence their lack of internal (or regional) demand that would buffer them against fluctuations in the relatively narrow range of raw materials on whose export Africa depends.

The pattern is consistent across a variety of countries (Figures 9b and 9c), although an oil producer such as Nigeria grew in the late 1970s when others were beginning to falter, and itself faltered later on when the oil price fell (a pattern repeated after 2014). Ghana's economy grew at nearly 2 percent per year in the 1950s, but growth rates turned negative in the 1960s, as the cocoa sector all but collapsed. Kenya grew slowly in the 1950s, then at an impressive rate of 3.2 percent annually in the 1960s. Zambia's mineral economy did well in both decades: 2.7 percent annual growth in the 1950s, 3.2 percent in the 1960s. Botswana, Cameroon, and a number of other countries – unlike Senegal and Ghana – grew quite modestly in the last decade of colonial rule and quite rapidly in the first decade of independence.

Then came the 1970s. The spike in oil prices of 1973 and 1976, the subsequent world recession and drop in demand for tropical products, and the rise of world interest rates sent Africa into a tailspin. For nearly twenty years after 1976, GDP per capita growth rates were below zero. For Africa as a whole, GDP per capita fell some 20 percent. In 1996 the figure stood barely ahead of where it was in 1966. In Zambia, where the copper market collapsed, GDP per capita fell 36 percent in ten years and stagnated for another ten. The 1970s was a terrible decade for Tanzania, for Ghana, and for Senegal.

The statistical boom of the 2000s is impressive in relation to both the previous half-century of African history and to growth patterns around the world in the same time period, and like previous growth spurts it was uneven, among and within countries – no more so than Nigeria, where oil wealth – which grew by leaps and bounds until it peaked around 2014 – has produced a fabulously wealthy elite and a substantial middle class, but left millions of people in poverty, including in the very regions that produce the oil. Cities juxtapose a swollen population of the poor with an ostentatious presence of wealth.

Where conflict has become endemic, as in Somalia or the Central African Republic, many people live at the edge of starvation or take refuge in neighboring countries. Impressive gains and significant poverty reduction has occurred in Ethiopia (which had experienced a devastating famine in the 1980s) and Rwanda, and recovery from civil war has reduced poverty in Liberia. In Zimbabwe the economy all but collapsed in 2000–08 – in no small measure because of mismanagement and conflict – but then recovered, but not to the levels it had attained in its best years after it had come out from the rule of a white minority government in 1980. The big question is what will happen in the future given Africa's relationship to a fluctuating world economy, the possibilities of diversification, and the dangers of becoming ever more firmly locked into the existing structure driven by primary-product exports.

The Promise and Limits of Peasant Production

Much of Africa's economic performance after World War II came from the efforts of small-scale farmers. In Kenya, the lifting of the ban on Africans growing coffee led to a pattern of growth that changed the nature of the colonial economy. Smallholder output rose at an average of 7.3 percent per year between 1954 and 1964, and the smallholder became the backbone of an economy once dominated by white settlers. Kenya's economy proved dynamic in the decade after independence in 1963: GDP per capita rose almost 30 percent in the following decade, even as population grew. African planters similarly displaced white settlers in the coffee and cocoa sectors of Côte d'Ivoire beginning in the late 1940s, and this territory became the economic star of French West Africa; after independence in 1960 it doubled its real per capita GDP in twenty years. When Zimbabwe finally rid itself of white rule in 1979, marketed output from peasants went in a decade from 10 percent of total production to over 50 percent. In much of Africa the stalwarts of earlier smallholder agriculture – Yoruba cocoa farmers in Nigeria and Chagga coffee planters in Tanganyika – increased their output, income, and political in influence in the 1950s.

Such success stories, nonetheless, were based on crops that were produced in many parts of the world. The favorable prices of the post-war years weakened by the late 1950s and early 1960s, badly hurting the economy of Ghana. The more drastic fall in the price of cocoa in the 1980s cut Côte d'Ivoire's GDP per capita in half, erasing the

FIGURE 10A Cocoa production, 1961–2014

FIGURE 10B Coffee production, 1953–2014

impressive gains of the two previous decades; it would bounce back and fall again. Overall, Africa's cocoa farmers were producing three times as much in the 2000s as in the 1950s, but their share of the world market remained about the same. Coffee production had a big period of growth in the 1960s, and fluctuated after that, while Africa's world market share declined (Figures 10a and 10b).

One of the virtues of peasant agriculture is its flexibility. Using family labor, producers could increase or decrease export-crop output while insuring their own food supply. African peasants were able to survive periods of low world prices because they engaged in "self-exploitation," making use of the unpaid labor of women and children to maintain production even when sales prices could not have justified paying hired labor a market wage. In the relatively prosperous zones, farmers – and their wives and children – kept their options open: members engaged in food production, export-crop production, off-farm wage labor, and off-farm enterprises. Many used earnings not just to reinvest in the agricultural enterprise but also to pay children's school fees or to participate actively in local politics, in the hope that more career options would open up.

In much of the world, agricultural expansion has been a brutal process, built on the dispossession of rural people by an elite capable of managing land and labor to maximize profits. In much of Africa, however, agricultural relations more often entailed what Sara Berry (1993) calls "exploitation without dispossession." In cocoa production, for instance, family labor was indeed exploited, as was the labor of immigrants seeking to move into the cocoa zone, but there was not a rigid line between a planter class and an agricultural laborer class. As new land was brought under cocoa cultivation, junior family members or immigrant workers who became clients of established planters could aspire to become planters themselves. Claims to land could only be sustained with community support, softening any cleavage between a planter class and the rest of the population. Berry argues that employers in such circumstances found labor hard to discipline and hence lacked the coordination to make full use of productivity-enhancing inputs such as fertilizer and irrigation. None of this was an obstacle to productive agriculture, or indeed to considerable inequality in the resources for agriculture and pastoralism, but it did stop short of transformation into the kind of ruthless capital accumulation and continuous pressure to enhance productivity characteristic of capitalist agriculture in Europe, North America, and parts of Asia and Latin America.

It is easier for a scholar to say that incremental improvements in small-scale farming may be the best that can be done in African circumstances than it is for a new state to accept such limitations. African leaders wanted a farming sector that was economically strong and politically weak and feared they would get exactly the reverse: that cocoa or coffee producers, well networked among themselves, would constitute a political challenge without delivering the "modern" agriculture that the leadership sought.

This helps to explain some of the apparently self-destructive tendencies of both the colonial and post-colonial eras. Colonial states in the 1940s and 1950s spent vast sums of money on centrally directed agricultural schemes, such as the cotton and rice systems of the Niger Valley in what is now Mali or the "ground nut scheme" to grow peanuts on a vast tract of land in Tanganyika, using wage labor and heavy war-surplus equipment. Later, Kwame Nkrumah and Sékou Touré tried to create state-run collective farms, which – like the colonial ventures – failed to become reliable producers of agricultural commodities. So, too, did schemes such as the Tanzanian government's "villagization," which made farmers live in clusters, so that they could both be provided with government services and be observed, while they devoted time to growing crops prescribed by the government.

Colonial governments after the war used marketing boards to take much of the earnings of the commodities boom out of farmers' hands, creating stabilization funds to support farmers in case prices declined. Nationalist parties in the Gold Coast, Nigeria, and elsewhere fought the marketing boards, but once in power kept them in place, this time emphasizing the importance of using agricultural income in an activist fashion rather than as a hedge against market fluctuations.

For a time in Ghana, Nigeria, Côte d'Ivoire, and Kenya, cocoa or coffee revenues remained buoyant enough to make possible a measure of state-centered growth in a variety of industries, the rapid Africanization of the bureaucracy, the expansion of the educational system, and the provision of other services. State-centered development perpetuated the tendency of colonial states to appear distant, extractive, and imposing. The centrality of import and export tariffs, as opposed to other kinds of taxes, to state revenue perpetuated the quality of the colonial state as a gatekeeper, policing the intersection of internal and external economies. This is a point to which I will return in Chapter 7.

During the last years of the colonial era and the early years of independent governments, particular attention was given to integrating more rural producers into market relations through road networks. Progress was made and has periodically been renewed, but transportation remains one of the major obstacles to agricultural development. According to specialists, Africa has half the road density of Latin America and a third of that of Asia, although unevenness is as much an issue as the overall density. Africa has, for centuries, supplied the rest of the world with specific commodities through relatively narrow channels; what has been and remains a problem is creating a web-like pattern of interconnections capable of moving high-volume, low-value commodities within and across territories, and that requires a larger investment in infrastructure than colonial or post-colonial regimes have been able and willing to provide.

So far, I have been writing about countries with strong cash-crop sectors. Some regions *should* fit this picture – good land not too far from ports – but do not: Liberia, Guinea, parts of Congo/Zaire. Foreign-owned plantations took over some of the best land, paying miserable wages. At times, violent conflict or heavy-handed state oppression prevented such regions from living up to their potential. Some regions have had less opportunity. In areas of marginal rainfall or other environmental difficulties, trying to produce commercial crops while feeding a growing population and maintaining cattle herds severely strained resources. Deforestation, accelerated by the use of wood fuel in the face of the scarcity and high cost of alternatives had deleterious ecological effects. In the 1970s the prolonged drought in the Sahel, the large region south of the Sahara, led to famine, and was widely seen as a warning of ecological dangers ahead. Widespread droughts have been repeated in parts of eastern and southern Africa.

Ecological problems are rarely purely "natural"; the confining of growing populations of Africans to "reserves" in parts of southern Africa where white settlers had expropriated extensive land caused profound degradation in many areas. The extension of Africa's largest cities into the surrounding areas has taken a great deal of farmland out of production. Worst of all have been the war zones, where insecurity compounded environmental vulnerability and produced devastating famines. A million people may have died in Ethiopia in 1984–85 in a famine induced by government oppression and civil strife. The food supply in the war zones of southern Sudan has been dangerously meager since the 1970s, and the new civil war in South Sudan that erupted shortly after it seceded from Sudan in 2011 led to a still ongoing crisis of famine and malnutrition.

The late colonial era witnessed often heavy-handed efforts by agricultural experts to counter allegedly neglectful African practices with scientific conservation practices. Such interventions have produced as much conflict and uncertainty as "improvement." Ecological history reveals evidence of thoughtful adaptation by African farmers to environmental stress. Recently, experts discovered that in areas of marginal rainfall zones intercropping trees and food crops produced better crop yields than clearing entire fields of trees, something farmers in those regions have known for years.

Many experts have insisted since the 1950s that secure title to specific plots of land would give farmers more incentives and means to improve their land. Clear title, they argue, would give farmers a basis on which to secure loans to obtain fertilizer or other inputs and provide the most effective farmers with better opportunities to enlarge their farms. Since the 1990s the World Bank has been particularly eager to convince African states that individual ownership and registered titles will mean enhanced productivity in agriculture compared to tenure systems where land allocation is controlled by the local community, by kinship elders, and by chiefs. Kenya, Tanzania, Ethiopia, Mozambique, and Ghana, among others, have encouraged affluent Africans and foreign corporations to purchase tracts of land with the goal of enhancing export production through large, modernized, and market-oriented agricultural units. They have made some headway in land consolidation and titling, but estimates are that between 5 and 10 percent of sub-Saharan Africa's arable land is held under registered titles. The figure varies from 72 percent in South Africa to 2 percent in Tanzania.

Some experts, however, think that "land-grabbing" has accelerated since the 2000s, as investors from China, South Korea, India, and the Persian Gulf want to insure food security for the future and as corporations invest in large-scale biofuel production. Foreign equity firms have been willing to finance some projects that alienate large amounts of land, and governments have been so eager for investment that they sign off on vast tracts, alleging – a questionable proposition – that the land is little or poorly utilized by indigenous people. The sale by the government of Madagascar to a Korean corporation of land amounting to a significant percentage of the entire island produced so much anger that it led to a coup that overthrew the government in 2009.

Both land titling favoring indigenous owners and investment in corporate agriculture have had mixed results at best, and continued

flows of investment and government support for the necessary infrastructure have not been consistently forthcoming. In the case of
foreign agricultural investment, much of the land has not even been
brought under cultivation, but is being held as a contingency for the
future. The failure of projects does not necessarily result in the return
of land to original users. Relatively few jobs have been created; even
the stronger investment projects have not produced the linkages to
other sectors in the region or the technology transfer to African
entrepreneurs that advocates, with their generic vision of the virtues
of free markets, have promised.

Critics of such approaches fear that wholesale privatization would
unleash uncontrollable conflict in rural areas and will likely increase
rather than diminish rural poverty. Where land fertility is poor, flexible
land allocation within a community might make more sense, allowing
farmers to use small plots in slightly different ecological zones and
land to lie fallow for a number of years while cultivating new areas.
Privatization might result in land speculation rather than more efficient use, as urban elites and foreigners gobble up land. People
already living at the margins of subsistence may find themselves
hemmed in by alienated land, unable to practice crop rotation,
forced – even more than at present – to overuse forests and grazing
land. At the same time, the evidence we have of innovation and
expanded cultivation within indigenous systems of property and labor
allocation provides alternative ways of thinking to the standard formulas of Western experts.

We should not, however, romanticize "communal land tenure" as
an egalitarian alternative to cut-throat capitalism. Elders and chiefs
had considerable power to allocate land in many instances, and they
had personal interests as well as communal responsibilities. They
might want to exploit land themselves or rent it to outsiders. Rural
elites might be in cahoots with state officials rather than providing a
defense against government or foreign predation. Women might fare
no better under patriarchal local elites than in a competitive land
market. In short, chiefly authority might be a defense against land
accumulation, but is also a potential source of inequality in its distribution. Nor can one have confidence that national governments will
protect people's access to land from the dangers intrinsic to both
"custom" and "the market."

Where people migrated in search of land suitable for marketable
crops, tensions between "autochthone" and "stranger" farmers could

become acute, as they did for example in Côte d'Ivoire, Cameroon, and parts of Kenya from the 1980s onward. Such tensions have often become ethnicized, as competition for land access mediated through political patrons could be seen as the clash of "tribes." When international financial institutions pushed African governments to downsize urban employment in the 1980s and 1990s, and with rural populations growing, people falling back on the land for subsistence were in conflict with better-off farmers trying to produce export crops.

Drought, conflict, and inadequate facilities for marketing crops have all encouraged families to send some members – mainly young men – to seek wage employment in cities, or even outside the continent. The combination of the need to diversify economic strategies and agricultural systems that require periodic clearing of new land encourages large families. Otherwise, the loss of labor power from migration would disrupt the farming cycle. The money sent back by migrants is critical both to survival in the worst areas and to breaking out of low-intensity agriculture in zones of more potential. In colonial and post-colonial Kenya, for instance, urban wage labor was a source of capital for agricultural improvements, since banks provided little credit to small-scale African farmers. Because young men were the most likely to migrate, the effect on women was above all to increase not only their workload on the farms but also their vulnerability, for their fate depended on remittances a man chose to send back, on his not finding a "city wife," and on his staying healthy.

The Industrialization that Didn't Happen

The cure for a colonial economy dependent on sales of a narrow range of agricultural products and on purchase from outside of manufactured goods seemed to economists and political leaders in the 1950s and 1960s to be industrialization. It didn't work out so simply.

In Ghana, for example, the quest was to find alternatives to cocoa exports. Nkrumah took over the colonial project to build a huge dam over the Volta River which would produce the electricity to transform Ghana's abundant bauxite into aluminum. That thousands of Ghanaians lost their land to the lake behind the dam was to be offset by a claim that they would be relocated into areas where they could begin "modern" farming. The project was constrained by shortages of finance and the need to raise money from foreign enterprises and banks, the nexus Nkrumah was hoping to escape. The multinational aluminum companies were in a strong position to demand exacting terms. Ghana gained export income, but it did not achieve economic autonomy, least of all from multinational aluminum companies. The new modern farming sector did not live up to its billing.

Africa has long had great difficulty in attracting capital investment, given its spread-out population divided by colonial and post-colonial borders, the continent's generally low income levels, and the uncertainties of labor-force development among people whose long and bitter experience encouraged them to avoid subordination to an employer by keeping other options open. The mining industry – in gold, copper, diamonds, and other minerals – has been the biggest exception, but only in South Africa and, to an extent, in Southern Rhodesia did it spawn broad regional industrial development. Even in the early 1950s French and British officials were noticing that private overseas investment was not following in the wake of their public development investments. African political leaders thought that independence would make a decisive difference; they could build their own industries.

To an extent they did. States used tariff barriers, taxing imported finished products heavily and capital inputs lightly, to get investors to manufacture products within their borders. Much investment in the 1960s was import-substitution industrialization (ISI), relying on transnational corporations headquartered in the United States, Europe, and Japan that wanted to establish production inside the tariff walls put up by African states. States also founded parastatal corporations in sectors that they hoped would stimulate a wide range of private activity or else built industries intended to constitute the core of a socialist economy. In either case, the constraints were severe: industry demands technical knowledge as well as finance, and that is highly concentrated in the world economy. Transnational companies often bargained to keep competitors out, and state-owned industries were given protected markets, so that ISI often meant that producers were sheltered and inefficient. Citizens were then stuck with products more expensive and of lower quality than those available on the world market. Continual importation of machinery and supplies was necessary for industry to function. The economics of industrialization in countries with small markets and little infrastructure were bad enough; the politics were worse, for politicians were tempted to use protected industries to enrich themselves and their clients and to distribute relatively well-paying jobs.

Industrialization nonetheless had its moment: between 1965 and the mid-1970s, industry expanded twice as fast as GDP. Much of this was in mining, but manufacturing, albeit from a low base, grew at nearly 7 percent per year between 1960 and 1980. Growth was concentrated in food processing and textiles. Except for South Africa, where industrialization stretched back to the nineteenth century, it was concentrated around a few centers: in Zimbabwe near Harare or Bulawayo, and in Kenya near Nairobi, for example.

After the oil shocks, growth in manufacturing declined, and by 1980 it was negative: Africa was slowly deindustrializing. Mauritius, a tiny island country, was a rare African country able to follow the Southeast Asian pattern of producing textiles for export markets. Nigeria, Botswana, Kenya, and for a time Zambia could build industry to service a significant mining or agricultural economy, but they were vulnerable to the loss of demand for their usual exports. By the 1970s most African countries were having difficulty competing with low-cost exporters in world markets or supplying their own people with manufactured imports at competitive prices.

During the 1970s a debate took place among experts on the economy of Kenya, particularly at the University of Nairobi, over whether the economy was remaining dependent on foreign firms or whether a Kenyan elite, branching out from its control over the best land and government resources, was developing a national form of capitalism, in manufacturing as well as commerce and agriculture. The question was resolved not by scholarly debate but by a change of regime after the death of Jomo Kenyatta. The new government, led by Daniel arap Moi, set out after 1978 to undermine the allies and clients of its predecessor. It also undermined the dynamism of both national and foreign capital. But the problem was more general than that. Between 1970 and 1997 investment per capita declined in Africa, while it doubled in South Asia and went up seven-fold in East Asia.

South Africa, with the most industrialized economy in Africa, had an opportunity after the end of apartheid to make itself into a regional pole of development. To a certain extent it did, and South African entrepreneurs can be found in many African countries. But in manufacturing, it could not match the market power of China, whose exports of manufactured goods were growing by leaps and bounds in the 1990s. South Africa, meanwhile, remained vulnerable to the fluctuating gold price. While it had a larger domestic market than other

African countries, the poverty of a large portion of its population weakened its possibilities for industrial growth.

The economic growth of the 2000s and the heightened capacity for consumption enhanced markets for manufactured goods, but once again China and Southeast Asia have been so efficient in this domain that market opportunities for the kinds of goods that most Africans can afford are limited. The rising cost of labor in China may create new possibilities, and there has been Chinese investment in textile industries in Ethiopia, for instance, but it is hard to see that the intense worldwide competition in that sector offers opportunities for a breakthrough when Africa's main advantage in manufacturing would be the low cost of labor. In the current configuration of ideology and power in the world economy, tariff protections for infant industries are less available than before the era of structural adjustment.

Building an industrial center requires more than cheap labor, or even natural resources. Good communications, reliable electricity and water, linkages among firms, skilled labor, and management capacity are all factors that tend to encourage industrialization where it is already advanced and where states are capable of delivering consistent services. A glance at a railway map of Europe and Africa (Map 4) suggests the enormity of the gap between a densely networked region and a zone (with the single exception of South Africa) of limited connections, mostly directed toward evacuation of products rather than regional interaction. Manufacturing in Africa is also limited by the scarcity and irregularity of electric power, even in South Africa. Industrialization proceeds most easily when integrated into a complex regional system that connects different kinds of industries. Some economists think that the increasing density of some African cities and their immediate surrounds will create circumstances more like those of newly industrializing zones in Asia, but Asian experience suggests that the efforts of states to provide infrastructural improvements and coordination to industrialization are important ingredients as well. The period in the 1980s and 1990s when most African governments were in financial difficulties and outside agencies were imposing austerity did not help, despite claims from those agencies that imposing financial rigor would produce a favorable investment climate. Today, it is still not evident that the focus of investors – from China and elsewhere – on extractive industries will help the diversification of African economies. In fact, the oil-rich African countries of Nigeria and Angola lead the way in

——— Railways

MAP 4 Railways

exporting capital *out* of Africa, so much so that some experts consider that Africa is a "net creditor" to the rest of the world. Angola and Nigeria have tried to introduce "local content" laws to insure that local capitalists will have a role in servicing the oil industry – and Angola has a powerful state-controlled oil company – but it remains to be seen how far these measures will go beyond providing sinecures to friends of the regime.

Over the last half-century, mining has been an important but fluctuating source of revenue and provider of jobs. From the early 1940s to the mid-1960s copper output from Northern Rhodesia climbed more or less steadily from under 200,000 tons per year to over 700,000. Copper brought enormous wealth to the Belgian Congo as well. Gold enriched South Africa over many decades, and the country boomed in the late 1970s.

Other minerals have had their moments: iron ore in Liberia; bauxite in Guinea and Ghana; uranium in Niger, Gabon, Namibia, and Madagascar; diamonds in Botswana. These export peaks (with the partial exception of gold) have only rarely been sustained, and even more rarely have they had effects beyond the mining enclaves and the labor reservoirs that supplied them. Multinational mining corporations play off the diverse locations of supplies around the world and sometimes the substitutability of products; mining enclaves in Africa are vulnerable to state incapacity and disorder. Botswana stands out as an instance where a government consolidated itself before large-scale production of a valuable resource – in this case diamonds – began, and it was able to negotiate effectively and make a resource work for it rather than the other way around. At the other extreme was Sierra Leone, unable to control illicit diamond mining since the 1950s, overwhelmed in the 1990s by conflict over diamond mining between a predatory government and equally predatory rebels trying to claim the diamond fields.

Two of the world's leading copper producers, Zambia and Zaire/ Congo, experienced, after the 1970s, plunging prices, declining output, and growing unemployment. Zambia's output fell as steadily in the period 1970–93 as it had risen in the previous twenty-three years, declining from 700,000 tons per year to around 250,000 tons. Copper revived in the 2000s, enticing investment especially from China. Zambia's export income from copper went from a little over $500 million in 2001 to over $7 billion in 2014, then fell to a little over $4 billion in 2016. Not least of the problems has been that mining corporations can play Africa's copper mines off against mines in other regions; African copper producers' market share has fallen from 25 percent in 1960 to 10 percent in 2015.

This volatility is not surprising in primary-product exports, but its effect on workers can be devastating. The copper miners of Zambia were such an important source of profits and dangers that they were the focus of the efforts of the British government and the mining corporations to "stabilize" labor in the 1940s and 1950s (Chapter 2), and miners' hopes for a new sort of life were partially fulfilled: better wages, a chance to live with families and raise children in the mine towns, pensions for retirement, and the support of a recognized trade union. The independent Zambian government saw the mines as the key to the country's development and miners as a key constituency. As James Ferguson (1999) poignantly demonstrated, the miners' hopes were dashed in the 1980s when copper prices plummeted and the industry all but collapsed. Jobs disappeared, pensions evaporated in inflation. Will there be a new cycle? As far as workers are concerned, the upswing of the 2000s has been tempered by a more difficult social and political climate: poverty and unemployment in the region, an ideological climate hostile to social benefits, and often harsh treatment of miners at the hands of managers, with grievances particularly focused on Chinese-owned mines. The next downswing, if it materializes, will likely find workers with even less of a cushion than they had in the last cycle.

Then there are the oil-producing states, which in some ways became caricatures of state-centered development. Africa came somewhat late to the world of oil, discovered in southeastern Nigeria in the 1950s and coming into production in the 1960s. Angola, Gabon, Equatorial Guinea, Cameroon, and Sudan are now major producers, but recent discoveries are pulling other parts of coastal West Africa into the picture. Oil producers are spigot economies. They require large investment from multinational companies and highly skilled labor to develop the wells and open the taps. Then a small number of workers – a significant number of them expatriates – manage the wells. The governments collect vast rents. Oil production thus differs from the mining of copper, gold, and other minerals in that it involves far fewer workers and has fewer links to regional economies. Oil production represents the extreme of an economic situation in which the crucial relationship is that between a state that asserts sovereign control of a resource and foreign corporations that have the capacity to exploit it.

The revenue could of course have been used to diversify productive resources, but it was more likely used to enrich an elite that collects the rent and for symbolically important projects, as oil-fed governments built roads and schools in the home villages of leading members or prestige projects in capital cities. In Nigeria oil nearly ruined cocoa – a product which had the virtue of involving thousands of Nigerians in production and marketing – and over time Nigeria became more dependent, not less, on exporting its oil for government revenue and foreign exchange (Figure 11). Gabon, with a small population and large oil reserves, could in principle have come to resemble a low-key version of Abu Dhabi, where the local population prospers and

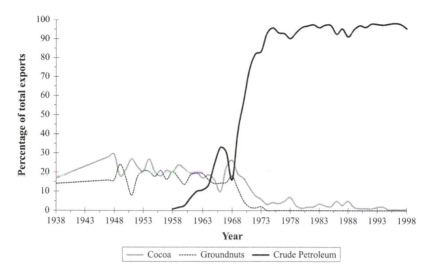

FIGURE 11 Commodity dependence in the Nigerian economy, 1938–1998

foreigners are brought in to do the work, but its rulers have chosen to keep most of the country's earnings to themselves.

For most of Africa the harsh times of the 1980s and 1990s had wider effects than those felt by the elite of wage workers: deteriorating health services in cities and countryside, higher fees for the education of children, unreliable electricity and water supplies, and few social services provided by governments. The export boom of the 2000s has led to extremes: Luanda, the capital of Angola, is now one of the most expensive cities in the world, with high-end accommodation focused on foreigners in the oil and related industries and the Angolan elite, while miserable conditions in the surrounding slums are mitigated mainly by relations of clientage with members of the ruling political party.

Such conditions do not necessarily encourage investment in a broad range of economic activities, but rather narrowly focused, often high-cost, services, including private security and private electricity generation for elite enclaves. Chinese corporations interested in investing in Africa have sometimes built their own infrastructure, including railroads, but such investment represents a far cry from the multifaceted networks of communications and inter-business links that drive development elsewhere.

Chinese investment in Africa as of 2013 was well over $100 billion, nearly 80 percent of which was in transportation, energy, and raw

materials – little in manufacturing. What China wanted from Africa
was overwhelmingly minerals, including oil. Chinese interest in Africa
was not new, and not just a quest to feed the industrial powerhouse of
the late twentieth century. In the 1960s and early 1970s Mao's China
provided an alternative source of inspiration and a modest amount of
material support to African countries that claimed to pursue a socialist
pathway (see Chapter 7), including to varying degrees Guinea, Ghana,
Mali, Tanzania, and Zambia. It was in 1968 that China began construction of the Tazara Railway, a line of over 1,000 miles linking the
port of Dar es Salaam in Tanzania to the inland country – with its
copper mines – of Zambia. The project was intended to get around the
stranglehold that Portugal and Rhodesia, still ruled by whites, had
over Zambia's links to the world economy. This mammoth project
was financed and planned by Chinese corporations and staffed by
Chinese personnel – up to 40,000 of them – with Africans in the least
skilled positions. The railroad was designed both for a political purpose and to bring out raw materials that China needed.

After the death of Mao in 1976 and the rapid expansion of the
Chinese economy through both state-controlled mechanisms and
private investors, China's involvement in Africa escalated. China was
willing to invest in large-scale infrastructure projects in different parts
of Africa, as well as to buy and exploit copper mines and other
productive industries. China became the key to what many hoped
would be Africa's renewed dynamism. But just as Africa has long
been vulnerable to the fluctuations of demand from Europe, it owes
much of its export increase in the past two decades to China and the
vagaries of Chinese demand.

The weakness of industrialization has meant that the expansion of
wage-labor forces that most observers in the 1950s and 1960s expected
would continue did not do so. Some speculate that the stabilization
policies of those years were in part to blame: encouraging employers to
rely on a small but relatively well-paid labor force instead of a large but
ill-paid one. But the approach of the 1920s and 1930s – when wages
were kept low – did not exactly dynamize industrial employment, nor
did the period of structural adjustment in the 1980s and 1990s do so.
People still kept coming to the cities, living off irregular employment,
small-scale marketing, or more successful family members. Seeking an
urban job did not reflect so much a careful calculation of rural and
urban alternatives as a logic akin to gambling – the hope that persistence, family networks, or finding a patron would produce a big leap

FIGURE 12 Migrants from West Africa trying to reach the Canary Islands, 2007. Since the islands were part of Spain, entering them would give migrants access to the European Union. Using small boats to cross a large stretch of the Atlantic Ocean from Mauritania or Senegal, many were drowned and others taken into custody by border police, and often sent home. Other Africans tried to cross the Mediterranean from Libya to Sicily, giving rise to a humanitarian crisis for the refugees and an immigration crisis for European states. Desirée Martin/ AFP/Getty Images

out of the poverty trap. As in most incursions into gambling, failure was more likely than success.

One consequence has been for job seekers to look further afield, especially to Europe. The former citizens of French Africa had the right, under the treaties that gave their countries independence, to seek work and to reside in France until French policy changed in 1974. Britain was also relatively open to immigration into the 1960s. Migration has continued ever since, through clandestine routes and otherwise. In the 2000s the attempts of young, largely male, Africans to reach Europe – although less than migration within Africa – became a drama. Some Europeans were shocked by the tragedy of thousands of people drowning as they tried to reach the Canary Islands, Sicily, or southern Spain in overcrowded, unsafe boats under the thumb of unscrupulous human traffickers; others propagated racialized images of hordes of Africans invading Europe.

In Africa the migratory wave had other meanings: it had a great deal to do with family solidarity, with the support that a migrant who made it to Europe or North America could give to relatives back home, and it was a reflection of the acute disjuncture in the world economy that induced young men to look beyond the continent to support themselves and their families. Although the largest number of would-be workers were and remain poor and unskilled –especially in impoverished or conflict-torn regions – skilled and highly educated Africans have also sought jobs elsewhere, where sophisticated industries or professional opportunities (including for engineers and doctors) could provide possibilities commensurate with their talent and training. The result of the presence in Europe and North America of large numbers of Africans – from street cleaners to professionals – has been a high volume of remittances sent back to Africa.

African countries in 2014, according to the World Bank, received nearly $35 billion in remittances from their citizens abroad, a figure somewhat lower than the total that African countries received in overseas development assistance: $47 billion. Other studies suggest that remittances exceed the level of foreign aid. In some countries the dependence on remittances is strikingly high: Liberia gets 25 percent of GDP from remittances, Lesotho 17 percent, Senegal 10 percent. In some arid areas near the Senegal River, remittances make up to 20–50 percent of family budgets. A newly endowed mosque, a new family dwelling on the outskirts of an African city, or an expanded cattle herd tended by relatives could be the sign of a successful migrant laborer in France; the unsuccessful migrant may be too embarrassed to return.

Remittances are a factor in migration within Africa, as migrants stream from Zimbabwe or Lesotho to South Africa, from Burkina Faso to Côte d'Ivoire. Within South Africa, the dependence of rural women on the insecure urban earnings of men worsened in the 1950s, and again in the 1970s, as expulsions of women from cities under apartheid regulations exacerbated the pressure on land. Such areas were no longer seen as resources for the social reproduction of a workforce; they were dumping grounds. Even after the end of apartheid, it has been hard for people caught between rural areas with exhausted soil and too-dense population and urban slums where job opportunities are lacking.

That migration, within or beyond Africa, appears to so many to be the only path out of poverty points to the profound consequences of inequality both among and within states. China and parts of Southeast Asia provide examples of improved incomes in recent decades, but overall the hopes expressed in the 1960s that political liberation would allow the poor countries of the world to level themselves upward have only in part been met, and assertions by economists in the 1980s and 1990s that market-oriented policies would lead to economic opportunities in Africa have not been realized. Instead of convergence upward, economists have observed widening gaps: between "First" and "Third" Worlds; within each of those worlds; within African countries. The connectedness of different regions continues in spite of obstacles to immigration in Europe and North America, the vulnerabilities of illegal migrants to exploitative employers, and the loss of earning potential of migrant workers whenever there was a recession in the industrial economies.

In the face of the disappointing chronology of industrial development in Africa, are there technologies that have offered possibilities in the past and potentially for the future? The most promising have not been the capital-intensive technologies once favored by development profession-als, but those that are divisible, that are compatible with small individual investments and demand for products of low per-unit cost. Two cases in point, from different time periods, are the automobile and the cell phone, when compared to the railroad and the fixed-phone network. A businessman with a little capital could start a trucking, taxi, or minibus business; drivers could be readily found; patron–client relations could provide a measure of control over the seemingly anarchic growth of the transportation market. Roads required more concentrated effort, but during the colonial period forced labor was often used, and after World War II development funds became available. So if railroads were limited in coverage or capacity and constituted little more than a drain-age network connecting the interior to ports, roads not only fed the rail lines but constituted a more web-like set of linkages. The horrific traffic that clogs many African cities is a sign that the marriage of divisible technology, cheap labor, and entrepreneurial vigor could have an effect.

The cell phone has had a rapid ascendancy: subscriptions in sub-Saharan Africa have gone from 2.5 per 100 people in 2000 to 66 in 2013. Because it requires less investment in fixed facilities than land lines – notoriously lacking and unreliable in most of Africa – this technology has made instant communication much more available. Individuals can buy phone cards with a small amount of money. African entrepreneurs – especially with state connections – have made fortunes in the business, and young men, with no resources or training, could eke out a meager living by hawking phone cards on the streets of African cities. Cell phones not only allow people to talk to each other, but also to engage in banking operations and receive remittances or aid. Although cell phones provide a service in a way that fits the realities of poor and dispersed populations and facilitate a range of economic activities, it is not in itself a technology that produces something or provides export revenue.

Africa's access to up-to-date communications still lags behind other continents: less than a fifth of Africans use the internet, compared to two-fifths in Latin America and four-fifths in the most industrialized countries. Electricity is often unavailable or unreliable, and the weakness of the grid is a major obstacle to industrial investment as well as household consumption: only a third of Africans have access to electric power. And what makes the phone-card business so successful is the availability of young men to sell the cards, a reflection of the underlying poverty of African countries.

For many years, activists in and beyond Africa have argued for a more self-reliant industrialization, using "appropriate technology" and concentrating on product lines based on domestic supplies of raw materials. So far, these possibilities have been more hope than strategy. Meanwhile, it is less than clear that the enormous entrepreneurial energy that the visitor can observe in any African town or city is moving beyond the provision of low-cost services to low-income populations.

Economics beyond Borders

Another solution for Africa's economic ills that has repeatedly been proposed is unification: increasing the size of markets. Some Africans had thought that including France's and Belgium's colonies in what became the European Common Market could have brought a large part of Africa into a large and complex commercial bloc, but in the end the European powers decided to keep the primary benefits of economic integration for themselves and not include the former colonies of some of those powers (Chapter 4).

Decades earlier, colonial borders reshaped the varied spatial linkages that African trading groups had forged before colonization. Official and unofficial appropriations take place at borders. An ambitious experiment to transcend this problem was the East African Community, the common market and common services arrangements among Kenya, Tanzania, and Uganda, begun under the British and continuing in altered forms until 1977. This experiment had its accomplishments, but it couldn't overcome the rigidities of the state system, including leadership rivalries (especially after the eccentric and repressive Idi Amin became dictator of Uganda in 1971) and differing ideologies (self-reliance and socialism in Tanzania and Africanized capitalism in Kenya). Given the unevenness of physical and human resources in the region, the common markets produced conflict: the tendency of industries to locate in Nairobi, the best-equipped city, was unacceptable to Kenya's partners, and issues of favoritism in transportation services proved equally divisive. The East African Community broke up amidst acrimony. There is now talk of reviving it.

The more modest goals of the Economic Community of West African States (ECOWAS) have led to common action, particularly in banking, and remain promising for the future. The Southern African Development Coordination Conference (SADCC), originally created by southern African states to provide an alternative to cooperation with apartheid South Africa, now tries to play a similar role in southern Africa. Both organizations have been constrained by concern about domination by the regional powerhouse in each instance, Nigeria and South Africa. ECOWAS has been the more successful in facilitating cooperation both in economic affairs and in intervention in some of the more catastrophic cases of governmental abuse or conflict, sometimes in cooperation with European powers (Liberia, 1990; Sierra Leone, 1998; Côte d'Ivoire, 2011; Gambia, 2017).

One of the most concrete results of transnational action came from a more compromised sort of cooperation – that is, between France and its former colonies. The common currency (the CFA franc) has been pegged to the French (now European) currency and supported by France. This structure injected external discipline into financial policy in the region, since printing more money when the till ran empty has not been an option, and these states have been less troubled by inflation than others. Yet the CFA franc gives power to France, and its decision to devalue the currency by half in 1994, although regarded as overdue by most economists, brought home the fact that crucial decisions about African economies were being made in Paris.

That dreams of African unity in the closing years of colonial rule did not come to pass left African states without a continent-wide structure to defend African interests in a world in which economic power lay elsewhere. The Organization of African Unity, established in 1963, was from the start limited by member states' desire to guard their recently obtained sovereignty (see Chapter 7). It transformed itself in 2001 into the African Union (AU), which faces the same problem while trying to articulate a more ambitious economic agenda. Meanwhile, the task of sharing economic information, working to lower trade barriers, and making capital available across the continent was taken up, most notably, by the Economic Commission for Africa and the African Development Bank. In 2001 several countries created the New Partnership for Africa's Development, to which twenty countries now belong, with the object of coordinating development plans and encouraging sustainable technologies, environmental stewardship, and the alleviation of poverty. Its declaration affirming the control of each nation-state "over all its wealth, natural resources and economic activity" was both a warning to outside investors who claimed rights to African resources by virtue of "free trade" and an acknowledgment of constraint on international action imposed by deference to the principle of national sovereignty and the power of incumbent rulers. In practice, negotiations over trade regulation and other issues between European and North American partners take a bilateral form – country to country – rather than going through Africa-wide institutions or regional ones such as ECOWAS or SADCC. The AU envisions, over the 2020s, moving toward something more like the European Common Market and has taken preliminary steps in that direction, but at present it has neither the power nor the institutions to carry out common economic governance; the European Commission has nearly forty times the personnel of its African equivalent, even though the AU has more member states.

African states did participate in negotiations with the European Economic Community at different times to try to improve terms of access to European markets (the Conventions of Yaoundé of 1963 and 1969 and of Lomé of 1975, plus later agreements), to determine the degree to which African states could protect infant industries, and to find means of encouraging investment without trampling on states' management of their resources. They cooperated in the 1960s with other "developing countries" in the United Nations Commission on Trade and Development, which tried to improve the terms of trade of primary producers, and they helped to formulate during the 1970s the demand for a New International Economic Order. They voted in 1986 for a United Nations resolution on the "right to development." But the cards were not in the hands of the world's poorer countries, each of which needed aid and investment from the countries on which they were making demands. Moreover, international cooperation assumes that state leaders are disinterested advocates of African or at least national interests, and many are anything but.

As Senghor predicted in the 1950s, the form of decolonization that emerged – devolving power to individual territories and weakening supra-territorial federations – left each territory with limited resources and created a vested interest among political elites in keeping borders the way they were (Chapter 4). African economies are at least as likely to compete as to complement each other's strengths; most are trying to get narrow ranges of goods into "developed world" markets; all want to buy the same manufactured goods from Asia or Europe. Intraregional trade in Africa as a percentage of total trade is much less important than in Europe.

Interstate agreements are only one way in which people try to deal with the border problem. Unofficial cross-border trading networks – smuggling – may well be doing more to create regional trading relations than official efforts, albeit with high transaction costs in the profits of middlemen and bribes to officials. Smuggling is not necessarily incongruent with state interests, since officials sometimes take the lead in undercutting, for a price, their own trade regulations. A border gives rise to specialists who figure out how to cross it; such people constitute a community as much as any people located firmly within a given set of boundaries.

Traffic in drugs across the Sahara – including a route that takes narcotics from South America through Guinea-Bissau, then to North Africa, then to Europe – helps to finance guerrilla groups in the Sahel, including Islamists who have caused havoc in Mali and its neighbors. Decades of violent conflict among warlords in the eastern Democratic Republic of the Congo was, most observers believe, exacerbated by small-scale and illicit mining operations, smuggling coltan, cobalt, gold, and other minerals out through Indian Ocean ports – with the complicity, most likely, of Rwandan and Ugandan officials. Both insurgencies and counterinsurgency operations by governments have in Congo, Sierra Leone, Angola, and other cases been funded by agreements with corporations or shady networks to provide future rights to exploit minerals.

The other side of connections across borders is closure. There have been numerous border closings and expulsions of aliens – Ghanaians from Nigeria, Burkinabé from Côte d'Ivoire, Mozambicans and Zimbabweans from South Africa. Those expelled were often following the paths of migrant labor and regional trade that their fathers took during the colonial era. Particularly notorious was Ghana's expulsion of 100,000 aliens, mostly from Nigeria or Burkina Faso, in 1968. In

2008 there were waves of violence in South African cities against Africans from other countries. An escalating instance of xenophobic politics occurred in Côte d'Ivoire during the 1990s and 2000s. The government promoted the notion of *ivoirité*, aimed at excluding from full participation in national life people regarded as not completely Ivorian, including many who had come generations back from Burkina Faso or Mali. The *ivoirité* crusade developed in the context of rivalries for presidential succession after the death in 1993 of Félix Houphouët-Boigny. It culminated in a north–south civil war in 2011, ending only with the intervention of ECOWAS and France. The exclusionary politics stood in contrast with the dynamic that had decades earlier made Côte d'Ivoire the wealthiest state in the region: the movement of labor from the relatively arid and transport-poor north to the fertile and well-connected south.

If the Africa of sovereign nations has at times moved away from its own history of migration and regional trade, the internal conflicts of some states have spilled across the borders of others. Many more refugees are being sheltered in African countries other than their own than have crossed the Mediterranean into Europe, despite the publicity the latter has been receiving since the mid-2010s. What is allegedly the world's largest refugee camp, Dadaab in Kenya, houses an estimated quarter of a million people, mostly Somalis fleeing the disorder in their country that has raged for over two decades. Distinctions between "political refugees" – fleeing violence – and "economic refugees" – fleeing poverty – are hard to sustain in practice, since violence and economic dislocation often reinforce each other, and the refugee risking his life to cross the Mediterranean in a small boat is, in any case, fleeing a desperate situation.

Africa's interconnections are old, but they are not necessarily getting ever stronger. Economists think that Africa's share in world trade has diminished since 1960, although the figures aren't very precise. Foreign aid declined to a minuscule 0.23 percent of donor-country GDP in the 1990s – well below targets advocated by international organizations – but in Africa this still represented over 13 percent of GDP, higher than in any other "developing" region; governments such as those of Tanzania and Mozambique would close down overnight without donor support. Africa's connections with the rest of the world are neither as intense nor as balanced as those of other regions, but they are essential to the welfare of its people and to prospects for the future.

Escaping the Underdevelopment Trap

For sixty years, since the independence of Ghana, African countries have been trying to escape the trap of underdevelopment. Poverty can be a vicious circle; capital needed to improve productivity must come from savings, but poor countries save with difficulty. In a competitive world, the advantages of cheap labor can be seized by countries with labor costs almost as low but with better infrastructure or easier access to transportation. The efforts of African states to get out of the position in which they found themselves at independence have followed a particular arc: modest if uneven progress, followed after 1975 by a reversal of fortune that in much of the continent set back further economic and social progress for nearly a quarter century. The kinds of measures that in the long run are most vital to a developing economy – security, health, education – were disabled by austerity measures implemented by governments or imposed on them by international financial institutions in the face of the revenue shortfalls brought about by the world recession. The export dependence of African economies made them particularly vulnerable, and in that sense much of Africa suffered from the inability of the first generation of rulers to make good on what, for most of them, was an explicit goal: to develop national economies. The immediate crisis of declining export income was prolonged by the debts acquired as leaders tried to maintain their political position in the face of loss of revenue. The problem of these years lies at the center, in a thematic as well as chronological sense, of the history of Africa since 1940.

Most African regimes after 1975 tried as long as they could to hold down outlays while continuing politically necessary expenditures, such as paying off clients and providing visible services to political constituencies. It didn't always work. By 1980 many countries faced huge and mounting indebtedness to international banks (which had been all too willing to lend in an earlier era) and to organizations such as the IMF. They had to devote an increasing percentage of export revenues to debt repayment, leaving little for necessary imports, let alone for investment. Uganda devoted 5 percent of its exports to debt service in 1980, and 66 percent around 1990; Kenya's debt service went from 16 percent of exports to 34 percent, and Côte d'Ivoire's from 25 percent to 60 percent. Facing bankruptcy, the majority of African countries appealed to the IMF for further loans to enable them to stretch out payments. The IMF imposed stern conditions under a policy that became known as structural adjustment.

IMF economists blamed the crisis on bad policies of African governments. African leaders stood accused of technical mistakes – for example, of overvaluing their currencies, which discourages exports and encourages imports – and of misguided social policies. Above all, they were accused of creating too many sinecures in the civil service and state-owned businesses, paying urban wage workers too much, and setting agricultural prices too low. Officials were accused, sometimes accurately, of "rent-seeking" behavior: establishing restrictions on doing business, then collecting bribes for exceptions or allocating monopolies to friends and relatives. The remedy for this was held to be the market: shrink government; remove regulations; lower trade barriers; and let the market work its magic, especially by stimulating agricultural production and exports. Some thirty-six African countries took out loans from the IMF during the 1980s and were subject to the conditions it imposed.

Critics contended that the premises of the program were wrong. African governments were not bloated; they had many fewer civil servants per capita than any other developing region; the level of social services was hardly sufficient to provide a minimally educated, reasonably healthy workforce. The IMF formulas did more to insure that African countries focused on repaying debts owed to the affluent part of the world economy than on rebuilding basic economic structures in Africa. Critics contended that the IMF approach had less to do with saving Africa than with writing off the continent.

Defenders of the IMF claimed some success where IMF prescriptions were followed, in Ghana and Uganda most notably, while the critics claimed that this success was defined in self-fulfilling terms – that budgets shrank and debts ceased to mount – while evidence that market-oriented policies improved social welfare or built structures capable of sustaining growth was less clear. Further, the critics argued that if a major cause of difficulties was the overpayment of urban workers in relation to rural farmers, the precipitous decline in urban wages since 1980 should have resulted in economic advance. But the record of the low-wage 1980s was worse than that of the "high"-wage 1960s, which suggests that the so-called urban bias was a mistaken target from the beginning. While advocates of structural adjustment claimed that privatization of state corporations and deregulation gave corrupt politicians less room for rent seeking, critics argued that, faced with shrinking resources, politicians cut necessary services and useful investments first and politically useful rents last, so that IMF policy undermined the numbers and salaries of teachers and health-care professionals (too few to begin with) and set back the development of a workforce able to develop skills over a lifetime, but it did not stop corruption.

The World Bank and leading development economists began in the late 1990s to take a more self-critical view of the effects of structural adjustment and to return to something more like the developmentalist thinking of the 1960s. The World Bank itself declared in 2003 that it had moved its priority from structural adjustment to "poverty reduction." On the eve of the year 2000 leading figures in development circles proclaimed Millennium 2015, with the objective of eradicating poverty in fifteen years. Despite a variety of new initiatives to promote agriculture, industry, and commerce with the goal of bettering the condition of the poorest of the poor, 2015 has come and gone and poverty is still with us. When journalists celebrate the reduction of global poverty, most of what they cite is accounted for by China's remarkable development since the 1970s.

Now, the European Union intends to support development for another reason: to discourage migration from Africa to Europe by targeted efforts to improve job opportunities in African countries such as Mali from which the largest number of clandestine migrants are coming. But the sums in question are trivial in comparison to the problem. Some changes that might help African countries export, such as ending the subsidies given to certain crops by the European Union, have been discussed but not put into effect.

Meanwhile, the cause of poverty, ill-health, and social ills in Africa has been taken up by a host of non-governmental organizations (NGOs). They operate in many domains: health provision, population policy, childhood development, elementary and secondary education, prevention of human trafficking, empowerment of women. Some of them fill gaps in service provision that neither African governments nor official development programs take care of. Some commentators worry that NGOs have become an industry in themselves, providing careers for North Americans and Europeans the way colonial service once did. Some NGOs are better than others in forging common projects with African organizations. In any case, NGOs are more accountable to their donors than to the people they serve, and the fact that they do useful work testifies to the dashed hopes that governments elected by citizens of African states would be responsible for safeguarding the security and welfare of those citizens.

Social Change in Independent Africa: Health

We need to look beyond the ups and downs of economic indicators and the possibilities and constraints of transforming economic structures. When we turn to some of the most important dimensions of African social life – health and the education of a new generation – we find, once again, evidence of real progress and serious limitations.

The most important of these concerns life itself. Life expectancy since the late colonial period has increased, infant mortality is down, and populations have been growing. The ever-larger generations are having more access to education than previous generations. Literacy levels have improved. All this suggests that some conditions of life have become significantly better in the last seventy-five years.

In the early colonial years, because of the traumas of colonization and exposure to a wider range of diseases, Africa lost population. The taming of epidemic diseases (but not endemic ones such as malaria or sleeping sickness) as well as lowered infant mortality and higher birth rates turned the decades after World War II into years of burgeoning population growth. Rates of population growth moved from about 1 percent at war's end to 3 percent in the 1970s, leveling off or falling slightly since then (Figure 13a). The modernization project required better health facilities, and some independent African governments, like Tanzania's, made a strong effort to bring clinics to rural areas.

In sub-Saharan Africa as a whole, life expectancy rose from forty to over fifty years between 1960 and 1990, before falling off slightly and then rising again in the 2000s. Infant mortality fell by 2015 to a third of what it had been in 1960 (Figure 14a), although in some countries there was an uptick in infant mortality in the 1980s and 1990s, probably due to AIDS. The long-term improvements were linked not only to medical care, but to other social services: whereas 27 percent of Africans had access to safe water in 1975, 40 percent did so in 1990.

Once considered underpopulated, Africa is now seen as the opposite. Rural population density has increased enormously, while Africa has rapidly urbanized (see below). The issue is in fact complex – as a closer look at the ups and downs in Figures 13a, 13b, and

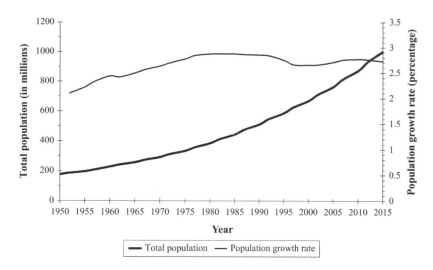

FIGURE 13A Total population and population growth rate in sub-Saharan Africa, 1950–2015

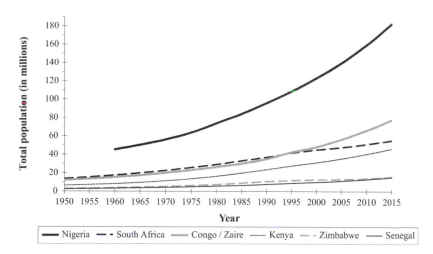

FIGURE 13B Total population in selected African countries, 1950–2015

14a–14c begins to suggest – and high population growth reflects not just the accomplishments of modern medicine, but also its limitations. Childhood mortality is still sufficiently high for families needing assurance that a young generation will survive to have more children than experts consider optimum, and the importance of diversifying options – given the risks of farming, wage labor,

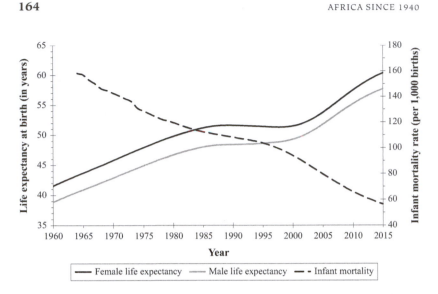

FIGURE 14A Life expectancy at birth and infant mortality rate in sub-Saharan Africa, 1960–2015

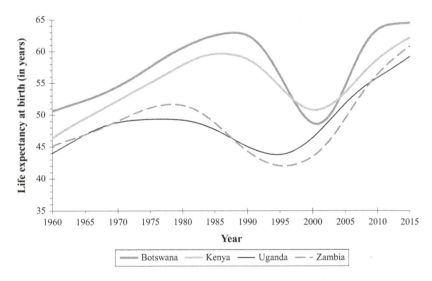

FIGURE 14B Life expectancy at birth in selected African countries, 1960–2015

migration, or any other survival strategy – also encourages larger families. Improved infant and child mortality might well, in the long run, lower population growth rates, as would better schooling and job opportunities for women. These are all areas where governments in the early years of independence made considerable, but

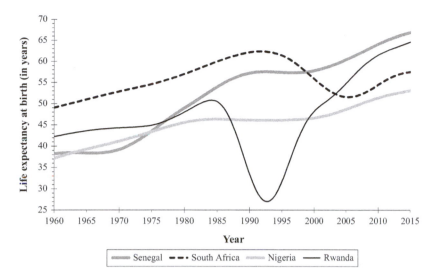

FIGURE 14C Life expectancy at birth in selected African countries, 1960–2015

insufficient and unsustained, progress. The percentage of African women using modern contraception is less than a third that of Latin America and Asia – partly a result of choice, partly of the uneven distribution of health care. As a result of high birth rates, Africa's population is younger than that of other continents: two-thirds of Africans are under twenty-five, over double the percentage in Europe. Experts think that by 2100 the population of Africa as a whole will surpass that of China.

The economic crisis of the 1970s and 1980s had powerful effects on welfare beyond the stagnation of GDP. Efforts to build health and sanitation facilities in many countries lost ground. In some countries there are fewer physicians per capita now than in the 1970s. Preventable and curable diseases are still killing people, particularly children. Thousands of children die every day of malaria, and large numbers die of diarrhea. With improved economies in the 2000s, some countries have improved their health-care systems. Rwanda, for example, now provides health insurance and decent maternity services to most of its population.

Looking at country-specific life-expectancy data (Figures 14b and 14c) for Botswana, Kenya, Uganda, Zambia, and South Africa, one sees a very large drop in the 1990s, wiping out most if not all of the gains since 1960, before recovering and pushing upward in the 2000s.

The principal cause of the reversal was the AIDS epidemic, although economic difficulties and poor funding for health services are factors too. In the case of Rwanda, a sudden drop in life expectancy in 1994–95 was caused by the genocide that began in April 1994 (Chapter 1).

AIDS is not a uniquely African scourge, but its extent and its particular pattern reflect post-1970s African conditions. Africa was hit harder than any other part of the world by AIDS. In the last two decades of the twentieth century it claimed nearly 14 million African lives. An estimated 12 million children were orphaned. Skilled workforces were particularly affected, and workers who become sick have children, partners, siblings, and other relatives who also suffer. In South Africa 19 percent of the population was infected as of 2014; in Botswana the figure was 25 percent. Mortality finally began to decline in the new century, from around 1.5 million deaths in 2004 to just under 800,000 in 2014.

The incidence of AIDS in Africa follows a distinctive pattern: most cases appear to be transmitted by heterosexual contact rather than by homosexual contact or syringes shared among drug users. A majority of HIV-infected Africans have been women, whereas in the United States and Europe at the height of the scourge, women accounted for under a quarter of infections. Heterosexual transmission has something to do with the importance of migration – especially male labor migration – across much of the continent, and the high rates of HIV infection in a relatively prosperous country such as Botswana suggest that a more active exchange economy can produce more infections.

The pattern has much to do with gender inequality, for many women, lacking resources of their own, are dependent on a male miner, truck driver, or even a high-school teacher, who has multiple partners. The pattern of the epidemic also reveals the failure of governments to provide routine health care and living conditions. HIV infection is rendered more likely by poor basic health: inadequate nutrition, endemic diseases, and lack of treatment for curable venereal infections. The AIDS epidemic reveals what Didier Fassin (2007: 274) calls "inequality in the face of death." With a crisis – and especially worries of disease spreading to Europe and North America – a panicked international medical establishment intervened in Africa to try to contain AIDS, but part of the cause of this pattern of infection lay earlier in the shortfalls and reversal of an effort to provide routine medical care and nutrition, as well as the social conditions that facilitated transmission of the virus.

Mortality due to AIDS decreased from the 1990s because of the introduction of effective antiretroviral medicines (ARVs) and in some cases (such as Uganda) safe-sex campaigns. But one of the underlying problems was revealed once again in 2014, when an epidemic of Ebola – a viral infection with a mortality rate over 50 percent – in Guinea, Sierra Leone, and Liberia spread in a region where health services had lapsed, as a result of budget cuts, and in the latter two cases civil war. Because of the lack of rural clinics to sound the alarm, the response of international health organizations was slow, but when it came it focused intensely (with local caregivers playing a courageous and essential part) on isolating infected people and stopping the spread. The epidemic ended – and it never had the feared effect outside this region of Africa – but the underlying problem remains: the lack of routine medical care in much of the continent and a tendency of outside agencies – including such active health-minded philanthropists as the Gates Foundation – to focus on whatever disease touches their concerns or fears at a particular moment. Although thoughtful members of the international health field appreciate the difficulty, they run into the problem that the provision of routine health services to a population that cannot afford private care is fundamentally a state concern, and some states lack the means (or the will) to confront it. At present we lack international mechanisms capable of approaching the issue at a global level. This failure should be considered in the light of the progress that had been made from the late 1940s through at least the 1970s in much of Africa. Providing medical care in a dispersed and relatively poor population is not an impossible task.

Social Change in Independent Africa: Education

Education was arguably an even greater priority than health services to new African governments. In the 1950s, before formal independence, transitional governments in southern Nigeria made "universal primary education" a key element of their platform. Over sixty years later the promise remains unfulfilled, but the effort was impressive, as it was in most African countries. Education was often the largest item in the state budget (as high as 20 percent). When Kenya became

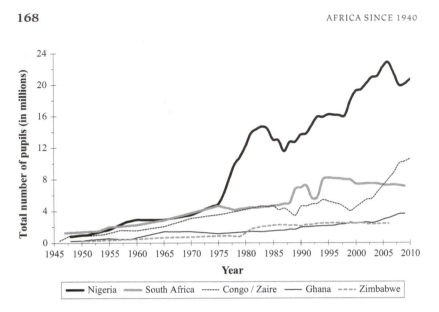

FIGURE 15A Primary education: total number of pupils in selected African countries, 1946–2010

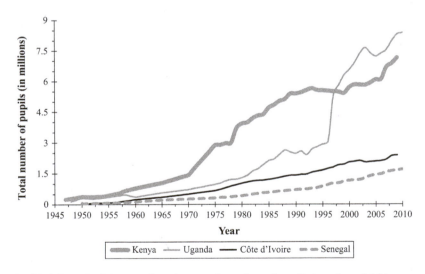

FIGURE 15B Primary education: total number of pupils in selected African countries, 1946–2010

independent, 900,000 students were in primary school; thirty years later, there were 5.5 million. Figures 15a–15d point to the efforts of African countries to get more and more children and young adults into classrooms, and Table 1 shows the effort in select countries in relation to

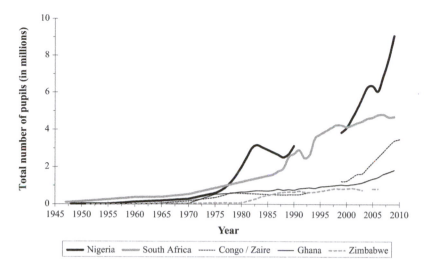

FIGURE 15C Secondary education: total number of pupils in selected African countries, 1946–2010

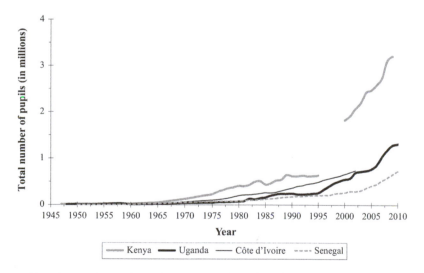

FIGURE 15D Secondary education: total number of pupils in selected African countries, 1946–2010

their age-appropriate populations. In sub-Saharan Africa as a whole, gross primary enrollments went from 43 percent of the school-age population in 1960 to 98 percent in 2014, secondary from 3 percent to 43 percent, university from practically nil to 9 percent. Adult literacy

Table 1 *Education: gross enrollment rates in sub-Saharan Africa, 1960–2014 (percent)*

Year	Primary			Secondary			Tertiary		
	Male	Female	Total	Male	Female	Total	Male	Female	Total
1960	54	32	43	4.2	2.0	3.1	0.4	0.1	0.2
1970	63	45	54	15	11	13	1.7	1.1	1.4
1980	86	68	77	23	15	19	2.7	1.5	2.1
1990	79	66	73	27	20	23	4.2	2.2	3.2
2000	88	75	82	29	23	26	5.2	3.6	4.4
2010	100	93	97	44	36	40	9.2	6.5	7.9
2014	102	95	98	46	40	43	10	7.2	8.6

Source: For 1960, World Bank, *Can Africa Claim the 21st Century?* (Washington: World Bank, 2000), p. 106.
Since 1970, World Bank, *World Development Index* (Washington: World Bank, 2017).

Note: Gross enrollment rate is the number of students *enrolled* in a given level of education, regardless of age, expressed as a percentage of the official school-age population. It can be above 100 percent if a significant number of people not of conventionally defined school age are enrolled.

Table 2 *Literacy rates in selected African countries, c.1960–2015 (percent of males and females aged fifteen and above)*

Country	c.1960		c.1970		c.1980		c.1990		c.2000		c.2010		2015	
	Male	Female	Male	Female	Male	Female	Male	Female	Male	Female	Male	Female	Male	Female
Congo/Zaire	49	14	35	11	48	21	62	34	81	54	88	46	89	66
Côte d'Ivoire	8	2	25	6	34	13	44	24	61	39	52	30	53	33
Ethiopia							36	19	50	23	49	29	57	41
Ghana	30	10	43	17	58	31	70	47	66	50	78	65	82	71
Kenya	25	6	56	26	70	43	81	61	87	78	79	67	81	75
Nigeria			31	10	45	22	60	38	67	43	61	41	69	50
Rwanda					51	27	68	49	71	60	71	62	75	68
Senegal	10	1	23	6	31	12	38	19	51	29	62	40	68	44
South Africa	41	40	72	68	78	75	82	80	84	81	94	92	96	93
Uganda	44	26	51	22	61	31	69	43	78	59	83	65	81	67
Zambia	53	30	64	32	72	47	79	59	76	60	89	78	90	81
Zimbabwe	48	31	66	49	78	62	87	75	89	79	88	80	89	85

Source: World Bank, *World Development Indicators* (Washington: World Bank, 2000, 2017); United Nations, *Demographic Yearbook* (New York: United Nations, 1960, 1963, 1964, 1970); United Nations Educational, Scientific and Cultural Organization (UNESCO), *Statistical Yearbook* (Paris: UNESCO Publishing, 1980), pp. 44–46.
Note: Some dates are approximate

(Table 2) rose from 27 percent in 1970 to 45 percent in 1990 to 63 percent in 2015. In some countries, progress stopped during the period of structural adjustment; in others, school enrollment continued to advance.

Yet it is the unevenness of education across the continent that stands out. This pattern is particularly striking in recent statistics on literacy. In Zimbabwe between 80 and 90 percent of men and women can read and write, in Burkina Faso 22 percent. South Africa – which cut illiteracy in half between 2000 and 2015 – and Kenya are near the top of the literacy range, Guinea and Niger near the bottom. Senegal educates a portion of its population quite well – it has one of the continent's leading universities and a long history of training teachers – but the majority of its female population still does not know how to read. Despite considerable progress, a third of the African population – the majority of them women – are illiterate. At higher levels, women's access to education often remains below that of men despite improvements in recent years.

South Africa experienced a variant on this pattern: it had long provided high-quality education to a portion of its population – whites, that is – and it provided significant, but lower-quality, educational facilities to a portion of its black majority. After 1994 the government was confronted with the political necessity of providing equal education – or at least a facsimile of it – to all citizens without diluting too much the training of a well-educated elite that its sophisticated economy demanded. Resources were put into the system, but finding adequately trained teachers, given the bottlenecks of previous decades, has made it difficult to insure that access to schools would mean quality education. As inadequately educated students emerge from primary schools, tension mounts over the difficulties of many students at secondary and tertiary levels.

Providing university education for more than a handful of Africans entered the colonial imagination quite late. After World War II British and French officials thought they could get away with one university each for their West African colonies (Ibadan, founded in 1948, and Dakar, in 1957). With independence, universities became national projects. Most African states have at least one; Nigeria has many. Some African countries, notably South Africa and Ghana, supply medical personnel to more affluent countries; more African engineers work in the United States than in Africa. Despite the overall weakness of university education in Africa one can still speak of a "brain drain" from Africa, a sign that inequality in the world tends to perpetuate itself as people move to where there are opportunities to use their talents.

The austerity epidemic of the 1980s affected schools. Government spending per pupil declined around 20 percent by 2000. Recovery has been uneven – impressive in some places, disastrous in countries beset by violent conflict. In the years of structural adjustment, teachers' salaries plummeted, forcing many to do other work alongside their primary jobs; sometimes they went unpaid. Class sizes increased – to seventy-five in Dakar, for instance – and facilities became degraded. Many schools in Africa still do not have blackboards and most lack books. Studies of schooling in some rural areas reveal the discouragement of students and parents and declining enrollments: too many primary-school graduates cannot get jobs, and families no longer put so much faith in education. Nevertheless, self-help efforts are organized at the village level to promote schooling, sometimes with results that credit the effort more than the accomplishment. Private schools – church related or secular – took on increasing importance in some places, for those who could afford them.

The sudden effort to promote secondary and university education in the 1950s and 1960s gave Africa a substantial class of people conversant in literature, science, and technology, and with ambitions to know more. Many of them came from very modest backgrounds. Toward the end of colonial rule came belated efforts to "Africanize" the civil service in African countries, and this generation of students had career opportunities open to them. The French government, for example, admitted Africans into its school that trained colonial civil servants, then turned the school into an institution specifically for training people from its former colonies for service in their own countries. Since this generation entered such positions at a relatively young age, they could stay in their positions for some time, making upward mobility more difficult for the next generation. The turndown in economic fortunes – at a time when educational improvement was showing results – created a major obstacle for the generation that came of age twenty years after independence. Not surprisingly, the people entrenched in good positions were doing their best to pass them on to their own children. By the early twenty-first century education of sufficient quality to lead to professional opportunities has increasingly become a privilege for the children of those already in such a position.

The development drive of the late colonial and early post-colonial years had been intended, among other goals, to put in place a workforce capable of attracting investors and making production efficient, orderly, and predictable. The uneven results, particularly in the hard years of the 1980s and 1990s, have produced a situation where would-be investors and employers complain of the inadequacy of an educated labor force, and primary and secondary school graduates complain of a lack of jobs.

Many people have been left out altogether. For them, poverty means not only material suffering, but the inability to achieve adulthood – to marry and start a family – or to fully participate in a "modern" society whose attractions are visible and unattainable. "Youth" has become a problematic category in Africa – a source of hope for a more prosperous future and for politically aware participants in democratic governance, and concern over an alienated generation prone to be recruited to dubious causes. As the Senegalese historian Mamadou Diouf (2003: 9) puts it: "For many youths, idealism, nihilism, and sometimes even pure, childish naughtiness seem to coexist."

Cities, Countryside, and Beyond

Change in economic structure, health, and education from the middle of the twentieth century onward was part of a transformation of the way Africans lived that is difficult to grasp, not least because Africans were in motion, geographically and socially. However much the image of "tribes" has figured in outsiders' perceptions of Africa, the continent has a long history of movement: trade diasporas, religious pilgrimages, kingdoms incorporating their neighbors, the movement of expanding lineages into new regions, and labor migration, coerced and voluntary. The movement of people accelerated in the post-war era.

Colonial officials, national leaders, scholars, and intellectuals were caught up in the ferment of a rapidly changing continent. In the 1950s and 1960s many of them were attracted to the notion of "modernization." Modernization seemed like a complete package of transformations: people from backward villages would move to dynamic cities; nuclear families would replace extended ones; rigid social hierarchies would give way to openness and to individual achievement. Other African intellectuals saw modernization as "Westernization" and as a danger to a uniquely African way of life. Still others thought that Africans could adapt and change without becoming Western. Meanwhile, ordinary people were trying to live their lives: to use resources that were new and others that were old, to struggle against the oppressiveness of the new by using the old and against the oppressiveness of the old by using the new. What they were producing did not fit a pre-packaged modernity, nor did it constitute "tradition" or "community." People were fashioning and refashioning forms of connections and association.

In the early 1950s anthropologists were introducing concepts such as "social situation," "social field," and "social network" to emphasize that Africans did not live within a bounded universe but created new patterns of social and cultural relations as they moved into different sorts of places. Africans were not merely molded by being "urbanized"; they were bringing something to the city as well and weaving together city and country in different ways.

More recent scholarship has emphasized the vibrancy of urban social and cultural life: the wide range of associations that people formed among themselves; the importance of new patterns of leisure and consumption; the vitality of sociability and conversation in tea houses and bars; the ways in which African writers, artists, and musicians took in influences from around the world and projected their own creativity to other continents (Chapter 7).

Africa certainly became a much more urban continent in the post-war years. As late as 1960 only 15 percent of its people lived in cities. By 1975 this figure had passed 20 percent, and by 2014 it was around 37 percent. Given that total population had grown over those years, that meant a lot of people living in cities. Africa is still the least urbanized continent in the world, but is urbanizing at the most rapid rate. In 1950 only one sub-Saharan city, Johannesburg, harbored over a million people; now forty do so. The process has been very uneven. Lagos and Kinshasa became "megacities," with over 10 million inhabitants. Each country seemed to have at least one pole of attraction for rural dwellers, although some countries remained overwhelmingly rural.

How can one think of the changes in urban life in the post-war decades? The gap between what French scholars call the "legal city" and the "real city" is a place to start: a distinction between the regulated, controlled space of planners' imagination versus the lived realities of city-dwellers. Pre-war colonial cities were supposed to be nodes of government administration and symbols of imperial power; they were more often rude and haphazard. Africans were supposed to be temporary residents, with only a few exceptions: the old Yoruba

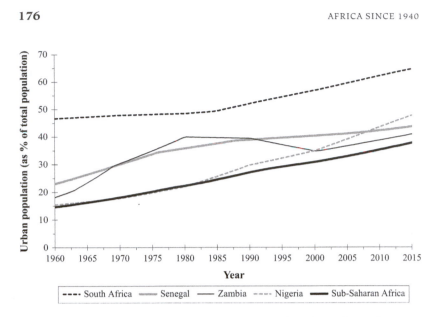

FIGURE 16A Urban population as a percentage of total population for selected African countries and sub-Saharan Africa, 1960–2015

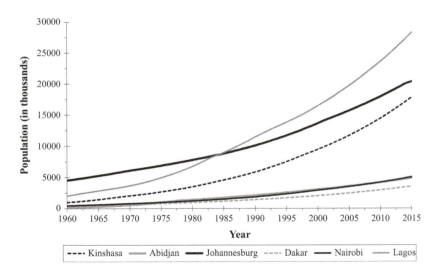

FIGURE 16B Population of selected African urban agglomerations, 1960–2015

cities; established commercial centers along the coasts with established urban elites; and certain South African cities where the historical presence of an African population was grudgingly acknowledged. In reality, Africans had been making their own cities for many years

(Chapter 2), and while the housing they built was often rude, settlements sprang up where they were not supposed to be and women entered spaces that were supposed to be for males. The city was not the bastion of white society that colonial officials imagined, nor was it the haven of the "detribalized native" that they feared. What appeared chaotic to Europeans was often the fruit of well-organized networks of rural–urban connection.

After the war French and British officials imagined a different sort of city, segregated more by class than by race, and above all a material and symbolic expression of their wish to incorporate of Africans into a "modern" urban space, organized in accordance with the best ideas of sanitation and urban planning. There was much new construction, and this proved the model for the post-independence fashion in the building of downtown high-rises, grid-like urban layouts, and wide streets. Colonial regimes at times forcibly removed Africans from downtown neighborhoods to rebuild them in proper fashion. Sex ratios moved toward equality, both as women moved in from rural areas and as more and more urbanites were city born.

Serious struggles took place in the 1940s and 1950s over restrictions on residence. Where city-center space was coercively modernized, peri-urban settlements – in Dakar, in Mombasa, in Lagos – spread outwards, sometimes on the basis of land that was simply occupied, sometimes via understandings between older and newer residents. The struggles were most severe in white-dominated cities in southern Africa. In Johannesburg in South Africa, in the late 1940s, where urban industry was expanding much more rapidly than housing, up to 90,000 people organized to occupy vacant land and build shack settlements on the periphery of the city, confronting authorities with a fait accompli. The apartheid state, especially from the 1950s onwards, removed Africans from other locations, where they had constructed a too-threatening associative life and attempted to sort people into different sites within a racially defined urban space. Migrant men, meanwhile, were shuttled in and out of single-sex hostels and compounds on the mines and in Johannesburg. The apartheid state was sophisticated enough to grant certain categories of people rights to live permanently as families in segregated sections of cities, set against the hostels, the illegal encampments, and the whims of authorities to change the rules.

When the apartheid system began to fall apart in the 1980s, the spatial structure of Johannesburg changed. The Central Business

District with its imposing skyscrapers began to be hollowed out as businesses and white residents moved to the suburbs, creating multiple poles of urban concentration, segregated by class if not by race. Once-fashionable neighborhoods nearer the center were allowed to decay and became attractive to migrants from other parts of South Africa or Africa more generally, living in increasingly tawdry conditions but helping new waves of migrants work their way into the fabric of the city. The gated communities and shopping malls of the elite – no longer purely white – growing up in the suburbs provided protection as well as isolation from what was perceived, with some reason, as the dangerous spaces of what had once been a city center catering to whites. Johannesburg has become a city of barriers, enclosed spaces, and fragmented neighborhoods. It is lacking in public spaces.

The kind of life Africans built for themselves within the port cities, state capitals, mining towns, commercial hubs, railway junctions, and other concentrations of employment did not fit the expectations of colonial rulers or their African successors. Colonial thinking in the 1950s had emphasized the "stabilization" of urban labor. The reality – even then, but more so in the present – has been that regulated, relatively secure, unionized jobs were a minority. By the 1960s stabilized employment was not growing in most of Africa. In 1988, the International Labour Office estimates, "modern" wage workers constituted only 8 percent of the labor force.

What was growing most rapidly was what colonial regimes had once feared and labeled as detribalized or floating populations. By the 1970s scholars had given this category a new name: urban informal sector. What they were trying to describe wasn't specifically urban, for it referred to people moving into and out of cities; it wasn't literally informal, since a variety of relationships – from apprenticeship to Islamic brotherhoods to control by local power-brokers – regulated it; and it wasn't a sector, because people within it interacted closely with those in regulated employment.

The term most usefully refers not to a particular socio-economic category but to a domain outside state regulation: a heterogeneous world of small and often transitory workshops, of traders working in the streets, of illegal activities. While job security has been under assault worldwide in recent decades, some observers consider Africa to be the most "informalized" continent, not surprising given the weakness of investment in large-scale enterprises. Where official economies all but collapsed, as in Mobutu's Zaire or Sékou Touré's

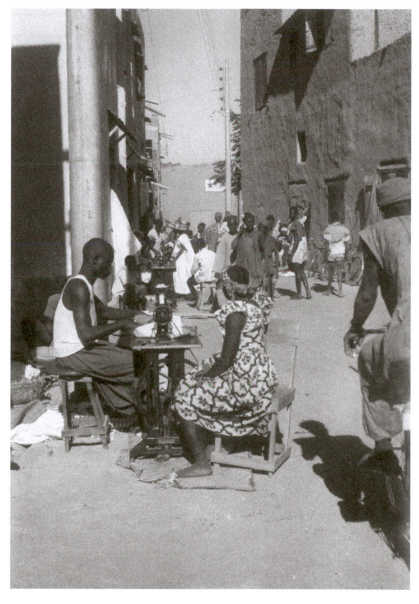

FIGURE 17 Tailors working in a street, Mopti, Mali, 1962. Artisanal production and small-scale marketing remained the backbone of the "real" economies of urban Africa, even when colonial and post-colonial planners thought in terms of state-dominated economies or modern corporations. ©ECPAD/La Documentation Française

Guinea, informal economic relationships were what kept people alive. The extent to which "self-employment" – another euphemism for people outside of regular wage labor – dominated the economic scene has varied greatly: in the early 2000s, 90 percent of Tanzanian workers were considered self-employed, in Zambia (once the scene of stabilization efforts in the mines) 82 percent. In comparison, only 15 percent of the workforce in South Africa was self-employed, 18 percent in Namibia.

In some ways the "illegal" city, whether in Mathare Valley outside Nairobi or Pikine outside Dakar, was well organized, because the legal insecurity of tenure required cultivating relationships with state officials. Non-regulated activities delivered low-cost services, and in that sense they "worked." Some observers thought that here was a model that the overregulated, corrupt, and inefficient legal sector should emulate. But it worked in particular ways. Such activities were organized more on the basis of relationships than routines. They were a sign that the project which independent states had taken over from their predecessors – of building a seemingly rational, modern economy, of making that economy and society truly national, truly incorporative of all its citizens – had failed, and that an Africa of less visible and more personal connections had emerged in its stead.

In the 2010s what used to be called "informal" labor was being called "precarious" labor. As a specification of a particular form of labor the term is problematic, for the precariousness of wage employment is intrinsic to any capitalist economy. The term does suggest that the salience of workers who had reasonable expectations of a career in wage employment – if not a specific job – has diminished in relation to workers who lived off short-term and irregular employment. At the extreme, the men who take the risky voyage across the Sahara and the Mediterranean to seek illegal – hence precarious – work in Europe underscore the large numbers of Africans who find themselves in a desperate situation.

Stabilized labor never did replace the relations Africans made for themselves. The circulation of workers between villages and cities or workplaces was enabled by kinship groups wider than the individual family. People used family connections to find jobs in cities and to preserve access to farmland in villages of origin. Families could have more than one residence. They had to think strategically about placing members in different locations. While kinship solidarity could help people cope with the precariousness of wage labor, and in the best situations lead to decent incomes from a combination of salaries, farm earnings, and trade, the risks were severe, above all to women and children. The ill-health or desertion of a male wage earner could set a rural family spinning downward into poverty, or the breakup of family bonds in a city could leave children without support networks and with no state services to help. Child beggars, "parking boys," very young hawkers, and youthful petty criminals are a feature of every African city. Youth gangs are common.

Today's fragmented and precarious situations emerge from a particular historical sequence: in the 1950s and 1960s stabilization policies and relatively high wages seemed to offer to railway families of Nigeria or the mine families of Zambia new possibilities over the life cycle, giving a worker and his family the hope of living off a pension and trade income late in life. By the 1980s in both cases, men's wages and pensions had eroded. What saved many – but not all – such families from penury was the continued viability of kinship and other forms of personal connection. Moreover, in cities from Accra to Dar es Salaam, the strong presence of women in "informal" economic activities became increasingly vital to family survival. The male wage earner, despite the dreams of post-war colonial officials and African planners and trade unionists, has not led the African family into a "modern" prosperity. Women and children have been hit hard by the reversals on Africa's economic pathway, while the persistence and diversity of social ties in African communities have softened, if only partially, the pain of an unrealized project of social change.

Decolonizing Gender?

Women remain the bedrock of food production: hoeing and weeding, processing food, hauling water and firewood, and harvesting and marketing food. In some areas, but far from all, women in the early colonial era extended their role in agriculture into cash crops and, for a time at least, acquired better access to cash, especially as younger men's roles in warfare, hunting, and porterage were undercut. Women's centrality to both agricultural production and household reproduction accentuated the pressures on them, especially from male elders, to leave out-migration to the more dispensable young males.

African and European gender biases intersected in slotting men into education, and thus placing them in a privileged position as more roles in "modern" society opened to Africans after the war. While men's advantage in schooling persists to this day, the extent of the gap has slowly diminished (see Table 1, p. 170). Women's roles in crop production and food marketing are being complemented by a significant presence in teaching, health care, and other professional roles, a source of anxiety for "big men" as well of vital sustenance for the entire society.

The stabilization concept, when it flourished, had a particular gender ideology implicit in it: that of the male breadwinner, with wife at home. The worker would learn the ways of industry; his wife would be taught modern homemaking and child-rearing. Trade unionists drew on such notions to claim wages sufficient to support a family. But even where wages improved – or when, as in French Africa after 1956, wage workers received family allowances for each child – the effects of male wages were not necessarily as anticipated. As Lisa Lindsay (2003) has shown in regard to the "stabilized" railwaymen of Nigeria, better wages did not support a nuclear family so much as reinforce the notion of the "big man" who used his resources to make himself the center of a wider kin grouping. The family might be polygynous, but more generally it involved the wage owner's contribution to a wider network of kin, whom he helped in a variety of ways and whom he expected to contribute to his social, and perhaps political, stature. Women did not necessarily adapt to roles assigned them; railway wives, using their own resources and those of their husbands, frequently followed the Yoruba pattern of engaging in marketing, which brought them not only into intense participation in the market but also into close association with other women. There were many variations on such patterns in West Africa, some involving cooperation between husband and wife, others considerable autonomy between spouses.

The political openings of the 1940s and 1950s had ambiguous effects on women. Women participated actively in nationalist movements in places as varied as Tanzania and Guinea. In local politics in West African cities, women often played a political role stemming from their importance in marketing: female market leaders had an important constituency. In Nigeria the well-born and well-educated Funmilayo Ransome-Kuti brought market women into what had been a ladies' club and then helped turn it into the Abeokuta Women's Union, with 20,000 dues-paying members, and then the Nigerian Women's Union. These organizations became the nucleus of large demonstrations and played a role in both local and Nigeria-wide politics.

In other ways, politics in the 1950s became more of a male domain as it became an open, public one. Because men were predominant in formal employment, trade union leadership was virtually all male. Party politics might present certain roles for women, but in no case at the time were women the top leaders, and in some cases as African men entered formal hierarchies in the civil service or in politics, they saw their own status in relation to how "their" women maintained a respectable and deferential position.

Susan Geiger (1997) describes the importance of women in "performing nationalism" in Tanganyika during the 1950s – playing a public role in rallies and organizing – but when it came to governing, the less-educated female activists were marginalized and their organizations subordinated to the national party. One of the leading activists, Bibi Titi, was pushed out of the political party and in 1969 jailed by the Tanzanian government for treason, only to be released and retrospectively turned into a heroine of the struggle against colonial rule.

Later, as more women became educated and professional, explicitly feminist movements developed in such countries as Senegal and Kenya, and they forced public debate on issues of particular concern to women. A few countries banned polygamous marriages; others accepted the parallel existence of different marital regimes. The UN Decade for Women, which ended in a conference in Nairobi in 1985, with its vigorous debates and strong resolutions, marked the integration of African women activists in worldwide feminist mobilization.

Women's organizations have often fought uphill battles against formidable male backlash. In Zimbabwe a Women's League that had been an active promoter of gender equality was turned into a part of the apparatus of the ruling party, and when the latter moved toward a defense of its power as an advocate of African "tradition" against the imperialist West, criticism of male dominance was reinterpreted as a Western imposition. A Zimbabwe Supreme Court decision in 1999 declared that the integrity of African cultural norms outweighed constitutional provisions against discrimination and meant that women could not claim equal rights of inheritance to men. Elsewhere in Africa the possibilities of women acquiring control of land in their own right has run up against arguments for chiefly power in land allocation and the unassailable position of the male head of household. Legal efforts to restrict polygyny or to make men responsible for the children they have fathered by "outside wives" have encountered – in Kenya for example – male legislators' refusal to surrender the prerogatives of the "big man."

The supposed dichotomy of African and Western values has in some countries, including Uganda and Zimbabwe, become the basis of government efforts to stigmatize homosexuality. Colonial laws criminalizing homosexual acts have in some cases been made more draconian, and international campaigns for gay marriage have encountered strong resistance. The importance of a deeper consideration of different forms of sexuality has, however, gained attention in Africa as well as in international organizations.

In the case of women's organizations, international connections became stronger in the 1990s and 2000s. Criticism from outside the continent stood little chance of getting anywhere without strong leadership and organization within African countries, but movements in Africa stood to gain in support and visibility from linkage to worldwide concerns. The award of the Nobel Peace Prize in 2004 to Wangari Maathai of Kenya for her work as an environmental and feminist activist gave broad recognition to assertions that such causes transcend state borders.

Women have become more present in seeking political office since the 1990s, even as elections became more frequent and legislative authority more consequential. In Mozambique, South Africa, Tanzania, Uganda, Rwanda, and Burundi over 30 percent of the seats in the legislature (as of the early 2000s) were occupied by women. The first woman to become head of state in Africa was Ellen Johnson Sirleaf, who became President of Liberia in 2006; she served until the beginning of 2018. Malawi has also had a female head of state, Joyce Banda, from 2012 to 2014, and an experienced woman diplomat, Sahle-Work Zewde, became president of Ethiopia in October 2018. An African Feminist Forum was held in Ghana in 2006, Uganda in 2008, Senegal in 2010, and Zimbabwe in 2016, and it gave rise to national and regional fora that explicitly embraced a feminist agenda for Africa.

Feminists have tough issues to address, particularly in relation to claims that African "tradition" supports patriarchy and that criticisms of male privilege are a "Western" import. Legal and customary practices that limit women's property rights remain in place in some states. Even in a country such as South Africa, whose constitution is among the world's most egalitarian and where women sit in the legislature and cabinet, women in poorer socio-economic situations are subject to discrimination and harassment in daily life, including a high incidence of rape. A man with modest access to resources is often able to keep women in a situation of dependence on him.

State regulation of reproduction has been an acute issue at key moments. Before World War II colonial states had sought to "retraditionalize" marriage, in order to strengthen the ability of indigenous elites and courts to regulate family life and inheritance. In the 1950s colonial rulers began to stress "modern" marriage, regulated by state law, hopefully producing the kind of monogamous household that would insure that children went to school and grew up to contribute to the market economy. Independent states sometimes acknowledged the intrinsic value of "customary" forms of marriage and inheritance, but insisted that those who chose other arrangements should be regulated by formal laws. There has been another reaction, too, at the core of state power. The "big man" concept has far from died out; indeed, given the importance of building networks of clients to political leaders, the place of the patriarch in politics has in many instances been strengthened. Big men do not necessarily want to be constrained by the nuclear emphasis of "modern" marriage and have fought against legal regulations that might prevent men from doing what they want to do. The ascendancy to the presidency of South Africa in 2009 of Jacob Zuma – an openly and boastfully polygamous man with children by different women – at least focused public attention on the big man's vision of gender relations.

During the controversy over clitoridectomy in Kenya in the 1930s, many men spoke in the name of Kikuyu women. Whatever Kikuyu women thought did not enter into the political arena. That is no longer the case. Women's organizations address issues such as polygyny, clitoridectomy, child custody and support, property rights, inheritance, and the prevalence of rape. Such concerns are the subject of political mobilization within Africa, not just intervention from outside. That has changed the politics of reproduction. But gender equality remains a long way off.

Religion in Times of Progress and Crisis

The relationship of religion to politics is often ambiguous. Around 1950 many Africans were worshiping in established Christian churches and trying to turn Christian universalism into an ideology of liberation and human progress. The Islamic brotherhoods of Senegal, having reached an accommodation with the French, were now forging relationships with the leaders of political parties. Powerful men such as Félix Houphouët-Boigny and Kenneth Kaunda emphasized in different ways their Christian beliefs. Houphouët-Boigny, near the end of his life, built in his home town at enormous expense a basilica modeled on Rome's St. Peter's. Others, like Nkrumah, channeled Christian messianic imagery into a cult of the leader and his modernizing mission. Still others, Mobutu for instance, cultivated a reputation as men well connected with sorcerers.

In other cases, prophets and cult leaders gathered followings that were highly personal and antagonistic to secular authority, whether of Europeans or Africans. In Northern Rhodesia the cult led by Alice Lenshina, known as "Lumpa," developed after 1953 from a mission station but broke away from Christian doctrine as well as mission organization, claiming that it was building an instant millennium on earth and trying to separate itself from all other institutions. It condemned polygamy and witchcraft. With some 65,000 followers living at the edge of the Copperbelt, the Lumpa Church clashed with the leading nationalist movement, the United National Independence Party (UNIP) of Kenneth Kaunda. After independence in 1964 Lenshina's attempt to control autonomous Lumpa villages challenged the UNIP's desire to make clear its authority. The result was a bloody episode of post-colonial state repression; some 700 Lumpa died, and Lenshina was jailed for over a decade. Like the colonial regimes before them, other newly independent countries cracked down on what they considered dangerously autonomous cults.

What of religion in the sequence of economic regression and recovery from the 1980s to the 2000s? An important new trend, unevenly present from Angola to Kenya, was the proliferation of evangelical Protestant churches, some following American leadership but all emphasizing a direct relationship between the individual and God. In Kenya during the 1980s the more orthodox Christian denominations challenged the authoritarian regime of Daniel arap Moi, but the increasingly numerous evangelicals spoke of salvation and had relatively little to say about the iniquities of the regime. Such churches both reflected and accentuated growing disillusionment with the national project. Building Kenyan society was not the point; their concerns were salvation and another sort of community. Elsewhere, evangelical or pentecostal churches have engaged directly in politics – pushing for the election of Frederick Chiluba in Zambia in 1991, for

FIGURE 18 Pentecostal mass at Redeemed Church of Christ, near Lagos–Ibadan road, Nigeria, 2003. Huge churches, some improvised, some with elaborate facilities, are found in many African countries, a growing trend in recent decades. Jacob Silberberg/Getty Images

instance – while in Ghana and other countries they have been a visible public presence, on the radio, on television, in cinemas, in the press.

If evangelical Christianity was once seen as the solace of the poor, it is now – in Africa and elsewhere – equally likely to be associated with the "prosperity gospel." People who have achieved a measure of prosperity seek a moral framework in which to place their success, while parishioners who have yet to do so well see a hopeful future in their participation in a worldwide Christian community in which success and salvation go together. Evangelical preachers have become media celebrities, and their displays of their own wealth are widely seen as a sign of their spiritual integrity rather than a contradiction of it. Neither solace nor prosperity, however, exhaust the different meanings found within evangelical Christianity in Africa. The quest for security, the desire for a personal relationship with the divinity, identification with local, regional, and worldwide communities, and different conceptions of how to confront evil in the world were behind not only variation among churches but flux and instability in many of them. Religious communities, as James Pritchett (2011: 45) puts it, helped people find the "courage to live with fragmentation, multiplicity and contingency."

Religious discourse often justified patriarchy, but some of the movements, with varying ties to Christianity, that have flourished in post-war Africa have been led by women prophets in the mode of Alice Lenshina. Parishioners in more conventional churches are dispropor-tionately female. Spirit-possession cults in a number of contexts allow a woman "possessed" by a spirit to make demands that would be seen as offensive to gender norms if she was in a non-possessed state.

African Islam is as varied as African Christianity. In the late eight-eenth and nineteenth centuries, in Sahelian West Africa, where Islam had been an influence for a millennium, a series of militant move-ments proclaimed *jihad*, trying to bring a more rigorous form of Islam to a region where local practices had influenced even self-proclaimed Islamic polities. While the appeal was to a universalistic vision of Islam – including strict enforcement of the Sharia – the movement was built on particularistic connections, notably networks of pastoral-ists and itinerant scholars, especially from the Fulani ethnic group. The large and powerful polities they established in what is now northern Nigeria or the Senegal–Mali border zone were hierarchical, with Fulani nobles on top and slaves on the bottom. In the case of Northern Nigeria the British began to work through the regional rulers – known under the Arabic title of emir – shortly after conquer-ing them militarily, and they even encouraged a Hausa–Fulani sub-imperialism, helping northern elites to establish de facto control over neighboring peoples within Nigeria. This elite (Chapter 4) was instru-mental to the conservative decolonization of Nigeria, and kept in place a hierarchical social structure in the region, while exercising strong influence over the Nigerian federation as a whole.

Not all people in northern Nigeria are Muslim, and the middle belt between northern and southern Nigeria is notable for the mixture of Christians, Muslims, and people practicing local religions. Tensions among these communities have waxed and waned, but in the last two decades they have become acute. Part of the Muslim elite has since the 1970s pushed for a more consistent practice of Sharia law in the provinces they dominate, but that was not enough for a radical fringe which has been influenced by the jihadist networks that have spread in parts of North Africa and the Middle East and across the desert into Sahelian Africa. These groups, mostly male, mostly young, see them-selves as detached from the social context of their region, have no hope in a future within a multiconfessional society, and seek to impose their version of Islam – which they see as rigorous – on their region.

FIGURE 19 Arrival of pilgrims from the Mouride Brotherhood at the holy city of Touba, Senegal, 1956. Although Mourides have migrated to many cities in Europe and North America as traders, their version of Islam is less universalistic than other versions of this religion. The focus is on the hierarchy of religious leaders (*marabouts*) and on their connection to the founder of the brotherhood, Ahmadu Bamba, and his city, Touba. ©ECPAD/La Documentation Française

The most vicious of these groups, Boko Haram, strongest in the northeastern regions of Nigeria, tried to destroy educational institutions, kidnapped young girls to turn them into "wives" (or sex slaves), and terrorized villages. The Nigerian army has, at the time of writing, been able to contain Boko Haram's spread, but not to end its capacity to inflict terror on villages, refugee camps, and cities. The army's undisciplined violence may have aided the movement's recruitment.

In Mali and the desert to its north, *jihadi* movements have overlapped with older networks of traffickers, in the trade in drugs and arms and in kidnapping, enabling them to maintain a considerable level of military prowess even though their tactics do more to alienate (and intimidate) than to incorporate people in the region. A barely functioning Mali government in 2014 called on French help to save itself and liberate several cities that had been taken over. Another radical and violent movement in Somalia – where state authority had collapsed – has helped to prevent the reconstitution of state authority in the country and staged violent attacks in neighboring Kenya. Just how much these movements emerge out of the failure of particular states to provide young people with a sense of belonging and of a future, and how much they are linked to international networks, is not entirely clear.

Elsewhere in Africa, Islam has established decidedly local roots, and the strength of those ties provides a degree of insulation against versions of Islam with universalistic pretensions. The Mouride brotherhood of Senegal (Chapter 2) ties its members into a religious hierarchy and network of connections closely linked to political and economic elites. Originally a rural movement, Mourides were beginning to dominate the central marketplace of Dakar by 1945. By the 1970s the Mouride traders' diaspora was extending to Paris and New York. Transnational without being Westernized, Mourides remained closely linked to a hierarchy of *marabouts* in Senegal itself. They looked not so much to Mecca as to Touba, the holy city created by the Mourides' founder, with its great mosque inaugurated in 1963 and visible for miles around. Mourides were once hostile to Western education, but by the 1970s Mouride student associations were strong in the University of Dakar. The *marabouts* had considerable influence on political parties, but also maintained a certain distance from the Senegalese state.

As Stephen Ellis and Gerrie ter Haar (1998: 185) comment, religious discourse – Christian, Muslim, or otherwise – has much to say about "manifestations of evil said to infest the main institutions of Africa's governance." This concern has led to public critiques of governments' abusive behavior, and it can also take the form of accusations that greedy or repressive politicians and businessmen are engaging in witchcraft or other occult practices. Leaders may play on this discourse, claiming to have access to dark powers. The vertical linkages between leaders and followers intrinsic to much politics in contemporary Africa (Chapter 7) produce jealousy, and attempts to use spiritual means to gain influence on top or to project it toward the bottom are part of the maneuvering surrounding patronage systems.

Witchcraft accusations may be a way in which a community, in the absence of a credible legal system, gains a measure of control over the invisible as well as the visible realm. Communities can call upon political leaders to protect them from supernatural forces acting against them, and when governments in South Africa and Mozambique failed to do so, for example, they could be portrayed, in Adam Ashforth's words (2005: 314), as "either ignoring dangers facing the community or in league with the evil forces themselves."

Religious zeal and accusations of witchcraft are not simply phe-
nomena of the village or of "traditional Africa." They are as much
part of the city as the countryside, of the twenty-first century as much
as the past. Men and women are facing forces that seem more difficult
than ever to control, and the complexity of religious and spiritual life is
indicative of a situation where people's needs are great, their means
compromised, and the solutions far from obvious. In a variety of ways,
religious communities and religious beliefs have provided a moral
compass for people to engage with the social order, at times to criticize
it directly, at times to find refuge from it, and in some situations to
enhance their own power within it.

Conclusion: On Blame and Debt, on Credit and Trade

The continued poverty, the high indebtedness, the inadequate infrastructure, and the absence of coherent strategies for improving
people's standard of living in post-colonial African states gave rise
after an initial period of hope in a new order to a blame game, and it
has not altogether gone away, even when signs of improvement have
appeared. Some argue that the damage colonialism did was permanent and that neo-colonial structures remain in place. Some African
intellectuals have called for a "second liberation."

The problem can be reframed by more attention to a historical
sequence. Both late colonial and African governments, after the stagnation of the previous decades, presided over real improvements in
certain conditions for certain portions of their populations: progress in
building schools, roads, hospitals, and port facilities; progress in
bringing Africans into positions in civil service and private employment where they could contribute more than unskilled labor and
where they could help a younger generation advance. The blame for
what went wrong, some would say, lies in the world economy that
turned so decisively against Africa in the 1970s and the policies of the
IMF and other international institutions that made it impossible for
Africa to "develop" its way out of its limitations.

Perhaps development did not go far enough, and an outside world
that had long treated Africa as a zone of extraction did not devote
sufficient resources to giving the continent a chance to find a different
vocation. But no, others argue, Africa benefited from the favorable
market conditions of the immediate post-war era, and if it had left

things to the market, it would have had better results than obtained by state-centered development in the 1950s and 1960s. No, still others say, the developers did too much: their solutions were too dependent on technology and capital, too centered on a male-oriented formal economic sphere. These are counter-factual propositions, and one must ask what the imagined alternative was. Africans never had the choice of simply entering "the market"; they were up against real markets, some of them controlled by giant foreign firms such as the United Africa Company or Union Minière d'Haut Katanga or De Beers, which concentrated capital and power and did not necessarily have an interest in widening the narrow channels of African econ-omies or building the institutions needed by a diverse and self-sustaining society. Would the fate of Africa's millions of small farmers have been better if they had been left alone to bargain with the multinational giants, and how would those farmers' children have fared without self-conscious efforts to equip them with skills for new careers and access to a wider world? Would a "community" left in splendid isolation have been a force for collective fulfillment or for the reinforcement of the power of local patriarchs over young men and women of all ages? Such questions do not have neat answers; indeed, they point to the importance of asking more precise questions, moving beyond a stark choice between pro-market and pro-state policies, between an authentic and bounded African community and an opening to the wider world.

A full bibliography for this book may be found on the website of Cambridge University Press www.cambridge.org/CooperAfrica2ed.

Bibliography

"Africa Rising." *The Economist*. December 3, 2011.
Alexander, Jocelyn. *The Unsettled Land: State-Making and the Politics of Land in Zimbabwe 1893–2003*. Athens: Ohio University Press, 2006.
Appiah, Kwame Anthony. *In My Father's House: Africa in the Philosophy of Culture*. New York: Oxford University Press, 1992.
Arndt, Channing, Andy McKay, and Finn Tarp, eds. *Growth and Poverty in Sub-Saharan Africa*. Oxford: Oxford University Press, 2016.

Ashforth, Adam. *Witchcraft, Violence and Democracy in South Africa*. Chicago: University of Chicago Press, 2005.

Austin, Gareth. *Labour, Land, and Capital in Ghana: From Slavery to Free Labor in Asante, 1807–1956*. Rochester: Rochester University Press, 2004.

Balandier, Georges. *The Sociology of Black Africa*. Trans. by Douglas Garman. London: André Deutsch, 1970.

Bamba, Abou. *African Miracle, African Mirage: Transnational Politics and the Paradox of Modernization in Ivory Coast*. Athens: Ohio University Press, 2016.

Barchiesi, Franco. *Precarious Liberation: Workers, the State, and Contested Social Citizenship in Postapartheid South Africa*. Albany: State University of New York Press, 2011.

Bayart, Jean-François. "Africa in the World: A History of Extroversion." *African Affairs* 99 (1999): 217–26.

Berger, Iris. *Women in Twentieth-Century Africa*. Cambridge: Cambridge University Press, 2016.

Berry, Sara. *No Condition is Permanent: The Social Dynamics of Agrarian Change in Sub-Saharan Africa*. Madison: University of Wisconsin Press, 1993.

Brautigam, Deborah. *The Dragon's Gift: The Real Story of China in Africa*. Oxford: Oxford University Press, 2011.

Cohen, Abner. *Custom and Politics in Urban Africa: A Study of Hausa Migrants in Yoruba Towns*. Berkeley: University of California Press, 1969.

Cooper, Frederick and Randall Packard, eds. *International Development and the Social Sciences: Essays on the History and Politics of Knowledge*. Berkeley: University of California Press, 1997.

Davie, Grace. *Poverty Knowledge in South Africa: A Social History of Human Science, 1855–2005*. Cambridge: Cambridge University Press, 2015.

Diouf, Mamadou. "Engaging Postcolonial Cultures: African Youth and Public Space." *African Studies Review* 46, 2 (2003): 1–12.

Diouf, Mamadou, ed. *Tolerance, Democracy, and Sufis in Senegal*. New York: Columbia University Press, 2011.

Ellis, Stephen, and Gerrie ter Haar, "Religion and Politics in Sub-Saharan Africa." *Journal of Modern African Studies* 36, 2 (1998): 175–20.

Worlds of Power: Religious Thought and Political Practice in Africa. New York: Oxford University Press, 2004.

Englund, Harri, ed. *Christianity and Public Culture in Africa*. Athens: Ohio University Press, 2011.

Enwezor, Okwui. *The Short Century: Independence and Liberation Movements in Africa 1945–1994*. Munich and New York: Prestel, 2001.

Fabian, Johannes. *Remembering the Present: Painting and Popular History in Zaire*. Berkeley: University of California Press, 1996.

Fassin, Didier. *When Bodies Remember: Experiences and Politics of Aids in South Africa.* Berkeley: University of California Press, 2007.

Ferguson, James. *The Anti-Politics Machine: "Development," Depoliticization, and Bureaucratic Power in Lesotho.* Cambridge: Cambridge University Press, 1990.

   Expectations of Modernity: Myths and Meanings of Urban Life on the Zambian Copperbelt. Berkeley: University of California Press, 1999.

Foster, Elizabeth. *African Catholic: Decolonization and the Transformation of the Church.* Cambridge, MA: Harvard University Press, 2019.

Freund, Bill. *The African City: A History.* Cambridge: Cambridge University Press, 2007.

Geiger, Susan. *TANU Women: Gender and Culture in the Making of Tanzanian Nationalism, 1955–1965.* Portsmouth, NH: Heinemann, 1997.

Geschiere, Peter. *The Modernity of Witchcraft: Politics and the Occult in Postcolonial Africa.* Trans. by Peter Geschiere and Janet Roitman. Charlottesville: University Press of Virginia, 1997.

Hall, Ruth, Ian Scoones, and Dzodzi Tsikata, eds. *Africa's Land Rush: Livelihoods and Agrarian Change.* Rochester: James Currey, 2015.

Hart, Jennifer. *Ghana on the Go: African Mobility in the Age of Motor Transport.* Bloomington: Indiana University Press, 2016.

Huillery, Elise. "History Matters: The Long-Term Impact of Colonial Public Investments in French West Africa." *American Economic Journal–Applied Economics* 1 (2009): 176–215.

Hunt, Nancy. *A Colonial Lexicon: Of Birth Ritual, Medicalization, and Mobility in the Congo.* Durham, NC: Duke University Press, 1999.

Jamal, Vali, and John Weeks, *Africa Misunderstood or Whatever Happened to the Rural-Urban Gap?* London: Macmillan for International Labour Office, 1993.

Jerven, Morten. *Poor Numbers: How We Are Misled by African Development Statistics and What to Do about It.* Ithaca: Cornell University Press, 2013.

   "African Economic Growth Recurring: An Economic History Perspective on African Growth Episodes, 1690–2010." *Economic History of Developing Regions* 25 (2010): 127–54.

Lee, Ching Kwan. "Raw Encounters: Chinese Managers, African Workers and the Politics of Casualization in Africa's Chinese Enclaves." *China Quarterly* (2009): 657–66.

Lentz, Carola. *Land, Mobility, and Belonging in West Africa.* Bloomington: Indiana University Press, 2013.

Lindsay, Lisa. *Working with Gender: Men, Women, and Wage Labor in Southwest Nigeria* Portsmouth, NH: Heinemann, 2003.

MacGaffey, Janet. *The Real Economy of Zaire: The Contribution of Smuggling and Other Unofficial Activities to the National Wealth of an African Country.* Philadelphia: University of Pennsylvania Press, 1991.

Magaziner, Daniel. *The Art of Life in South Africa*. Athens: Ohio University Press, 2016.

Manchuelle, François. *Willing Migrants: Soninke Labor Diasporas, 1848–1960*. Athens: Ohio University Press, 1997.

Meagher, Kate. *Identity Economics: Social Networks and the Informal Economy in Nigeria*. Woodbridge: James Currey, 2010.

Meyer, Birgit. *Translating the Devil: Religion and Modernity among the Ewe in Ghana*. Edinburgh: Edinburgh University Press, 1999.

Mkandawire, Thandika. *African Voices on Structural Adjustment: A Companion to our Continent, our Future*. Trenton: Third World Press, 2003.

Mudimbe, V. Y. *The Invention of Africa: Gnosis, Philosophy, and the Order of Knowledge*. Bloomington: Indiana University Press, 1988.

Murray, Martin. *City of Extremes: The Spatial Politics of Johannesburg*. Durham, NC: Duke University Press, 2011.

Pritchett, James. "Christian Mission Stations in South-Central Africa: Eddies in the Flow of Global Culture." In Harri Englund, ed., *Christianity and Public Culture in Africa*. Athens: Ohio University Press, 2011, 27–49.

Robertson, Claire. *Sharing the Same Bowl? A Socioeconomic History of Women and Class in Accra, Ghana*. Bloomington: Indiana University Press, 1984.

Sachs, Jeffrey. *The End of Poverty: Economic Possibilities for our Time*. New York: Penguin, 2005.

Seekings, Jeremy, and Nicoli Nattrass. *Class, Race, and Inequality in South Africa*. New Haven: Yale University Press, 2005.

Thomas, Lynn. *Politics of the Womb: Women, Reproduction, and the State in Kenya*. Berkeley: University of California Press, 2003.

Tripp, Aili Mari. *Changing the Rules: The Politics of Liberalization and the Urban Informal Economy in Tanzania*. Berkeley: University of California Press, 1997.

Tripp, Aili Mari, Isabel Casimiro, Joy Kwesiga, and Alice Mungwa. *African Women's Movements: Changing Political Landscapes*. Cambridge: Cambridge University Press, 2009.

Vaughan, Megan. *Curing their Ills: Colonial Power and African Illness*. Cambridge: Polity Press, 1991.

West, Harry G. *Kupilikula: Governance and the Invisible Realm in Mozambique*. Chicago: University of Chicago Press, 2005.

White, Luise. *The Comforts of Home: Prostitution in Colonial Nairobi*. Chicago: Chicago University Press, 1990.

World Bank. *Can Africa Claim the 21st Century?* Washington: World Bank, 2000.

CHAPTER 6

White Rule, Armed Struggle, and Beyond

The most important holdouts against the abdication of imperial power in the 1950s and 1960s were colonies with substantial white settlement. But despite the sustained efforts of settlers in Rhodesia and South Africa to retain power, and the determination of the Portuguese government to retain its centuries-old empire, their ultimate fate was determined by the regional and worldwide process that rendered empire indefensible. That process was slow; only in December 1960 did the United Nations officially recognize that world opinion had changed and colonial rule had become morally unacceptable. Rhodesia, South Africa, and Portuguese colonies became international pariahs, but it took over thirty more years before the last bastion of white domination in Africa fell.

In order to maintain white rule, Rhodesian settlers gave up their place in an empire that seemed intent on devolving power to black majorities. They claimed the same right of self-determination as exercised by other African countries; treating blacks as second-class citizens was a sovereign prerogative. The Unilateral Declaration of Independence (UDI) in 1965 kept in place colonial institutions – a bureaucracy and police apparatus that enforced white landownership and racial segregation – but cut them off from imperial power. When African political movements turned to guerrilla warfare the state fought back, but it faced a regional problem – armed groups finding sanctuary in now-free neighboring territories – and a global one – economic boycotts and isolation. In the end, colonialism could not be maintained without imperialism – without a global system of empires – not

196

least because white Rhodesians vitally depended on their sense of participation in "European civilization" and in the comforts, securities, and opportunities of a worldly bourgeoisie. Whatever the divisions and weaknesses of the guerrilla movements, they won the international battle to be identified with self-determination and progress.

The white population of Portugal did not experience democratic rule even for themselves. The country had been ruled by a dictatorship since 1926. Nevertheless, Portuguese Africa had participated in the developmentalist process of the 1950s. Its rulers tried to keep its benefits in white hands. Revolutionary wars beginning in the early 1960s in Mozambique, Angola, and Guinea-Bissau and dragging on without either side winning a decisive victory had such a negative effect on the morale of Portuguese soldiers and civilians that a faction within the army overthrew the dictatorship in 1974 and withdrew from the African continent. African rebels helped to bring democracy to a part of Europe, at enormous cost to themselves.

South Africa's white population, with its long history, was more entrenched. But the white nationalist government cracked by 1994. Although armed rebels could be killed, jailed, and exiled, its cities could not be made secure, and international boycotts meant that its white citizens could not participate in the Western world of which they felt themselves to be privileged members. The revolutions in Rhodesia/Zimbabwe, Angola, and Mozambique dashed the South African government's strategy of supporting a "white" southern Africa as a buffer against a "black" Africa to the north. South Africa had the wealth and military might to harrow its neighbors, and it caused much death and dislocation, but it remained isolated in Africa and despised around the world until it conceded power to an African majority. What surprised most knowledgeable observers was that the final stages of this political revolution were peaceful.

By looking at this entire half-century, one sees not only how long, fraught, and painful were the struggles to end empire and its racial consequences, but how much the process crossed national borders, involving connections within Africa and the engagement of Africans with international organizations. Then there is the role of the United States. It is only slightly too cynical to suggest that the high point of American contributions to decolonization came in 1943, when the State Department pressed its British allies to read the Atlantic Charter's invocation of a right to self-determination in general terms, not just as words meant to apply to the white victims of Hitler's invasions.

The USA pulled its punches, balancing its concern that the rising anger of colonized peoples could take a radical turn and its desire to "open" imperial markets to American competition against its fears of weakening friendly powers. From the late 1940s the USA helped to internationalize North–South relations by participating – directly and through international financial institutions – in the development effort, and it hoped for gradual development and political devolution rather than sharp breaks that might aid the wrong side in the Cold War. The USA would provide aid, but not too much of it, to friendly independent nations, and it would intervene, but not too often, when instability or left-wing politics threatened its interests. Its involvement in the Congo crisis and the assassination of Patrice Lumumba in 1961 signaled the American willingness to treat new African states as pawns in Cold War conflicts, and its reluctance to eject racially exclusive states from the community of democratic nations helped to allow the late decolonizations to occur even later. A low point of American post-war policy came in 1986 when the Reagan Administration, citing communist powers' military support of the Angolan government, joined South Africa in providing overt and covert support to anti-government guerrillas operating in Angola, putting the United States on the side of the apartheid state's effort to destabilize a neighboring country.

Within the United States, strong public sentiment linked the struggle against apartheid to the domestic civil rights movement, but government policy varied from official condemnation of apartheid to a "constructive engagement" that gave substantive support to the apartheid regime while claiming to influence it to behave like a normal state. American officials did little to aid the ANC in its quest for majority rule, but they celebrated the personality of Nelson Mandela when he came to power. Elsewhere in Africa, the United States has been eager to instruct African governments that they should support free markets and human rights, but not very eager to do anything about local tyrants (Mobutu, Abacha) who controlled important resources, or to put much money behind whatever economic policy it favored at a particular moment. Africa was only intermittently on the map of what really counted, most recently because of fear of terrorists associated with al-Qaeda or the Islamic State in the Sahelian region, Nigeria, and Somalia.

Meanwhile, NGOs – from Human Rights Watch to church groups to African-American rights groups – were part of the effort to liberate

South Africa from white domination. They were a resource available to Africans who sought foreign connections; but they also, whatever their intentions, tended to frame Africa as a region of famines, atrocities, and backwardness. In southern Africa, both formal organizations and mobilizations of students or unionized workers in different parts of the world helped to deny white-dominated regimes the place they coveted in international politics.

The next question is what happened after liberation. The argument, often heard during the period of armed struggle, that violent revolution would lead to popular mobilization and hence a solidaristic effort toward radical change in contrast to the too-easy takeovers by African politicians of other states, quickly showed itself to be wrong. Angola, Mozambique, and Zimbabwe experienced some of the most violent internecine conflicts the continent has seen. Certainly, South Africa, until the 1990s, did not make things easier for its liberated neighbors – nor was the world economy kind to socialist regimes – but whatever the degree of external constraint, no regime in southern Africa could demonstrate that it had enabled peasants and workers to flourish. The South African liberation movement had the most ambiguous relationship to violence, which was episodic – and sometimes internecine – rather than a unified struggle by military means. Its outcome has also been ambiguous: the end of racial domination and improved living conditions for an important portion of the population, but persistent inequality of a high degree. The trajectories that liberation movements took after their victories varied, but none has been able to demonstrate that armed struggle leads to democratic and socially just societies.

From Rhodesia to Zimbabwe

The colonial government in Southern Rhodesia, as in other British colonies, was challenged by a combination of urban workers and Western-educated elites in the late 1940s and 1950s. Urban and rural politics were linked by a form of capitalist development that deprived rural Africans of land and kept urban Africans under police eyes, and by a high level of state repression. The strike movements of post-war Africa hit Rhodesia in the form of a railway strike in 1945 and a general strike in 1948. Already, issues of family life – wages and housing for a male worker to support a family – were at the fore. State efforts to limit the presence of women in towns had the unintended effect of marking an illegal and disreputable female element set apart from respectable city-dwellers. A populist trade union, the Reformed Industrial and Commercial Workers' Union (RICU), led by Charles Mzingeli, put issues of gender and urban life at the center of urban politics, posing demands in terms of what Timothy Scarnecchia (2008: 13) calls "imperial working-class citizenship." The state, meanwhile, sought both to maintain racial segregation and to produce a trainable and tameable African working class in carefully policed quarters. There sprang up, however, communities led by charismatic leaders with an alternate vision of urban life in neighborhoods where the police did not come.

In rural areas the colonial government – with the approval of international experts – left little place for small-scale African farmers in its agricultural plans. Africans were to constitute a wage-labor force in agriculture and industry. Rhodesian Africans thus benefited little from the expanding production of maize, tobacco, beef, gold, and other minerals that was part of the post-war commodities boom, and Rhodesia, in the footsteps of its richer and whiter neighbor to the south, seemed on the road to a racially repressive version of capitalist development.

African politicians in Southern Rhodesia, as elsewhere, sought to establish their respectability and take advantage of the modest openings of the 1950s. This resulted in a loss of touch with the volatile politics of the neighborhoods, particularly in relation to women struggling at the margins. The RICU gave way in the mid-1950s to other organizations that increasingly reflected tension between a respectable, middle-class orientation and militant rejection of the possibility of working to expand the framework of imperial politics.

Meanwhile, the British creation (see Chapter 4) of the Central African Federation – Northern Rhodesia, Southern Rhodesia, and Nyasaland – enhanced the influence of Southern Rhodesia's white settlers, concentrated industrial and agricultural development in that territory, left limited opportunities for African workers and farmers in Southern Rhodesia, and produced powerful waves of mobilization against the Federation in Nyasaland and Northern Rhodesia. The agitation eventually led the British government to abandon the Federation and allow the two dissident colonies to become independent in 1964 as Malawi and Zambia.

As Rhodesia's white settlers consolidated power, its black politicians slowly realized that the kind of orderly political organization – punctuated by strikes, demonstrations, and occasional disorders – that had transformed politics in non-settler colonies would not work in Rhodesia. The political landscape changed when a succession of earlier political parties transformed themselves in 1963 into the Zimbabwe African People's Union (ZAPU), under the leadership of Joshua Nkomo, who had built his political career from a trade union base extended to the Ndebele region via his strong evocation of religious symbolism and his connections to the shrines of regional cults. Despite ZAPU's militant style and efforts to mobilize rural Africans, it could not effectively counter the repressive actions of the settler-dominated government. The opposition to white domination was far from unified, and in the early 1960s some previously important politicians were branded as "sellouts," while youthful thugs from different factions beat each other up, or worse. The Zimbabwe African National Union (ZANU) soon split off from ZAPU under the leadership of the Reverend Ndabaningi Sithole and later of Robert Mugabe, with considerable violence between supporters of the two groups. Both organizations were considering armed struggle and seeking arms from Egypt or other friendly foreign sources, and both were banned in 1964 (the year of Malawi's and Zambia's independence) and their leaders jailed.

Ian Smith and his radical white party, the Rhodesian Front, had a macho sense that settlers could do what soft colonial officials would not: keep their Africans down. The tension between London and Salisbury mounted until in 1965 Smith's government issued its Unilateral Declaration of Independence. Rhodesia would defend racial privilege in national rather than imperial terms. The government did not go as far as South Africa's in banning all black participation in voting, but manipulated the franchise in an unsuccessful effort to co-opt the most conservative elements of the African population and appease concerns abroad without weakening the control of Smith's white settler regime. White Rhodesians were in the ambiguous position of emphasizing their specificity as a people and as a nation and insisting that they were more British than the British, upholding British values when the mother country was turning over the rest of its empire to backward and dangerous demagogues.

The Labour government in Britain, convinced that UDI would fail and reluctant to kill white people, did little. The Rhodesian state, for nearly fifteen years, demonstrated that a minority government controlling an army and a bureaucracy could maintain security in urban areas, repression in the rural ones, and even foster a measure of industrialization and self-sufficiency in an economy that used cheap African labor to produce minerals and agricultural commodities for external markets. Rhodesia attracted a motley collection from around the world of white supremacists, mercenaries, and military adventurers willing to join the Rhodesian army's fight against African guerrillas, even as the actions of white Rhodesian men ranged from zealous participation in counterinsurgency to emigration.

ZAPU had guerrilla bases just over the frontier in Zambia. ZANU's big break came when the Front for the Liberation of Mozambique (FRELIMO) gained de facto control of neighboring parts of that colony, and especially after 1974 when FRELIMO took over Mozambique from the Portuguese and allowed ZANU to build bases from which it could work. ZANU's initiatives were concentrated in the African reserve areas of Rhodesia where people spoke Shona, the language of the ZANU leaders. ZAPU guerrillas made forays from Zambia. The more aggressive ZANU guerrillas from Mozambique faced a common bind: they had to live off the land in the very place where they were trying to mobilize peasants.

The insurgency offered hope to rural cultivators impoverished and oppressed by the Rhodesian state. At the same time, villagers had reason to fear guerrillas, who demanded food and at times coerced villagers into joining them, and who exposed people to revenge by the Rhodesian army. Young men and women of all ages could also find in the struggle alternatives to patriarchal domination.

The indecisive armed struggle proved costly to the increasingly isolated white government. As economic conditions in Rhodesia deteriorated in the early 1970s, guerrillas recruited more effectively among young men who had little at stake in the economy of white Rhodesia. Smith now began to cooperate with the British government to find a settlement that would bring black Rhodesians – hopefully of the less radical variety – into the government but protect the white minority. In a bizarre alternative to a vote, the British government sent a paternalistic commission to see for itself whether Africans supported the proposed agreement. Even the white sages could see the hostility of most Africans to a denigrating compromise. Religious leaders, released ex-detainees, and the African National Council, led by Bishop Abel Muzorewa, campaigned against the proposal. The war continued.

By 1977 Smith was trying to talk to nationalists like Muzorewa to forestall radicals such as Mugabe. Negotiations resulted in a second attempt at independence, a weak state with numerous guarantees for whites and little power for the new leader, Muzorewa. The white army continued to fight black guerrillas and Muzorewa couldn't get either side to stop, let alone tackle the demobilization of armies, the rebuilding of the economy, and the underlying questions of economic justice. More negotiations finally led to real elections, with the result that in 1980 ZANU and Robert Mugabe came to power, with Joshua Nkomo and ZAPU uneasily and briefly cooperating with the new regime. Armed struggle had not achieved a military victory, but it had trapped the settler regime in the limits of its own project and forced it to negotiate.

The people of Zimbabwe had fought for independence; much of the peasantry had been mobilized, and their leaders were courageous, socialist, and self-confident. Zimbabwe inherited from wartime Rhodesia an economic infrastructure that emphasized self-sufficiency; it had a mix of agricultural, mineral, and industrial possibilities. Zimbabwe may well have had more economic and political options than other African states, but the very mobilization of part of the Zimbabwean population also posed its dangers. Mugabe believed he had to demobilize people: trade unions that might strike for better wages and conditions after liberation, ex-fighters who could pose demands, and above all followers of his comrade and rival Joshua Nkomo, head of ZAPU.

Mugabe's socialist rhetoric came up against Zimbabwe's need for dependable revenue, not just for projects to relieve an exploited population, but for patronage to keep ZANU's network of supporters content. Although some white-owned land was redistributed, one of the conditions for ending the war was ZANU's agreement to respect private property. Mugabe was at first anxious to preserve the high-output agricultural sector, with its large, white-owned estates, and to keep the white-owned business sector intact. Zimbabwe's elite was Africanized by a kind of crony capitalism: the state did little to encourage an autonomous, African business class, but used its own strategic location to provide opportunities to clients. The initial years of ZANU rule had their successes: the dismantling of policies that privileged whites, an 80 percent increase in the number of schools in a decade, access to drinking water for most of the population, bargaining rights for workers. But, after an initial growth spurt, the economy began to deteriorate in the mid-1980s. The rural areas where most Africans lived suffered from soil erosion and lack of infrastructure.

Mugabe's former freedom fighters, meanwhile, were dealt with carefully: their history of mobilization turned out to signify not so much that they were a vanguard of social transformation as that they were an interest group that had to be placated. The regime ethnicized issues of patronage and of opposition, particularly in relation to the followers of Nkomo. Mugabe accused them of mobilizing Ndebele against Mugabe's primarily Shona base. Zimbabwe's security forces waged a bloody, repressive campaign in Ndebele regions. Some observers estimate that 20,000 people were killed. The state-led violence exacerbated whatever animosity existed, until an uneasy truce was reached in 1987. Press censorship, detention of opponents, and the banning of political parties other than ZANU were part of the regime's policies in the 1980s, eased for a time in the 1990s, and worsened again, as the declining economy, increasing anger at corruption, and the ability of the opposition to make good use of even small openings in the press and electoral system undermined the government's authority.

Mugabe was by the 1990s willing to make white landowners, whose contribution to the national economy he had once supported, the scapegoats for economic chaos. He meanwhile cracked down on domestic opponents and foreign journalists. Inflation was rampant; unemployment was as high as 80 percent; teachers and other civil services were paid irregularly. Within Zimbabwe, civil society produced contradictory pressures: from veterans of the revolution, to distribute land and resources to them and improve pensions; from labor and church organizations, for fair elections and the end to political repression and government corruption. People, including former freedom fighters, were taking things into their own hands by occupying large farms, but they had little capacity to make them productive. Government officials, including Mugabe's own family, were also helping themselves to the land of white farmers who were driven off or evicted. Not just white farmers, but African agricultural workers were forced off many of the large farms. With the agriculture sector in chaos, there was little food to be bought in cities, little medicine to be had, little pay even for people with jobs.

By the late 1990s international financial organizations as well as international NGOs were pressuring African governments to allow multiple political parties and hold elections, and Zimbabwe was a visible example of a political trajectory from liberation to oppression.

Mugabe made gestures to respond to such pressure while doing his best to avoid their substance. The most important opposition party to emerge was the Movement for Democratic Change (MDC), led by Morgan Tsvangirai. Tsvangirai was charged with treason after the 2002 elections; he was beaten up by police in 2005. The government seemed to have lost elections in 2008, but rigged the vote count enough to force a run-off, then carried out a campaign of beatings and murders against the MDC until Tsvangirai had to withdraw. Mugabe then pretended to cooperate with the opposition – itself weakened and divided – while controlling the security forces. The strategy worked for some years, aided by a modest recovery of the economy, the discovery of diamonds (mostly controlled by Mugabe's henchmen), and assistance from the foreigners Mugabe condemned. But Mugabe, clinging to power into his nineties, overplayed his hand by trying to groom his wife to succeed him. Elements in the military finally intervened in December 2017, put Mugabe under house arrest, and installed former general Emmerson Mnangagwa as President. The new President was a long-time member of Mugabe's regime, implicated in the massacres of Ndebele in the 1980s. Whether he and the military, which backs him, will set Zimbabwe on a new trajectory is far from clear, but the fall of Mugabe after thirty-seven years in power can only leave anyone who experienced the hopes vested in the end of white domination sad and frustrated at the long period in which the welfare of a reconfigured nation was sacrificed to a regime that above all wanted to cling to power.

Mozambique and Angola

Portugal's presence in parts of southern Africa lasted from the fif-teenth century to 1975. Mozambique and Angola had the misfortune to be colonized by what had by the late nineteenth century become one of Europe's least prosperous empires. The worldwide commod-ities boom of the post-war decade affected it in a particular way: a developmentalist colonialism directed by an authoritarian state, unmediated by the concerns for social progress and political stability in other colonies; and an influx of white workers from Portugal, who took a large share of the skilled jobs and civil service positions which were central to the new political and social dynamics elsewhere. In the 1960s Angola's white population was similar in proportion to that of

Rhodesia, but it was poorer and less educated. Roads, schools, and other services were miserable.

Trying to adapt to the new international climate, Portugal asserted that its African territories were not colonies but an integral part of Portugal, and that Portugal had a special genius for Christianizing and assimilating indigenous populations into a non-racial people. From 1961 Portuguese Africans were considered citizens with the same status as white Portuguese. The reality was different, however: although Africans could theoretically aspire to the status of *assimilado* (the assimilated one), only 1 percent ever got there, and racism characterized every dimension of the system, from the judiciary to labor recruitment.

Angola was the better endowed of the two southern African colonies, and it suffered accordingly. It had been integrated into the slave-trade routes linking the central–western coast of Africa with Brazil; in the early twentieth century it was a source for coerced labor for offshore islands; parts of its own interior were used, again via coercive methods, for cocoa and mineral production; and after 1975 its fate was shaped by oil and diamonds. The nucleus of African organized opposition emerged among educated Africans who were either racially mixed or *assimilado*, and especially among educated Angolans who met up with intellectuals from other Portuguese colonies living outside Africa. The Movimento Anti-Colonialista was founded in Paris in 1957, and it included Agostinho Neto, Eduardo Mondlane, and Amilcar Cabral, who would lead radical movements in Angola, Mozambique, and Guinea-Bissau. Peasant and worker unrest in Angola was for a time contained, until major peasant upheavals broke out in 1961.

Angolan politics was shaped by the sharp disarticulation of society. Whereas urban West Africans were linked by kinship networks and frequent movement to rural areas, the elite of Angola's capital, Luanda, constituted a small and relatively isolated social category: Portuguese-speaking, Catholic, educated. They stood in tension not only with Africans who had little chance of acquiring fluency in Portuguese, but also with the "new *assimilados*" whose education had not taken them into this social milieu. The old *assimilados* and racially mixed people formed the core of the Popular Movement for the Liberation of Angola (MPLA), founded in exile. The return of its key leaders in 1960 coincided with rural revolts and urban riots which they did not control.

The MPLA, led by Agostinho Neto, looked upon politics through nationalist and socialist lenses. Others, however, saw its leaders as mulattos who were remote from the social institutions and networks in which most people lived. Meanwhile, people from the Bakongo ethnic group, living on both sides of the border with the Belgian Congo and connected to Bakongo who had been active in politics in the Congo, began to organize themselves in Angola. At the center of a rural insurrection in 1961, they eventually formed the National Front for the Liberation of Angola (FNLA) under Holden Roberto. Then came UNITA, led by Jonas Savimbi, who was from an Ovimbundu-speaking region and had been in leftist student circles in Europe. His small cadre of followers, mostly from Protestant mission schools, had a base in the Central Plateau of the Angolan interior. Savimbi at first espoused a Maoist ideology that emphasized peasant revolution, whereas the MPLA's Marxism focused more on a vanguard leading the nation to modernization and social justice.

Angola's three nationalist factions were not ethnic parties, but their relationship became ethnicized. UNITA developed its rural base among Ovimbundu speakers in a region that had been left with few resources by Portuguese development policy, extensive out-migration of laborers, and a sense of an Ovimbundu way of life that was under threat both by Portuguese oppression and the more worldly Angolans of the cities. Many people from the Central Plateau perceived the MPLA as not fully African, although it saw itself as nationalist and internationalist. The three movements followed separate paths: the FNLA gained support from now-independent Zaire, UNITA from Zambia, and the MPLA from the Soviet Union and Cuba.

The anti-colonial struggle in Angola was long and harsh, and the three armed movements had limited military success. But Portugal was not rich and its conscript army was not motivated, while the settler population was too diverse, poor, and dependent on the state to go it alone, UDI style. The Portuguese empire came to an end when an army coup overthrew the dictatorship and opened up a twisty road to democratization in Portugal itself. The coup leaders came to see that the African wars were draining Portugal of its strength, and they set their eyes on becoming fuller participants in relations among European states. To do so, they would wash their hands of colonies – and of Africans. They began a negotiation process with the liberation forces in Angola, Mozambique, and Guinea-Bissau which resulted in independence for all three in 1975. Independence resulted in a mass flight – not anticipated by the Portuguese government – of white Portuguese from all three territories. Some 800,000 went to Portugal, including nine-tenths of the whites of Angola.

Portugal ceded sovereignty to the "Angolan people" without making clear who represented them. The anti-colonial war immediately became a civil war that lasted twenty-seven years. The FNLA was supported by Zaire and the CIA, which saw it as the least Marxist of the three, but it never got out of its regional confines and soon faded. UNITA had support from Zambia and South Africa, the latter anxious to keep an independent Angola too weak to threaten its dominance over the region, especially in its dependency of neighboring South West Africa (now Namibia). The United States added its support to UNITA in 1986. Savimbi's political style remained what it had always been: centralizing, personalized, and brutal, his Maoism now reduced to organizing a rural area rather than a socialist agenda. UNITA, although it had popular support within its regional base, was the tightly controlled and frequently purged satrapy of a warlord. In addition to garnering support from South Africa and the United States, UNITA organized diamond smuggling into Zaire, getting guns and spoils for Savimbi's henchmen in return. Most important for those in the region, UNITA provided rewards for young men who would smuggle and fight (and it coerced others into joining), and this provided the only means of earning a livelihood in an area otherwise devastated by terror and counter-terror.

The MPLA won the first round of the civil war by holding Luanda and pushing outward, aided by Cuban troops and indirect Soviet support. Both sides saw their goal as forging a state that would create a nation. UNITA and the MPLA, whatever their ideological attractions, asserted power by acting as the only potential state within their respective regions. As oil deposits near the coast came into production, the MPLA began to enjoy revenues from French and American oil companies, which were willing to pay what in the oil-rich region passed for "the state" regardless of its rhetoric. That rhetoric was Marxist–Leninist, and it represented, at some level and at least at first, the desire of an educated elite, familiar with the European ideals of socialist revolution, to be the agent of transformation of an impoverished, ill-educated population. Its stance also reflected the support it received from Cuba and the Soviet Union.

The MPLA combined the features of a Soviet party and an African gatekeeper state, whose power derives from controlling the interface of

FIGURE 20 The faces of war: a very young soldier for the MPLA beneath a poster of the party's leader, Agostinho Neto, in the city of Huambo, Angola, 1976. AFP/Getty Images

national and world economies. Its main source of power was oil revenue coming from militarized enclaves and, after gestures at revolutionizing agriculture, it did little in the countryside other than recruit soldiers. Thanks to oil revenues, it was able to import food. Education, health, and other state services languished. The illegal urban economy supplied consumers, and rural distribution followed regional lines of clientage.

When the Cold War wound down the United States and Russia lost interest, and left Angolans with the mess that their intervention had exacerbated. Cuba and South Africa pulled out their soldiers in 1988. A UN-brokered peace agreement in 1992 was patched together so incompetently that it soon failed. Meanwhile, the MPLA discarded its Marxism–Leninism in favor of cooperation with the West, and it made gestures toward allowing multiparty elections. The MPLA government, with its oil revenues, and UNITA, evading the state gatekeepers through diamond smuggling into Zaire and Zambia, continued their war. A small civic movement, associated with the Catholic Church, tried to mediate. The conflict ended, after several aborted attempts at negotiations under international auspices, only when government forces finally got to Savimbi in 2002, killing him and pushing his followers to abandon his failing cause.

MPLA socialism never was fully oriented toward making life better for the masses, and, without even the veneer of pretending to share the country's oil wealth, the family of President Jose Eduardo dos Santos enriched itself. The capital, Luanda, has become one of the world's most expensive cities, to be enjoyed by expatriate investors and government-associated oligarchs; Chinese investors have joined European and American corporations in the oil and infrastructure sectors. The exodus of white Portuguese of the 1970s has to a certain extent been reversed as Portuguese find niches in the oil-fed urban economy, and the majority of the Angolan population gets by as best it can. The retirement of dos Santos from the presidency at the end of 2017 offers the hope of moving beyond dynastic government, but not necessarily beyond that of a small elite distant from ordinary Angolans.

Mozambique was once the preserve of European companies that administered large segments of territory on concessions from the Portuguese government and built plantations for export crops, including sugar, cotton, and cashew nuts. The concession companies made heavy use of forced labor. In southern Mozambique stints of migratory labor in the gold mines of the Witwatersrand in neighboring South

Africa were preferable to coerced labor within Mozambique. The region's port, Lourenço Marques (later Maputo), catered to the Witwatersrand's need for an outlet to the sea. In comparison to Angola, the lack of highly concentrated sources of wealth, the smaller size of the *assimilado* elite, and the way related languages and cultural patterns overlapped discouraged sharp rivalries among political movements. FRELIMO emerged in 1962 under the leadership of American-educated Eduardo Mondlane in the northern region, where Tanganyika (later Tanzania) provided a haven and a base. Northern peoples predominated in its membership. FRELIMO's advance was slow and painful, but its army did establish liberated zones in the north, where it tried to involve peasants in their own governance, and it infiltrated parts of the south. The uncertainties of guerrilla warfare contributed to the demoralization of the Portuguese army and the 1974 coup. In 1975 FRELIMO came to power, under the leadership of Samora Machel, who had succeeded Mondlane after the latter was murdered by the Portuguese.

FRELIMO did not constitute an isolated state elite like the MPLA; Mozambique lacked resources that could be produced and marketed without the active participation of a large proportion of the population. The party did have serious ambitions to transform society, and its vision of a post-revolutionary future captured the imagination of many people in Mozambique. But FRELIMO made mistakes: its leaders assumed that they would lead the way to remaking rural society, often ignoring the wisdom of people who knew their environments and their fatigue at having long been told by others what to do. FRELIMO faced the basic dilemma of having to extract from agricultural production the resources it needed to improve education, health, and urban welfare. Independence was accompanied by the destruction of some of the facilities the Portuguese had built and an exodus of skilled workers; Portugal had done little to train its successors in running railway yards, let alone ministries.

Much of FRELIMO's attempts to rid urban areas of "marginal" people and revitalize agriculture seemed too familiar to people who had lived through colonial rule. FRELIMO's brittle authoritarianism was rooted both in the urgency of the situation – the perceived need to use the tools of the state to forge a unified and homogeneous nation in the face of enemies within and without – and the elite's experience through its international connections of a brand of Marxism that stressed a one-party state that managed workers and peasants in a single-minded effort at social transformation.

It also had South Africa and Rhodesia for neighbors. The apartheid regime engaged in economic and other forms of sabotage. The plane crash that killed President Machel in 1986 may well have been caused by the South African secret services. Because the FRELIMO government helped the rebels fighting white Rhodesia until 1979, Rhodesia worked with South Africa to develop a rebel movement to destabilize Mozambique. Although RENAMO began that way, and was continually supported by South Africa until the early 1990s, its relative success also reflected FRELIMO's failure to build support in parts of the countryside. Many peasants saw themselves not as committed and loyal participants in FRELIMO's socialist experiment but as people beset by government troops on one side and rebel troops on the other. The war, dragging on until 1992, displaced between 5 and 6 million refugees within and beyond Mozambique's borders, killed hundreds of thousands through violence and famine, and rendered much labor migration and other economic activity too dangerous to undertake.

FRELIMO's efforts to build a socialist economy also ran into a lack of skilled labor, managerial experience, and capital. Heavy-handed efforts to turn exploitative plantations and ill-equipped village producers into new forms of agricultural cooperation resulted in more confusion than production. The government had hoped to abolish chieftaincy, strong ethnic attachments, and local ritual practices in order to turn Mozambicans into citizens committed to socialist ideals and national goals, but many peasants did not see how those abstractions translated into a better life. Some people accused the government of failing to protect people against sorcery, which they believed lay behind commonly experienced misfortunes. In the absence of a pathway to a new society, Mozambicans were vulnerable to rebels who both encouraged their attachments to local authority structures and traditions and made threats against which the government could not protect them. In parts of the countryside, rebel rule became a reality, and then government counterattack became another menace. War and underlying political and economic weakness had devastating effects on people's livelihoods.

The weakening of the apartheid state by 1990 reduced its interest in ripping apart the region, and neither FRELIMO nor RENAMO could play the oil and diamond games that UNITA and MPLA did in Angola. There was, at least, a basis for a settlement, and in 1992 the two sides agreed to stop fighting, to allow participation of both movements in government bodies, and to hold elections. FRELIMO had, since 1989, dropped its Marxist–Leninist label (the substance had long been a mixed bag), won reasonably fair elections, privatized much of its state enterprises, reconnected its economy to South Africa, and cooperated with the World Bank and development agencies. The government had never been able to make socialist enterprises effective, and the new strategy of privatization produced state–capital alliances rather than a sharp break. Since the changes, Mozambique has had periods of significant growth – and been celebrated by international financial institutions – but that growth has been difficult to sustain or to make accessible to the country's poor. The country has been beset by floods and other climate-related disasters, and by continued fears that the RENAMO–FRELIMO conflict might recur.

The FRELIMO government has not only sought compromise on economic policy, but on administrative and judicial structures, cooperating with "traditional" elites in parts of the country. It accepted or encouraged multiple forms of justice, including "community courts" in rural and peri-urban areas that followed blends of custom and official law. Mozambique's effort to create a socialist, national citizen ended up reproducing what anthropologist Juan Obarrio (2011: 6) calls "customary citizenship," a layering of ethnic and national memberships. Mozambique remains a poor country, but one that has experienced a tenuous recovery from civil war and economic collapse.

South Africa

After World War II South Africa both epitomized and at the same time made a mockery of development goals. Its post-war boom resulted in extensive industrialization and the production of great wealth, and it left millions in misery. The government called its policy in the 13 percent of the country reserved for African cultivators and families, into which millions of people removed from cities were dumped, "separate development." Whereas around 1950 the ANC seemed similar to parties in other African territories, the latter were soon organizing for real elections that would soon confer real power, and the former could organize but not campaign, and frequently saw its members jailed. Black South Africans got to vote in their first meaningful election in 1994 – thirty-seven years after Ghana became independent.

The 1960s were grim years in South African politics. The escalating
militance of the ANC and the Pan-Africanist Congress (PAC) – mass
demonstrations and mass violations of pass laws, boycotts of buses and
shops – culminated in March 1960 in an anti-pass demonstration in the
town of Sharpeville, upon which police fired, killing scores of Africans.
The government response to the ensuing international outrage – coming
at a time when other African colonies were going free – was to ban the
ANC and the PAC. These parties moved their bases into exile, mostly in
Zambia and Tanzania, and founded armed branches, the ANC's
Umkhonto we Sizwe and the PAC's Poqo. Nelson Mandela and many
other leaders were soon arrested; Mandela would reside in prison for
twenty-seven years. After faltering for a time, the South African economy began to race forward; unlike almost all African countries, it
profited greatly from gold sales during the troubled years of the world
economy in the 1970s. Its industrial products didn't break into international markets, but its relative self-sufficiency prepared it for the
boycotts and sanctions that were to come. Whites in South Africa had
a standard of living equivalent to that of western Europe. Blacks and
Coloureds (as mixed-race people were called) did not.

The state managed racial distinction – and distinctions among
Africans – in a shrewd manner. Its ability to monitor the movements
of Africans, via pass laws and residential controls, enabled it to balance demands for labor against the desire to exclude from "white"
areas those Africans who were not immediately of service. Under the
Group Areas Act some Africans born in cities had a right to live there
permanently; others could in specified circumstances stay for long
periods; others lived temporarily (in principle) in single-sex hostels.
The best-paid, best-housed Africans still chafed at the impossibility of
obtaining the rights of citizens. The fivefold expansion of African high-
school enrollments between 1965 and 1975, as the industrial economy
demanded more educated labor, still left students with an inferior
curriculum, inferior job opportunities, and few legal means of political
expression. The migratory system divided families; and the combination of bitter rural poverty and urban discrimination left a large
number of young men and women excluded from opportunity or
hope, likely recruits to criminal gangs, the bo-tsotsi. Few people in
the early 1980s thought that apartheid would soon be dismantled;
fewer still that it would end via negotiations. Revolution seemed one
possibility, continued oppression a more likely one.

How did a negotiated resolution come to pass? Not because of
victory in the armed struggle that Umkhonto we Sizwe and Poqo

FIGURE 21 Forced removals, South Africa, 1987. A family in Soweto, near Johannesburg, collecting their belongings after police evicted them from their dwelling following a rent boycott. Walter Dhladhla/AFP/Getty Images

waged – a point made by Mandela himself. One has to understand the multiple basis of African mobilization as well as the particular vulnerability of the white elite. The multidimensional engagement of African political actors, as noted earlier, has deep roots: the politics of chieftaincy, of peaceful petition, of Gandhian peaceful resistance, of Christian universalism, of Pan-Africanism, of labor militance, and of youthful violence could coexist in a single township or rural district. These efforts could be conflictual or complementary, but they enhanced the possibilities of different networks among South Africans and different linkages outside of South Africa. After the 1958 All-African Peoples' Conference in newly independent Ghana, other African countries became a source of inspiration, and later independent southern African states could serve as guerrilla bases, places of exile and organization, and sources of support. Some movement leaders, from the 1950s onward, traveled to other African countries, to India, to the 1955 Bandung conference, to the UN, and to states in both the "Western" and "Soviet" blocs. Soviet support was important to the ANC's exile bases in Zambia and Tanzania. Even when repression within South Africa seemed solid, political and labor leaders had reason to maintain their efforts and their aspirations.

FIGURE 22 South Africa on strike, August 1987. Members of the National Union of Mineworkers at ERGO, a gold refinery near Johannesburg, during the major strike of 1987. Although this strike was not successful, it was one of many such events in the 1980s that convinced the white government that it was not in control. Trevor Samson/AFP/Getty Images

In the two decades after Sharpeville, the South African and international threads were spinning together in new ways. Take labor. For all the state effort at insisting that Africans were not really "of" the city, the growth of industry in places such as Durban proved otherwise; families were part of the city too and needed shelter, food, and schools. Underground organization of the workplace in Durban surfaced in January 1973 when workers at a brick factory went to a field instead of to work, beginning a series of strikes and demonstrations in advanced industrial sectors, including automobiles. In the absence of recognized unions, officials did not know with whom to negotiate or whom to jail. Zulu chiefs as well as unknown labor leaders became involved and negotiated with employers.

The strike wave occurred at a time when capital had been prospering for years, when wages were held in check and prices rising, and when Africans' rural resources were severely compromised by the forced removals of Africans from areas designated for whites. In 1974 there were 374 strikes, involving 58,000 African workers. They won significant wage increases. There were strikes and disturbances on the gold mines in 1975–77, and wages went up in the 1970s, after decades of stagnation, even as the mine owners tried to draw on the wider southern African region for labor. African miners broke into whites' control of more skilled positions, their share of semi-skilled and skilled roles moving from 22 percent to 39 percent. After recognition of the mineworkers' union in 1982, 60 percent of miners had joined by 1988.

The government vacillated between repressing the labor movement and trying to co-opt it into a system that would give it a measure of recognition. Employers tried to channel demands into "works committees" that could be readily controlled. Even small concessions gave African workers an opportunity for more shop-floor organization. Workers' anger was proving difficult to contain. Parts of the business elite feared that repressive industrialization was reaching its limits and that it would be better to channel militance into known channels when it could not be stopped. The government by the end of the 1970s grudgingly recognized that it had to allow Africans to participate in some kind of trade union system, and a trade union federation was recognized in 1979. That too proved difficult to control, and African unions soon became important actors in struggles for better wages, and for political change as well. The new policy echoed the policies in the African colonies of France and Britain thirty years before, when they had been rejected in South Africa. The new initiatives would – as in British and French Africa – have consequences more far-reaching than the calculations of officials.

The second thread came from youth – urban youth in particular. They were part of the city, but the city was not offering them a future. The Bantu Education system was humiliating, and the segmentation of housing and jobs meant that many stood little chance of getting even where their parents were. It was not just the city that was in question: the migratory system had spread urban culture and the appeal of urban lifestyles into the most remote parts of South Africa. The political significance of youth was by no means homogeneous. Some were satisfied with the pleasures and the expressiveness of music, drinking, and dance; others gravitated into gangs that preyed on African workers. Pass laws that made job seeking difficult actually fostered illicit activities.

In the schools and universities a new political movement was emerging: Black Consciousness. Steve Biko split off from a multiracial student organization to form the South African Student Organization (SASO) in 1969. SASO picked up the Africanist thread of all-black political movements from the banned PAC, inflected by strong Christian themes, an effort to forge in black South Africans a new

FIGURE 23 Soweto Revolt, June 1976. High-school students in the segregated township of Soweto, near Johannesburg, took to the streets to protest the quality of the education provided for blacks and their lack of future possibilities. The widespread protests were met with police violence, resulting in hundreds of deaths. Bongani Mnguni/City Press/Gallo Images/Getty Images

consciousness and confidence in themselves and their future. It was in the high schools that Black Consciousness caught on most strongly, appealing to young men and women who were far from the worst off in South African society, but whose imaginations and hopes were ground down by Bantu Education. Biko was arrested in 1973 and SASO banned. Biko was murdered by the police three years later.

In 1976 youthful anger spilled over in the biggest township outside of Johannesburg in what became known as the Soweto rising. Its immediate cause was an attempt by the Bantu Education authorities to make Afrikaans the language of instruction, which students took to be a demand for submission to the culture of their most immediate oppressors. Its underlying causes were the frustrations that young Africans had been experiencing for many years. In the townships the students forced the schools to close; they blockaded streets; they attacked police stations; they tried to force their elders not to work. Police fought back with bullets as well as tear gas. In official figures – understated – 575 people died and over 2,000 were injured. Riots took place in other cities as well. They not only shook the white population's sense of being in control, but defined an event whose anniversary would be marked every year with posters of a man carrying the dead body of the young Hector Pieterson, shot by the police.

South Africa at the beginning of the 1980s was a police state: banning organizations and individuals, jailing people for political offenses as well as for violations of pass laws and other apartheid regulations, assassinating opponents. It was a sophisticated police state, defining different categories of residential access in order to separate out an elite interested in stability. The government hoped that, with the iron fist in the background, a small incentive to cooperate would go a long way. But apartheid also meant that very few black South Africans would more than grudgingly accept the status quo, and the elaborate attempts of the state to build an ideology of acquiescence were ridiculed.

The apartheid system had tried to channel urban dwellers into townships such as Soweto, where it distinguished long-term residents in their small houses from short-term, male migrants in hostels. Some illegal settlements, such as Crossroads, near Cape Town, vigorously defended themselves and were tolerated; others were bulldozed. All this was breaking down as people poured into the crevices of the system, driven by the overwhelming degradation of rural conditions and the especially precarious condition of women, caught between the illegal status of most of them in the cities and the impossibility of survival in the countryside. People moved into backyard shacks, into squatter settlements, into rooms in other people's shacks. In the 1980s official strategy was to regain control by widening the zone of tolerance of shack settlements, while keeping them confined to certain areas. But shack dwellers also organized themselves. They provided another urban constituency of considerable volatility, a source both of gang violence and of organized, careful protest. Women leaders in shack settlements organized against lawless gangs as well as against the police.

The cracks were getting wider. The federation of trade unions founded in 1979 morphed in 1985 into a more militant and well-organized structure, the Congress of South African Trade Unions (COSATU). Its actions were not confined to the narrow terrain of "industrial relations." As Gay Seidman (1994) argues, "social movement" unionism took root in a situation where the problems workers faced were not specific to their place of employment. The state's regulation of housing and schooling and its policing of migration were all issues that a labor movement had to raise. With the ANC underground, COSATU became a surrogate political party as well, using its legal status to make claims and to threaten collective action, from strikes to mass demonstrations. The government had to live with COSATU, for it feared that the alternative was worse.

Despite waves and waves of arrests for illegal demonstrations and pass-law violations, the movement of people between cities, townships, shack settlements, and rural areas was not really under control. When the South African economy entered a recession in 1982, many people who had been drawn into the segmented wage-labor system, including high-school graduates, were left jobless. Urban violence escalated in the mid-1980s – some of it organized, some of it a mark of despair. The underground ANC was trying to channel militant action, calling on city-dwellers to make the cities "ungovernable." The reality preceded and exceeded the objective.

Beginning in 1959, government leaders asserted that the homelands (or Bantustans) were nascent "Black nations" – an attempt to portray South Africa as following some of the pathways out of empire opened up in French and British Africa. Starting with the Transkei region in 1962, the government proclaimed that Africans were citizens of their own countries, not citizens or potential citizens of South Africa. South African activists did not fall for this line, and other nations did not recognize the pseudo-nations. The reality was that these territories were closely controlled and economically unviable, but the policy did convey powers of patronage to rural African elites who identified themselves as "traditional."

The rural leader who appeared to be more than a stooge was Mangosuthu Buthelezi, the head of the KwaZulu administrative district. By refusing independent status for KwaZulu, he kept enough distance from the government to retain plausibility, while controlling a tight hierarchy of chiefs who had considerable power over returning migrants' access to land. He also drew on a form of Zulu neo-traditionalism developed by the bilingual elites of a previous generation, who in the 1920s gathered into a Zulu cultural organization called Inkatha – the name Buthelezi took for his revived Zulu association. For a time, Buthelezi positioned himself as an anti-apartheid leader, and while it has since been proven that in the 1980s and 1990s his organization cooperated with the secret police, including in the murder of opponents, he kept a certain public autonomy.

Inkatha represented more than Buthelezi's power mongering. There was a very real tension among Africans – especially strong among Zulu – between a moral vision focused on patriarchy and respect for elders and chiefs and a politics of individual freedom as exemplified by the ANC. Many Zulu feared that individualism and liberal ideals endangered kinship connections, the authority of household heads, bridewealth, the rural homestead, and a hierarchical vision of society. COSATU and the ANC – underground until 1990, visibly active after that – were increasingly focused on people in the townships, shack settlements, and other urban areas, where social life was more open and the value placed on the individual more salient. Each side often saw the other as representing antithetical values.

The ANC underground clashed more and more with Inkatha. In the Johannesburg area, where most Zulu workers were short-term migrants still dependent on the power apparatus in KwaZulu, young Zulu hostel-dwellers (known as *impis*) frequently fought with young ANC supporters, children of long-term residents for the most part (known as "comrades"). Gang violence got worse in the early 1990s. In Natal, near the Zulu homeland, much of the violence was Zulu on Zulu, for Inkatha's appeal was far from uniform across this group, and those Zulu well ensconced in Durban's strong industrial culture were likely to be COSATU and ANC supporters. Inkatha thugs tried to police the "exit option" of Zulus who were not willing to remain in the confines of a system of rural political authority linked to control of access to land (via chiefs) and peri-urban housing (via "shacklords"). As the secret police intrigued with Inkatha against common enemies, the violence became uglier and uglier.

The constitutionalist, non-racialist, nonviolent side of the ANC tradition, which had absorbed the "Africanist" initiatives of the 1940s and 1950s rather than give way to them, remained important even when the ANC itself was underground or in exile. In 1983 many of the local and regional organizations fighting apartheid founded a national, coordinating body, the United Democratic Front (UDF), initially aimed at combating a new Constitution that would have given Indians and Coloureds a small electoral presence and Africans none. The UDF was shaped by its ordinary members, notably Africans of working-class origin, radicalized in high school, then trapped in the segregated, stifling economy. The UDF, nevertheless, had a multi-racial membership and was committed to the democratic goals that had long characterized the ANC. "People's power" became a slogan at the national level, but sponsorship of neighborhood networks, con-sumer boycotts, school boycotts, rent boycotts, and attacks on African agents of local government made the UDF an important presence in the townships. Government banning orders and the declaration of a state of emergency in 1986 could not eliminate this mobilization. Meanwhile, the South African Communist Party, long linked to the trade union movement and the ANC, stood on the left flank, emphasizing both organization and economic justice. The ANC itself, from exile, organized a new round of armed attacks, more important for marking its continued presence than for their actual effects.

The international picture was opening up too. Since 1959 groups in England had organized boycotts of South African products, with limited economic effect but an important political one: underscoring that newly independent African countries constituted the international norm, while South Africa did not. African states maintained a steady critique at the United Nations and other international bodies, and tried to deny South Africa a place in international commercial, cultural, and athletic organizations. South African goods were at times refused entry by dockworkers in European or American ports; American university campuses were enlivened by demonstrations against endowment-fund investments in companies doing business in South Africa; religious organizations raised money for exiles and protested racial exclusion and violence; African-American organizations publicized South African issues and campaigned, with partial success, for official American sanctions against South Africa. The communist world provided aid and arms to the ANC, as well as a platform for some of its leaders and connections to other revolutionary movements.

South Africa had taken itself out of the British Commonwealth when it ceased to be white enough, and at Commonwealth meetings Africans painted the apartheid state as abnormal. South Africa tried to influence conservative African leaders such as Mobutu and Houphouët-Boigny to share in mutually beneficial trade relations, but others kept up the pressure to quarantine the apartheid state. The founding of the Southern African Development Coordination Conference (SADCC) in 1980 was intended to cement, through closer economic ties, the solidarity of southern African states against South Africa.

Two points are fundamental to understanding why these trends led to the unraveling of apartheid in the mid-1980s and a negotiated resolution between 1990 and 1994. First, the old radical line that the key to revolutionary mobilization is polarization – that absolute repression begets radicalization and revolution – is flawed. As in Gorbachev's Soviet Union, and indeed in the British and French empires a few decades previously, a little reform led to more demands, to a refusal to accept the all-powerful and inevitable nature of state power, and eventually to the breakdown of a system of domination. The legalization of trade unions for Africans in 1979 and the easing of some restrictions on urban residence in the mid-1980s were a start. The attempt of the government to gain ground by allowing Coloureds and Indians to vote only revealed that the regime was casting about for a way out of endless insecurity, isolation, and escalating repression.

Business was finding the cost excessive when there was no resolution in sight. In 1986 the regime – beset by riots, student protests, and strikes – tried to ease the burden on itself and gain a little legitimacy by abolishing the hated pass system. That gave the urban poor, both women and men, a better chance to set up shack settlements in bits of vacant land and to carry out the entrepreneurial (and sometimes criminal) activities typical of "informal" economies elsewhere in Africa, providing alternatives to the officially regulated economy. Meanwhile, COSATU and the UDF offered a democratic, apparently peaceful, alternative. The South African regime was losing its ability to frame politics.

The other point involves the nature of the South African elite itself. For a time, Afrikaners set themselves against English speakers, and enjoyed the pleasure of thinking themselves a struggling community. Afrikaner politicians had always emphasized the "Christian" nature of their society, and by that they evoked a connection to the history of Western civilization. By the 1970s or 1980s many Afrikaners had become too affluent and too worldly to be satisfied with proud isolation. They had become like most other participants in global capitalism. White South Africans wanted to travel, to have a national team in the Olympics, to have access to all the cultural and consumer resources to which their prosperity entitled them. Business leaders needed international sources of credit. They were hemmed in overseas for the same reason that there were demonstrations every week and a chronic atmosphere of crisis. The boycotts may not have actually isolated South Africa economically, but they did affect foreign investment and credit, and above all moral discourse. In terms of coercive power the regime could have gone on for years, maybe decades, but without international legitimacy and domestic order it is not clear for how long it could have carried along the majority of whites.

Political change is a process, not an event, and the South African government was slowly losing control over both discourse and action. The government made its first, conditional, offer of freedom to Mandela in 1985; it was refused. Cautious contacts between the famous prisoner and the administration led to Mandela's meeting with President P. W. Botha in 1989 and Mandela's release in February

1990, simultaneous with the unbanning of the ANC and the latter's renunciation of armed struggle. By this time the Cold War was no longer a factor, and the National Party could no longer hope that the United States would see it as a bastion against communism, while the ANC could no longer count on Soviet support. The two sides were even more exclusively focused on what had all along been their major concern: each other.

When F. W. de Klerk succeeded the aging Botha in late 1989, he seems to have thought that he could manage this process, but he had going against him the demoralization of the white elite, the alternative of endless strife and global isolation, economic difficulties, and the quiet self-confidence of Mandela, who could wait in prison for a while longer to get what he wanted and what his comrades in the street would accept. By 1990 Mandela not only had the organization of the ANC in exile to back him, but also COSATU and UDF, and able leaders such as Cyril Ramaphosa, the mine union leader, COSATU official, and UDF activist who became General Secretary of the ANC after it was legalized. With Mandela's release the UDF passed its torch back to the ANC, which took up negotiations with a South African state that was no longer what it had been.

The NP did not obtain what it thought it could out of negotiations, but settled for what it could get: the protection of minority rights and guarantees that property would be respected and certain electoral rules followed. It may be that NP leaders actually believed their own reasoning: that its reforms had separated out from the dangerous African masses an elite conservative enough to vote for it. But in the end, the NP leadership could only bargain on how it would give up power – a complicated process from late 1991 to early 1994. The ANC agreed to work with the NP in insuring interim government only when the latter had agreed to a date for elections: April 27, 1994. At that point, the ANC strove to curtail violence and capital flight.

The NP became so involved in its pas de deux with the ANC that it all but dropped its earlier connections with Inkatha, which for a time seemed to prefer violent confrontation in quest of regional autonomy to participation in the constitutional and electoral process. Inkatha realized just in time that electoral fever was high in KwaZulu, too. So, late in the game, Inkatha decided to contest the election as well. The violence in KwaZulu-Natal abated, and the last weeks of the campaign were both calm and enthusiastic.

In the end the NP learned that its status as the lone defender of white civilization was not what its constituents would accept any longer; they had to be part of an international system, and only majority rule would get them that. After years of denying Africans fair trials and access to property, whites' future security and prosperity now depended on whether the ANC majority would continue to take seriously a discourse on the rule of law and human rights that it had espoused since its founding in 1912. Mandela and his colleagues understood the irony: in offering to the NP the rights long denied the ANC, they could complete the long march to freedom.

When on April 27, 1994 black South Africans lined up in queues stretching around city blocks and country roads to cast their ballots, they revealed just how meaningful the act of voting can be. The ANC government then faced the burden of reforming one of the world's most unequal societies in an era of worldwide economic uncertainty.

It is, as of this writing, nearly twenty-five years since Africans in South Africa got the opportunity to choose their leaders. These have been years of hope, accomplishment, and disappointment. The ANC's promise to maintain the basic structures of electoral democracy have been maintained: elections have been held in 1999, 2004, 2009, and 2014, and they have been openly contested. Policies have been debated in the press and legislature. Presidents have not overstayed their terms: Mandela was followed by Thabo Mbeki, then by Jacob Zuma, and most recently by Cyril Ramaphosa.

The ANC has retained great credibility because of its leadership role in the long struggle, and that was both a virtue and a flaw in the political process. While veterans of the struggle were at the top of the hierarchy, the political situation was open enough to bring new people into the ANC – not least women, who became significant figures in the legislature and the cabinet. The party system, however, limited the openness of politics. Since ANC candidates were so likely to win in parliamentary elections, the real choice of candidates was made by the party; hence, the most important decisions were taking place in the obscurity of party institutions rather than in open electoral competition. The system tended to put patron–client relations within the ANC to the fore.

The danger is that patronage slides into the use of office for private gain. Particularly under the Zuma presidency, the elite's enrichment of itself – not least that of the President himself – was the focus of criticism in the press and periodic demonstrations. What was needed to call Zuma to account was for the party to abandon him, and it took until February 2018 for it to do so, the second time a president has had to resign because of the party's slow realization that he was not acting in its interest, let alone that of the country (Thabo Mbeki was pushed out in favor, ironically, of Zuma). The debate leading up to Zuma's resignation revealed that for his supporters a rhetorical strategy critical of South Africa's white capitalists still carries weight even when accompanied by both corruption and a failure to remedy the rampant inequality in South African society. This argument eventually (and barely) lost out to the appeal of honesty and competence, embodied in Cyril Ramaphosa, who had been a hero of the struggle against apartheid but who had become closely linked to the very capitalists Zuma's supporters were attacking, making himself one of the richest people in the country. Now that Ramaphosa has become President it remains to be seen whether he has the will and the capacity to reform the system from which he benefited. He will have to contend with one opposition party that takes a stand in favor of liberal reform measures fairly similar to his own and a radical faction critical of the power of capital, the Economic Freedom Fighters, led by a renegade former leader of the ANC Youth League, Julius Malema (who himself has been accused of giving into the temptations of personal enrichment).

Just how much room for maneuver the government has in social and economic policy is not clear. It controls the bulk of revenue, so that even though each province has its own elected government, those governments have limited power. The elites of the old homeland governments – those discredited collaborators of the apartheid regime – have, however, exhibited a certain resilience, for the central government needed the networks homeland elites had created and the experienced civil servants who had served them in order to bring its policies to the different regions of South Africa. At the bottom of the territorial administrative–political hierarchy are nearly 800 chiefdoms, each with its territory, inhabitants, and claim to represent a "tradition." The forward-looking, liberal, democratic ethos of the ANC had to adapt not just to the entrenched intermediaries that the apartheid state had left in place, but to a widely held belief in the importance of local communities, patriarchal social relations, and the role of chiefs in settling disputes and taking responsibility for the welfare of local people. The role – at times arbitrary – of chiefs in distributing land in the former Bantustans did not disappear with the end of apartheid, and the defense of "culture" remained a means of preserving entrenched hierarchies of traditional status, age, and gender which many people saw as protecting them against misfortune. But now, young men and women who don't share such beliefs can leave for the cities without risking arrest under the apartheid laws, so people locate themselves in different kinds of political communities – or find themselves alienated from all of them.

Inequality – within South Africa as well as within the world economy – has been an extremely difficult problem for even the most progressive members of the ANC elite to tackle. The grand bargain of 1994 depended on South Africa's abstention from a large-scale redistribution of property, and the government did not want to take the risk – which would have had serious consequences – of repudiating debt to foreign lenders or taking action that would deter investments needed to maintain or expand production, in the context of an economy weakened during the final decades of apartheid. The ANC considered itself constrained – over the opposition of many of its supporters – to restrain its initially ambitious development goals in order to keep expenditures under control and not to frighten international financial markets. Successive South African Presidents have walked a fine line between reforming without putting at risk a powerful economic structure and responding to the aspirations of a significant portion of its following who expected the ANC to stick to its previously expressed egalitarian and socialist thinking.

The fact was that the task was huge. About 15 percent of South Africa's population were used to a standard of living – including public services such as education and health care – at the same level as those enjoyed by North Americans or western Europeans. It was not politically possible to level the entire society downward. Suddenly to expand public services to include 100 percent of the population was both a political necessity and a practical impossibility. What South Africa accomplished was credible: large-scale programs to provide millions of South Africans with access to electricity and running water in their homes, and extensive construction of homes themselves. More and more Africans are going to school, so much so that there are not enough adequately trained teachers or good enough facilities to give those students a quality education. Students who get to university often find that they are not prepared to meet its challenges, a frustration that lies behind demonstrations and riots on several campuses that, at least on the surface, focus on complaints over fees and lack of African staff.

In the domain of health, efforts to make the world-class medical services long available to whites capable of caring for the entire population led to the opening of numerous clinics, but were made more difficult by the HIV–AIDS epidemic that was at its peak at the time of liberation. The conditions of the South African economy fostered the spread of the virus: the prevalence of labor migration and hence the separation of families; the vulnerability of women whose access to land, food, and shelter had been deteriorating. Under the presidency of Thabo Mbeki the government delayed the introduction of anti-AIDS medication. The eventual introduction of antiretroviral medicines increased survival rates but did not get at the root causes of the problem. Neighboring Botswana, where an active mining sector produced men with enough cash to command sexual services, also had a high rate of HIV infection, but its government responded more promptly and more vigorously with medical services, and hence experienced a lower mortality rate and a less devastating impact on the families of those infected. These are the problems of a society coming out of extreme, state-enforced inequality, and the post-1994 government has addressed but not solved them.

Not least of the social interventions of the ANC government has been cash payments: pensions, disability payments, and different sorts of grants to families in great need, particularly to women, who are especially likely to be without resources. Some of these redistributive efforts were directed specifically at the poor, while others were intended to narrow the racial gap, for example in the pensions that black and white workers received. As many as 30 percent of South Africans receive some sort of government payment. Nevertheless, much of the welfare provision comes not from the state but from families and kinship groups. Experts estimate that up to six people are supported by the wages of one worker. The extreme unevenness of people's life chances and people's access to treatment for illness or remedies for injustice leads to tensions, accusations of sorcery, the formation of gangs by future-less youth, and vigilante organization to combat the high rate of crime.

Some had hoped that once South Africa became an acceptable African state, it would become the hub of a manufacturing economy serving the rest of the continent. By the 1990s, however, inexpensive manufactured goods from China and Southeast Asia were widely available, making a radical breakthrough in market share unlikely, even in South Africa itself. South African firms did extend their reach into other African countries, but their activities were not generating many jobs at home. South African industry, faced with skills shortages fostered by racial discrimination, and agriculture, faced with Africans moving to cities, had over many years moved toward a capital-intensive model, limiting employment. All this was occurring in an economic structure – quite different from that found in most of

Africa – where a working class had been detached from the land. The post-apartheid government thus faced unemployment, of the order of magnitude of 30 percent in much of the post-1994 years.

On the other end of the spectrum, the most affluent South Africans are no longer exclusively white. ANC stalwarts, including Ramaphosa, have become some of the wealthiest men in Africa. There is a growing professional class of Africans who share in what used to be an all-white niche, and a substantial category of skilled and unionized workers with decent wages and job security. Some experts argue that South Africa should promote labor-intensive, low-wage, export-oriented industry rather than this highly differentiated economic structure, but it is not evident what South Africa's advantage over other low-wage economies would be. Others think that the economy will never absorb the unemployed and that some form of basic income grant should go to all citizens, regardless of the work they do, to provide a minimum subsistence to all and a platform from which to strive for some.

Now that all South Africans are citizens – with claims on the same social entitlements – they are more sharply differentiated than before from "foreigners." The mining industry and other activities in South Africa depended, since the nineteenth century, on getting labor from neighboring countries. South Africa's wealth was thus the product of many hands from across southern Africa. Since liberation, and with the mounting tensions over unemployment, the distinction between the citizen and the non-citizen has become more acute. Xenophobic violence against migrants, particularly those from Mozambique and Zimbabwe, has become frequent, most notoriously in a wave of violence against migrants to South African cities in 2008.

That so many refugees from political and economic crises in southern Africa have sought refuge in South Africa points to the continued unevenness that characterizes the region since its liberation from white domination over the years 1975–94. South Africa is not only more prosperous than its neighbors, but it – along with much-less-populated Botswana and Namibia – has avoided civil war and followed the norms of electoral democracy. South Africa since the nineteenth century developed a form of capitalism capable of sustaining a relatively high level of investment, industrialization, and the provision of a high-level standard of living for a portion of its population. That the ANC leadership exhibits a tendency toward crony capitalism – opportunities and sinecures developed with government protection – does not neatly distinguish it from its predecessor, but the capitalist elite is no longer lily white. The poor remain poor, but South Africa has more resources than its neighbors to distribute if it so chooses. Liberation from white rule in southern Africa has reduced the impact of racism, but arguably increased the prevalence of xenophobia. The tensions within South African society – between men and women, rural and urban communities with divergent values, rich and poor, clients of different elites – and among the peoples of the states of southern Africa are part of a regional structure that has changed drastically since the 1970s, but remains unequal and uneven in new ways.

The Aftermaths of Liberation Struggle

The argument, associated with Frantz Fanon, that revolutionary violence would purge societies of the psychological complexes induced by colonialism and form the basis for social and economic progress for the people as a whole has not borne fruit. None of the liberation movements was able to pursue over a substantial period of time an alternative to participation in a capitalist world economy, although Mozambique in particular gave it a try. They were caught between a world economy that, in the conjuncture of the late twentieth century, was hardly favorable to such a project, and a significant portion of the rural population that feared that making the countryside socialist would be yet another imposition from outside. Socialist projects also came up against their own limitations: the lack of personnel and infrastructure to provide a plausible alternative to the more flexible structures of a mixed economy. In more developed sectors of the economy, in Zimbabwe and South Africa especially, the risk of destroying what economic resources there were was a serious one – as indeed the sad history of Mugabe's Zimbabwe demonstrated. In all the territories, the emphasis on reversing the domination of whites gave an opportunity for the first generation of black leaders to claim that it was fulfilling the goals of liberation by transferring the fruits of empowerment to themselves.

If the economics of liberation are constrained, the politics are not necessarily conducive to ensuring that the citizen would actually be politically free and the government responsive. Liberation movements of necessity developed top-down structures of command and an insistence that their ideology constituted a fundamental truth. They worried, with reason, about infiltration by government spies. They therefore had a tendency to treat disagreement over goals and strategies and contestation of the position of leaders not as legitimate opposition, but as treason. Once in power, victorious liberation movements have not necessarily turned off such orientations. As Elisio Macamo (2017: 198) points out, FRELIMO, when it came to power in Mozambique, thought its task was to educate the people, not to listen to them. It brought with it a "political culture which is deeply hostile to citizenship." In Zimbabwe, Mugabe moved quickly to purge his allies in the struggle and continued to equate any opposition to himself as a resurrection of the white-dominated regime his movement had overthrown, even at the cost of driving a once relatively strong economy into chaos and peasants into poverty. In South Africa, the long and arduous struggle of the ANC against apartheid gave it a legitimacy that was both wide and deep, with more freedom of movement than its neighbors enjoyed. Its leadership was intent on not destroying the economic structures that gave it the possibility of both maintaining itself in power and transforming the racially encoded structure of society. It was able to make a series of compromises without losing its ability to tolerate debate and win elections, compromises with the outgoing government and capitalist elite to maintain the security of property, with the powers that be in the world economy to enhance access to finance, with its own influential members who wanted access to patronage and the resources of a wealthy economy, with trade unions that sought to protect a relatively well-off segment of the labor force, with citizens who wanted to break down the barriers of racial discrimination, and with the large majority of its citizens who needed access to the most basic resources – housing, water, electricity, health care, education – and who feared that trying to get it all at once might leave them with nothing. But it is now a serious possibility that the crony capitalism and clientelism that has gone along with ANC's strong position in politics will eclipse the democratic and distributive dimensions that have so far been part of its mode of action.

As Roger Southall (2016) argues, the alternatives that liberation movements faced when coming to power were not a dichotomy between the orthodoxy of free-market economics and turning the control of the means of production upside down. The "mantras" of the proponents of liberal capitalism can be as facile as those of a prefabricated socialism. There were options in between, compromises other than the ones that were made. Those options, as in the rest of the world, were not being exercised by people who were disinterested advocates of a cause. They were in the hands of people who had led struggles and believed that their ideals and their leadership were the only way forward. Nelson Mandela, who chose not to run for a second presidential term that he could have legitimately and easily won, was the conspicuous exception to the tendency of leaders to entrench themselves. Most people coming into authority had an interest in power and wealth, and had families and networks that supported their advancement and expected something in return. The political parties that came to power through the struggles of the 1970s through the 1990s faced a similar question to that faced by leaders who took over African countries, in less violent ways, in the 1950s and 1960s: could they develop and apply to themselves institutions and a political culture that fostered social progress and at the same time respected multiple voices and constraints on their own power?

A full bibliography for this book may be found on the website of Cambridge University Press at www.cambridge.org/CooperAfrica2ed.

Bibliography

Alexander, Jocelyn. *The Unsettled Land: The Politics of Land and State-Making in Zimbabwe, 1893–2003*. London: James Currey, 2006.

Ashforth, Adam. *Witchcraft, Violence, and Democracy in South Africa*. Chicago: University of Chicago Press, 2005.

Barchiesi, Franco. *Precarious Liberation: Workers, the State, and Contested Social Citizenship in Postapartheid South Africa*. Albany: State University of New York Press, 2011

Birmingham, David, and Phyllis Martin, eds. *History of Central Africa: The Contemporary Years since 1960*. London: Longman, 1998.

Donham, Donald. *Violence in a Time of Liberation: Murder and Ethnicity at a South African Gold Mine, 1994*. Durham, NC: Duke University Press, 2011.

Dorman, Sara Rich. *Understanding Zimbabwe: From Liberation to Authoritarianism and Beyond*. London: Hurst, 2016.

Gerhart, Gail. *Black Power in South Africa: The Evolution of an Ideology*. Berkeley: University of California Press, 1978.

Habib, Adam. *South Africa's Suspended Revolution: Hopes and Prospects*. Athens: Ohio University Press, 2013.

Hickel, Jason. *Democracy as Death: The Moral Order of Anti-Liberal Politics in South Africa*. Berkeley: University of California Press, 2015.

Klotz, Audie. *Migration and National Identity in South Africa, 1860–2010*. Cambridge: Cambridge University Press, 2013.

Kriger, Norma. *Zimbabwe's Guerrilla War: Peasant Voices*. Cambridge: Cambridge University Press, 1992.

Lodge, Tom. *Politics in South Africa: From Mandela to Mbeki*. Bloomington: Indiana University Press, 2002.

Macamo, Elisio. "Power, Conflict, and Citizenship: Mozambique's Contemporary Struggles." *Citizenship Studies* 21 (2017): 196–209.

Magaziner, Daniel. *The Law and the Prophets: Black Consciousness in South Africa, 1968–1977*. Athens: Ohio University Press, 2010.

Morier-Genoud, Eric, ed. *Sure Road? Nationalisms in Angola, Mozambique, and Guinea-Bissau*. Leiden: Brill, 2012.

Obarrio, Juan. *The Spirit of the Laws in Mozambique*. Chicago: University of Chicago Press, 2014.

Pitcher, M. Ann. *Transforming Mozambique: The Politics of Privatization, 1975–2000*. Cambridge: Cambridge University Press, 2002.

Ramphele, Mamphela. *A Bed Called Home: Life in the Migrant Labour Hostels of Cape Town*. Athens: Ohio University Press, 1993.

Ranger, T. O. *Peasant Consciousness and Guerrilla War in Zimbabwe*. Berkeley: University of California Press, 1985.

Ross, Robert, Anne Kelk Mager, and Bill Nasson, eds. *Cambridge History of South Africa Volume 2: 1885–1994*. Cambridge: Cambridge University Press, 2011.

Scarnecchia, Timothy. *The Urban Roots of Democracy and Political Violence in Zimbabwe: Harare and Highfield, 1940–1964*. Rochester: Rochester University Press, 2008.

Seekings, Jeremy, and Nicoli Nattrass. *Class, Race, and Inequality in South Africa*. New Haven: Yale University Press, 2005.

Seidman, Gay. *Manufacturing Militance: Workers' Movements in Brazil and South Africa, 1970–1985*. Berkeley: University of California Press, 1994.

Southall, Roger. *Liberation Movements in Power*. Oxford: James Currey, 2016.

Van Onselen, Charles. *The Seed Is Mine: The Life of Kas Maine, a South African Sharecropper*. New York: Hill & Wang, 1996.

West, Harry G. *Kupilikula: Governance and the Invisible Realm in Mozambique*. Chicago: University of Chicago Press, 2005.

White, Luise. *Unpopular Sovereignty: Rhodesian Independence and African Decolonization*. Chicago: University of Chicago Press, 2015.

Williams, J. Michael. *Chieftaincy, the State and Democracy: Political Legitimacy in Post-Apartheid South Africa*. Bloomington: Indiana University Press, 2010.

CHAPTER 7

The Recurrent Crises of the Gatekeeper State

African states were successors in a double sense. First, they were built on a set of institutions – bureaucracies, militaries, customs facilities, post offices, and (for a time at least) legislatures – set up by colonial regimes, as well as on a principle of state sovereignty sanctified by a community of already existing states. In this sense, African states have proven durable: borders have remained largely unchanged (with the notable exceptions of the secession of Eritrea from Ethiopia and South Sudan from Sudan). Almost every piece of Africa is recognized from outside as a territorial entity, regardless of the effective power of the actual government within that space. Even so-called failed states – those unable to provide order and minimal services for their citizens – are still states, and derive resources from outside for that reason.

Second, African states took up a particular and more recent form of the state project of colonialism: development. Political parties in the 1950s and 1960s insisted that only an African government could insure that development would serve the interests of "their" people. Yet by the end of the 1970s people in most African states had come to view such claims with either bitterness at the politicians who developed their own wealth at the people's expense or a continued yearning for development in the form of schools, hospitals, marketing facilities, and a chance for ordinary people to earn money and respect.

The early governments aspired both to define their authority over territory and to accomplish something with the authority they had. The dual project was born into the limitations of the old one, the colonial version of development. African states, like their predecessors, had great difficulty exercising power over territory and people within their borders. They had trouble collecting taxes, except on imports and exports; they had trouble setting economic priorities and policies for their citizens except for the distribution of resources that they could collect; they had trouble making the nation-state into a symbol that inspired loyalty. What they could do best was to sit astride the interface between a territory and the rest of the world, collecting and distributing resources that derived from that point itself: customs revenue and foreign aid; permits to do business in the territory; entry and exit visas; and permission to move currency in and out.

New rulers tried to break out of the limitations of the old – to enhance their economic, symbolic, and coercive power – but controlling the interface of the relatively impoverished territorial state and the concentration of power in the world economy fostered the development of gatekeeper states. The preeminence of gatekeeping strategies varied from place to place and over time, but they were a frequent recourse and a constant temptation.

Colonial states had ultimately derived their authority from their access to military force from outside; their coercive power was more effective at staging raids and terrorizing resistors than at routinizing authority throughout a territory; they had built garrison towns and railways to extend their capacities for such deployments; and they had come to rely on localized systems of "traditional" legitimacy and obedience. Their successors faced similar limitations, and often hesitated between alliances with the same decentralized authority structures, with the risk of reinforcing ethnic power brokers, or breaking them via another deployment of military power likely to provoke region-based opposition. They hesitated to intervene too radically to change the land-allocation regime for fear of disrupting the vertical relationships through local elites on which the maintenance of order depended (Chapter 5). That in turn meant that people's participation in national politics was to a significant extent mediated through local and regional power brokers.

Colonial states had been able to turn to the armed forces of the distant metropole to beat back challenges. Their successors could not be assured of such support. Keeping the gate was more ambition than actuality, and struggles for the gate – and efforts of some groups to get around it – bedeviled African states from the start. Independence added the possibility of weaving patron–client relationships within the state, something colonial officials did too, but not so well.

FIGURE 24 Self-representations of power, Zaire, 1984. President Mobutu
Sese Seko sitting on a throne, with the leopardskin that was his personal symbol
beneath his feet. Mobutu cultivated an image of the all-powerful, blending
symbols of European power (the throne) and African power (the leopard, his
reputation for command over sorcery). Martine Archembault/AFP/Getty Images

Power relations are more complicated than a "state" (bureaucracy, executive, military, legislature) attempting to rule over and interact with "civil society" (interconnections and collectivities formed among the people of a territory). At least as important are the vertical ties formed by a political elite, the connections between a "big man" and his supporters, who in turn have linkages to their own supporters. A person might hold an office – for example, as a commissioner in charge of a region – with certain duties and powers, but his daily reality might be to distribute rewards and cultivate support, shaping vertical ties that do not quite coincide with his official role. It is not enough to call that corruption, although many Africans as well as outsiders would do so.

Patron–client relations are not an intrinsically African characteristic. They are found throughout the world in varied relationships to formal institutions – elected legislatures, bureaucracies, police forces. The large gap between resources inside and outside of African states, and hence the importance of elite strategies of gatekeeping, give patronage a particular salience in most African states. Citizens may mobilize to demand that the state serve all its people, but many are likely to feel that the better strategy for advancement is to find a well-connected patron.

One of the origins of instability in Africa is the inability of gatekeepers to keep the gate. Too much is at stake in control of the gate. Traders could try to bypass customs collection, oppositional networks to establish connections with neighbors or with global powers, and get arms and support. People often try to live their lives within and across territorial borders as if the state had limited power over them. Some governing elites, in Senegal for instance, have managed patron–client systems and external relations with relative stability, whereas others, as in Zaire/-Congo, turned them into crude machines by which a leader and his shifting entourage extracted resources arbitrarily from poor peasants and rich merchants to such a degree that the formal dimension of state rule all but collapsed in parts of the country, and regional militias and warlords inflicted terror on villages. In Sierra Leone or Angola in the 1990s, rivals to state power developed cross-border networks that smuggled out valuable resources, notably diamonds, and smuggled in arms and luxury goods for the gate-evading leadership. But chaotic situations can evolve for the better: Ghana went through a series of short-lived military and civilian governments and experienced economic collapse from the mid-1960s into the 1990s, but has since achieved relatively democratic and effective government, considerable improvement in economic conditions, and a national sense of self-confidence.

It is possible, in theory, for political power to be exercised with no system of centralized state authority, and before colonization that was indeed the case in large parts of Africa, where kinship structures, village councils, small-scale chiefdoms, and shared religious beliefs and institutions maintained order. Today in some African cities and rural regions, associations of businessmen, market sellers, religious organizations, local defense communities, or leaders of ethnic associations cooperate in order to police and regulate local affairs, blurring the boundaries between state and civil society. They might even collect revenue, and they might also vie for control with gangs and other associations. But on a regional or national scale, a political order without an effective state to contain violence would be hard to reinstate today, given that arms are much more lethal and outside connections more available, giving power brokers the idea that they can upset whatever order people develop among themselves. A society run purely on networks may be the anarchist's dream, but experiences in Africa that lean in that direction have been more like a nightmare.

Since the downsizing of governments under international pressure in the 1980s and 1990s, international NGOs – sometimes with close linkages to national or regional organizations, sometimes operating on their own – have been of increasing importance in many African countries, providing medical care, promoting population control, mediating conflicts, helping farmers, and organizing micro-finance. At best, they function through local–external cooperation with shared goals. At worst, they provide the spectacle of foreigners driving around in their SUVs claiming to be doing what Africans are unable to do for themselves. International NGOs are responsible to their donors, so the question of who is accountable to the people most concerned remains, regardless of the good work they do. NGOs occupy part of the large space of what Gregory Mann calls (2014) "nongovernmentality."

During the struggles against colonial rule, leaders of parties, trade unions, farmers' organizations, merchants' groups, students, and intellectuals aspired to a view of state building with a strong "civic" and "social" dimension: the state would act in the interest of citizens through institutions accessible to all. Commerce, agriculture, and industry might be developed by government programs or regulated to allow reasonably fair market competition. Once in power, African regimes proved distrustful of the very social linkages and the vision of citizenship that they had ridden to power. Kwame Nkrumah set a dangerous and revealing precedent when he attacked trade unions and cocoa farmers' organizations in his first years in office. New presidents and prime ministers could use their control of access to import–export markets and revenues to reward followers and exclude rivals.

Gatekeeper states tended to allow local or provincial governments few resources and little autonomy. That made national politics even more of an all-or-nothing proposition. Leaders often saw opposition as "tribal," which could encourage regional leaders to accuse the "national" elite of being tribalist itself. Gatekeeper states' insistence on the unity of the people and the need for national discipline revealed the fragility of their control; they left little room for seeing opposition as legitimate.

A combination of predictable state institutions, a civic-minded political culture that emphasizes the accountability of leaders to the citizens, and a measure of personal politics and networking may produce tensions, but can also balance civic virtue and personal connections. What is problematic about gatekeeper states is the focus of patronage systems on a single point and the undermining, in the midst of rivalry for that point, of alternative mechanisms for influencing decisions and demanding accountability.

Foreign governments and international institutions were only too willing to work with gatekeeper states, which were permeable to their influence and useful in Cold War rivalries. Even a modest amount of economic or military aid could be a major patronage resource to a leader – or to an insurgency trying to topple or evade the gatekeeping state – when other forms of access to the world economy were weak. From the moment of independence, notably in the Congo crisis of 1960, Western states signaled that they might intervene against a radical national policy because they judged that its international implications were unfavorable to their interests. Some of Africa's most conflict-ridden states in the 1980s and 1990s had been among the largest recipients of economic and military aid intended to foster Cold War alliances: Angola, Zaire, Somalia, and Ethiopia. After the Cold War ended, both sides sometimes left in place former proxy combatants, either ruling cliques or insurgent movements, which in some cases resulted in continued havoc – in Angola and Somalia, for instance. They also left in place stocks of arms and supply networks to international weapons dealers that became available to would-be warlords, insurgent movements, and criminal gangs.

Arguably, a complex capitalist economy – and South Africa comes the closest among actually existing African states – makes gatekeeping strategies both less needed and less feasible, for it postulates a relatively wide range of economic connections within and beyond state boundaries. Business groups with a degree of autonomy can lobby and bargain with state officials, debating policy with labor organizations and developing alternatives for both economic and political activities.

Some observers speculate that the gatekeeper state is becoming less important under today's conditions, as some states solidify their fiscal position, economic growth and market-friendly policies allow some business people to entrench their position, NGOs bypass the state to provide resources to local organizations, and diasporas provide remittances to families in their place of origin. Ghana for example appears to have moved away from the gatekeeping model that predominated from independence into at least the 1990s. Nevertheless, the large place of extractive industries in the economic growth of recent years might have the reverse effect, giving gatekeepers more resources. Contracts for infrastructure projects or managing ports may outsource managerial control but keep the ultimate decisions in government hands.

If a country such as Ghana could move away from the strictures of the gatekeeper state in the 1990s, Zimbabwe moved in the opposite direction. After presiding over a relatively diverse economic structure (Chapter 6), Robert Mugabe moved against economic interests and civil society organizations he could not control, and concentrated resources in the hands of his clients. We should therefore think of the gatekeeper state not as an all-defining category into which to slot African states, but as a model of state structure in relation to the outside world that we can use to think about variation and change.

Outside interventions have not addressed the basic problem. Western development agencies and governments have been quick to blame the difficulties of African states on corruption and ill-considered policies of African governments. The remedies posed, notably under the rubric of structural adjustment, undermined governments' capacities to provide the kind of services that would tie the citizenry as a whole to state institutions – especially in education and health – without eliminating ruling elites' control of patronage. The democratic bargain found in many parts of the world by which states ask for votes, taxes, and obedience and provide needed services became even more difficult to sustain under structural adjustment, making gatekeeping and patronage even more attractive strategies. Gatekeeper states are thus not "African" institutions, nor are they "European" impositions; they emerged out of a Euro-African history.

In the 1990s the World Bank and the IMF, as well as Western governments, added political "conditionality" to the policies they were trying to impose on African governments that had accepted their bailout funds (as most had). The outside pressure was added to episodes of protest in African cities, sometimes led by youth groups, sometimes by middle-class professionals. The timing was both auspicious and constraining. After years of structural adjustment, few African governments had many resources to keep the patronage machines going, and they were hard put to secure their power by either coercion or co-optation. Gestures, at least, toward political dialogue and participation offered a way to try to reestablish legitimacy. At the same time, the economic situation was such that states had little with which to respond to the demands of their citizens. In some cases, Côte d'Ivoire for instance, educational spending – usually a concern of voters – had dropped drastically. So it was not clear that a renewed politics of citizenship would offer much to citizens, whatever the theoretical arguments about the positive relationship of liberal democracy and liberal economies might say.

Starting with a "national convention" in Benin in 1989, African governments undertook various experiments in public discussion of state structures, toward legalizing multiple parties, and toward holding elections. New constitutions were written, intended for the most part to restrain autocrats and enable voters. By one count, democratic elections occurred in sixteen African countries between 1990 and 1994, with more limited transitions in others, and improvement in civil liberties in some others. Not surprisingly, outcomes were mixed. One indicator of a changing political atmosphere is the means by which African leaders left office. In the period 1960–69 fifty-seven government leaders were thrown out in coups, three retired, and none was voted out of office. Between 1990 and 2007 twenty-seven were thrown out in coups, nineteen retired, and nineteen lost elections. The times were changing, enough to make elections a habit in some places and an example in others. But the trend was far from universal.

What follows is a series of short case studies of different African states from their emergence from colonial control into the early twenty-first century. They illustrate both how hard it is to escape effects of the historical trajectory this book has brought out and the variety of forms these processes have taken. One of the hazards in talking about African politics from the vantage point of the United States and Europe is that news stories about violence in Rwanda, Liberia, or Somalia – going back, indeed, to the Congo crisis of 1960 or the Biafran war of 1967–70 – turn into a single set of images applied to Africa as a whole. African realities should not be contrasted to an idealized picture of "democracy" elsewhere in the world;

there is not a polity on earth where every member has an equal chance to have his or her political opinion heard or where patronage and corruption are absent from political life. But there are differences, within and beyond Africa, in the degree to which people can express their views openly and without reprisals, in the capacity of government institutions to implement policies demanded by a voting public, and in the fairness with which government services and protection are provided to citizens. In many places across the continent African people are posing demands on government as citizens. Such demands, a number of African intellectuals have contended, amount to a call for a "second independence."

The Trials and Tribulations of States

Ghana: The Pioneer Guards the Gate

There is a particular poignancy to the history of Ghana because it was the pioneer. Kwame Nkrumah was more than a political leader; he was a prophet of independence, of anti-imperialism, of Pan-Africanism.

Even when Nkrumah became Leader of Government Business in 1951 and Prime Minister of an independent country in 1957, he was operating under difficult constraints. His government, like its colonial predecessor, depended on cocoa revenues for its projects to diversify the economy. A clash with cocoa farmers was virtually inevitable, as the government retained in its Cocoa Marketing Board accounts up to half of export earnings. As described in Chapter 4, Nkrumah had by 1959 suppressed the cocoa farmers' own organizations and banned all regional political parties, including the Asante-based National Liberation Movement. Meanwhile, the world price of cocoa was falling, farmers' income plummeting, and incentives to maintain and replant cocoa trees diminishing. After 1965 cocoa production fell by over half as farmers turned to growing food crops, depriving the Ghanaian state of its main source of revenue for everything it was trying to do. Nkrumah's biggest project to challenge the "neo-colonial" monocrop export economy, the Volta River dam and aluminum-processing industry, actually put much of the Ghanaian economy into the hands of multinational aluminum companies, which had the necessary technology, and international financial institutions, which had the money.

As early as 1958 Nkrumah was ruling by decree. He changed his political underlings frequently. His stature abroad, as the pioneer of

African independence and as a spokesman against imperialism, was high, but some of his most principled and ardent supporters at home were disillusioned. The autonomy of the trade union movement was severely curtailed; leftist trade unionists were detained or forced out, strikes made all but illegal. Nkrumah told workers that they were no longer "struggling against capitalists," and their task now was to "inculcate in our working people the love for labour and increased productivity." In 1961, nevertheless, a general strike erupted, led by railway workers. In 1966, while Nkrumah was abroad, he was thrown out by a military coup.

For many years afterwards Ghana underwent a cycle of military coups, of governmental efforts to deal with basic problems that neither the British nor Nkrumah had solved, of frustrated military governments turning rule over to civilians and frustrated civilian leaders falling to military coups, and of each generation of rulers accusing the previous

FIGURE 25 Demonstration in the streets of Accra after the military *coup d'état* that overthrew President Kwame Nkrumah, March 1966. Note especially the signs saying "Ghanaians are now free" – nine years after the country had become independent of Great Britain – and the one portraying him as "Sasabonsam," super-demon. AFP/Getty Images

one of corruption, repression, and failure to help the common people. Ghana was ruled by military governments in 1966–69, 1972–79, and 1981–92. In the late 1970s the economy was in a state of collapse.

Flight Lieutenant Jerry Rawlings was an unlikely architect of a transition to a system of choosing leaders by election. First taking power by a military coup in 1979, he soon allowed elections and a civilian government to take office, then staged a new coup in 1981. In 1992 he again allowed elections and was himself the successful candidate for president, as he was in the next election in 1996. After his term was up, Rawlings stepped down, and he accepted the defeat of his party's candidate for the succession, allowing a peaceful governmental transition to take place.

Government policy swung from Nkrumah's statist orientation in 1957–66 to a market-oriented economic approach under military and civilian rulers from 1966 to 1981, and then in a populist direction under Rawlings between 1981 and 1983. Rawlings was critical of wealthy Ghanaians and their foreign partners, using socialist rhetoric and seeking policies aimed at helping the poor. Then he changed his tune. He became the favorite of the International Monetary Fund for his willingness to cut back government expenditures, discard subsidies aimed at fostering urban consumption, privatize state-run corporations, and in general follow the rules of the structural adjustment policy. He had something to show for this: Ghana's debt burdens were reduced, its growth rate turned modestly upward after years of stagnation and regression, and it attracted outside investment. By some calculations, what Ghana had to show for its success was to bring the economy back by 2000 to the level it had been in the 1960s. Since then, except for a few difficult years, it has maintained impressive rates of growth – over 5 percent in some years.

By 1992 there was enough space for social movements to trouble the quest for budgetary rigor: strikes by nurses, doctors, Cocoa Board workers, and railway workers, to which the government responded with wage increases that ran contrary to IMF dictates. The government implemented policies specifically intended to reduce the adverse effects of structural adjustment on poor people and workers, and proclaimed at least a desire to alleviate poverty.

Ghana has not lacked for entrepreneurs, and its government has both implemented and softened structural adjustment policies with enough vigor to have been able to stabilize its finances and maintain a decent infrastructure in transport and education. Its export income remains dependent on cocoa and gold, and to a significant extent the contributions of its diaspora, for the counterpart of the loss of educated Ghanaians

FIGURE 26 Campaigning for the presidency, Ghana, 2004. Rally in support of John Atta Mills in Accra. Mills lost in 2004, but won in 2008. A series of close elections and reversals of fortune was a sign of democratic renewal in Ghana. Issouf Sanogo/AFP/Getty Images

who expatriated themselves has been a stream of remittances. In 2005 foreign aid amounted to over 10 percent of gross national income. By some measures, Ghana has passed (barely) the conventional threshold to be considered a "middle income" rather than a poor country, although some of its statistical success has been an artifact of changes in how GDP was calculated. Over half of Ghana's population now lives in cities, and supplying food has become a major source of income for farmers – whose cash incomes had long relied on exporting cocoa – but it is far from clear how urban populations will continue to support themselves.

After the mid-1990s Rawlings and his successor could make a plausible case for reelection on the basis of market-oriented economic reform. Most importantly, Ghana has since 2000 sustained an electoral democracy in which the incumbent party stands a chance of losing. In 2000 John Kufuor and his New Patriotic Party defeated the candidate of Rawlings's party. Kufuor was reelected in 2004 with 52 percent of the vote, and in 2008 John Atta Mills of the opposition party won a close election, not without controversy over the accuracy of the results. Mills died in office, and his successor, John Mahama, won in his own right in another close election in 2012. In the next cycle the opposition narrowly won, a sign that something like a two-party system and a norm of alternating between the two has been instilled in Ghana's voting public. The development in Ghana of two parties, each of which has a chance of winning, has built confidence in the normality of democratic institutions. Media in Ghana have been relatively open and vigorous. A National Reconciliation Commission, modeled on South Africa's Truth and Reconciliation Commission, opened a national discussion on past abuses of power, and in effect served as a warning to present-day rulers to behave differently.

Since the Rawlings era Ghana has tried, with mixed results, to develop various boards and local and regional committees to provide different mechanisms for participation in civic affairs. It remains a relatively centralized polity, with a strong President and a weak legislature. It has elected district assemblies, but they have few resources, so voters have lost interest in them. Whereas in Ghana's early years Nkrumah tried to implement a radical form of a gatekeeping strategy – a socialist vision of directed modernization, channeling agricultural and mineral exports through state mechanisms and trying to keep any other locus of civil and economic life from coalescing – his successors depended on their relations with international financial institutions. Only slowly has an economic structure emerged in which connections within and beyond the country are more diverse. But, after an economic and political breakdown that lasted from the mid-1960s to the mid-1990s, Ghana has come back with two decades of orderly political contestation and economic recovery. African states are not necessarily bound to one fate.

Congo/Zaire: The Unguardable Gate

The disastrous decolonization of the Belgian Congo in 1960 attached the word "crisis" to Africa in much of the world's press. Nearly sixty years later this vast and potentially wealthy territory remains as far removed from stability, democracy, and social progress as it was in the summer of 1960. Yet if the breaking up of the Congo has at times appeared to be imminent, the borders of the state remain the same.

This story crosses the frontier of independence. Belgium's hasty decolonization, in the footsteps of France and Britain and following the 1959 Leopoldville riots, came on the basis of inconclusive elections involving two regionally based political parties, the Bakongo-centered ABAKO and the Katanga-based Conakat, plus Patrice Lumumba's

Mouvement National Congolais (MNC), which was at least trying to offer a national vision and a critique of Belgian colonialism. Deal-making on the eve of independence made Lumumba the Congo's first Prime Minister and Joseph Kasavubu, the ABAKO leader, its President.

Whatever chance there was for Lumumba's national vision to be translated into concrete policies is hard to know, for he had no time. Some want to see him as a revolutionary hero, but his views fell within the 1950s African nationalism: liberation from an oppressive colonial regime, forging a sense of national purpose, and some kind of social and economic liberation beyond that, whose contours were not specified. He was catapulted to leadership without having the experience of a Kwame Nkrumah or a Sékou Touré. His speech at the ceremonies of independence, in front of the King of Belgium, which spelled out a devastating – and accurate – portrayal of the violence and exploitation of Belgian colonialism, encouraged Belgian intrigues against him and helped attach the labels of radical or communist to his name in Western capitals.

Within two weeks of independence the Congolese army mutinied, largely in revolt against the continued presence and arrogance of Belgian officers. Belgian civil servants left the central government en masse, having done little to train Congolese successors. Then Katanga, whose Governor, Moïse Tshombe, had excellent Belgian connections, seceded from the new state, and in this case Belgians stayed to help the secessionists. The copper-mining company that produced most of the Congo's export earnings began to pay taxes to the Katanga government. Here was a gatekeeper whose gate was being usurped. Lumumba scrambled for outside support, including from the Soviet Union and its allies, who proved of little help except to tie the label of Marxist more closely around his neck. Within a month a war of secession had started, alongside urban riots, the army mutiny, threats to Europeans, and the undermining of government capacity to act.

The UN, with Congolese consent, sent troops to restore order, but Lumumba and Kasavubu represented two different Congos. Kasavubu soon fired Lumumba, whether legally or not, and the UN – pressed by the United States and western European powers – cooperated with the President, not the Prime Minister. The UN tried to link peacekeeping with improving the Congo's administrative capacity, but the civil servants it sent were a small fraction of the Belgians who had left, and the Congo lacked the time to develop a capable government service.

Lumumba was placed under house arrest, but he escaped and fled toward his home base in eastern Congo. By then Joseph Mobutu, an

FIGURE 27 Patrice Lumumba under arrest in the Congo, 1960. After being ousted from the office of Prime Minister and placed under house arrest, Lumumba escaped and tried to flee to his home region in the eastern Congo. He was captured and, shortly after this picture was taken, he was murdered. Bettmann/Getty Images

army officer who had initially worked with Lumumba, was becoming the real strongman in the Congo. He played a decisive role in Lumumba's arrest and later in the effort to track him down. In January 1961 Lumumba was captured, apparently by Katangese militiamen, and murdered, with the apparent connivance of Belgium, the CIA, Mobutu, and local henchmen.

Mobutu acted in the background behind a series of weak prime ministers, and he displaced Kasavubu. UN troops played a crucial role in stabilizing this kind of state. By 1963 they had defeated Tshombe and restored Katanga, renamed Shaba Province, to the Congo. A semblance of order, albeit of an authoritarian sort, returned, and the copper revenues began to flow again.

The Congo's tradition of millenarian movements blended with its radical, Lumumbist one in a rebellion led by Pierre Mulele in 1964. Other regional rebellions broke out. The Congo was clearly not working as a nation-state. But the fact that it was a state was crucial, for outside interests feared a power vacuum or a turn to communism in so large, central, and well-endowed a space within Africa. Military forces (as well as mercenaries) from the Western world – including Belgian paratroopers flown in on American planes – helped to quell the Mulele rebellion, and others. Algeria, Egypt, and Cuba helped out rebels, particularly Lumumbists in the eastern region. The rebellions between 1960 and 1964 are thought to have cost a million people their lives.

In 1965 Mobutu put an end to the masquerade of the prime ministers. He ruled for the next thirty-two years as dictator. He did so with a great deal of Western support, both military and financial, from those who knew how corrupt and undemocratic his regime was but saw him as a bastion against communism or other destabilizing forces. Thomas Callaghy (1984: 5) argues that Mobutu went from running a "typical military autocracy" to another level of despotism. Formally, his system was "prefectoral": top-down rule by appointed representatives, hired and fired in order to keep them loyal and intimidated, plus efforts to attach each ethnic group, each locality, and each region directly to presidential authority.

This version of state building was not without its effects; even opponents saw Zaire, as Mobutu renamed the country in 1970, as a unit that they wished to rule. "Mobutuist" ideology emphasized the personality of the ruler and Zairian "authenticity," with everyone ordered to drop European names in favor of African ones. Mobutu renamed himself Mobutu Sese Seko. Frequent and arbitrary changes of administrative personnel and taking a personal cut out of all sorts of business activity were his hallmarks; he is thought to have sent billions of dollars into personal investments in Europe. He was shrewd at staying just one step away from behavior that Western powers would not tolerate, and he was bailed out by France, Belgium, and the United States in 1978 when exiles invaded Shaba Province.

Not only did Mobutu loot the treasury, but his security depended on his licensing others to do likewise. By the late 1970s, as copper prices fell, he was in trouble. The formal institutions of Zaire, from health facilities to transport, failed long before the system of clientelism and redistribution of spoils did. But by the 1990s Mobutu could no longer pay very much of his army, which for a time kept functioning by using its "state" authority as a license to pillage. The gatekeeping state limped along: copper revenues were funneled through the state, which took its official and unofficial cuts. This strategy became less reliable as copper prices declined and industrial capacity faltered. Industrial mining gave way to artisanal mining, including in diamonds and coltan, and those mines, with minimal capital requirements, were hard for the regime to control, offering revenue sources to autonomous – if not rebellious – factions, and temptations to outsiders to help out those groups in exchange for contracts or promises of future earnings from minerals. Zaire both provided a way around other states' gatekeeping efforts (allowing diamonds to be smuggled out of Angola) and saw its own wealth smuggled out in other directions, notably through East Africa. Most people lived off their own production and networks of social relations independent of the state. The other side of the parallel economy was a parallel society: a cultural dynamism in Kinshasa, with rich and critical forms of expression, particularly in painting and music.

Mobutu's downfall might not have come about if he had not lost his ability to insert himself into the social relations by which people survived. It might not have happened if he had kept paying his army, which stopped fighting before it stopped pillaging. Student protests in Lubumbashi in 1990 led to massacres by police; riots and looting took place in Zairian cities in 1991 and 1993. There was pressure starting in the 1990s from Western human rights organizations and then from governments; international financial institutions wanted him to clean up corruption. With the end of US–Soviet rivalry, the stakes for Western governments diminished. Mobutu probably could have survived all that: his gestures toward allowing opposition, debate, and political contestation opened a little space, and he outmaneuvered his domestic opponents and his foreign interlocutors. He turned an outside threat to his advantage, as the influx into Zaire of refugees from the genocide in Rwanda in 1994 (Chapter 1) meant that relief agencies had to deal with him. Sovereignty, once again, had its compensations.

But he could not control the situation. The presence of Hutu militias that had participated in the Rwanda genocide in the refugee camps led to clashes with Zairians from groups related to the Rwandan Tutsi, who organized to defend themselves. With opposition to the exactions of Mobutu's prefects and soldiers already strong in eastern Zaire, the multiple conflicts in the region spiraled out of control. Rebellion in eastern Zaire was supported by the new Tutsi-led regime in Rwanda, backed in turn by Uganda.

For reasons little understood, a man with a strange history put together, starting in eastern Zaire, the diverse elements into a coherent fighting force focused not just on the border region but on the state of Zaire itself. Laurent Desiré Kabila, originally from Shaba, had been a Lumumbist and then a regional warlord, running a small fiefdom isolated enough that Mobutu's army couldn't get to him, connected enough to run smuggling operations and to survive for decades. His rag-tag army, with Rwandan and Ugandan support, expelled Hutu refugees and militias alike from camps, at terrible human cost, and began an odyssey across Zaire. The long march was at least made possible by the unwillingness of Zaire's army to resist and much of the population's hope, after three decades of predation, that the young soldiers of Kabila offered a positive alternative to Mobutu. Kabila's entrance into Kinshasa in May 1997 was extraordinary. He was welcomed by the populace of a city in which an anti-Mobutuist popular culture had taken strong root. Kabila himself lacked strong ties to both his home province of Shaba and eastern Zaire, where his soldiers and backers came from.

His supporters were soon disappointed. Kabila was dubbed Mobutu II – even his renaming of the country as the Democratic Republic of the Congo had a Mobutuist tinge to it; he made similar deals with foreign mining firms to pass out the country's mineral wealth for uncertain long-term development prospects; he showed no patience with political debate and alternative organizations; he had few scruples about human rights; and he was not the man to turn personal and clientalistic authority relations into routine performance of state functions. His inability to control violence – including that of surviving Hutu militias – cost him the support of Uganda and Rwanda, and another rebellion, with parallels to the one Kabila himself had led, gave rise to escalating conflict, stoked by ethnic militias, warlords, and groups engaged in the predatory extraction of minerals in the eastern part of the country. Zimbabwe and Angola, meanwhile, provided key support to Kabila. They both wanted to defend the principle of sovereignty on which their own security depended and to preserve the connections that gave them a share in the spoils of the Congo. Congo was a fragmented society, with different groups in different regions making their own connections to neighboring states or smuggling networks that were all too willing to cooperate.

Kabila's end did not come from his regional enemies or principled opposition, but from one of his bodyguards, who, in 2001, shot him dead. He was succeeded by his son Joseph, who like the older Kabila was notably detached from the society he was trying to rule. After postponing promised elections for years, Kabila finally allowed them in December 2018, but outside observers and many Congolese believe the vote count was rigged to keep his most emphatic opponent out of office and maintain Kabila's ability to manipulate the political scene from his position as Senator for Life. It is not clear, in the months following the election, that the long-lasting pattern of violence, rape, and pillaging of resources in the eastern part of the country is abating.

Mobutu, with help from European and American allies and international financial institutions, had held something together that kept its borders even while it kept changing its name. Rather than forge a coherent and functioning state apparatus, he treated the country as a zone of predation, with echoes of Leopold II. While he for a time gathered enough coercive and redistributive capacity to prevent the emergence of an alternative way of doing things – as the more idealistic Lumumba had once proposed – he acted like a warlord, and faced down the threats of others who acted much like him. It was a long-lived act, but in 1997 it came apart. The Kabilas, father and son, have been more like Mobutu than a genuine alternative to his way of rule, but less able to maintain support abroad and tight control at home, hence offering little hope of reducing conflict. Here is a gate that hasn't been kept, a state system unable to use its potentially lucrative mineral base to finance another sort of society, prey to rival warlords who have their own mechanisms for exporting gold, cobalt, coltan, and other minerals while the state struggles to revive the industrial production of copper. The Democratic Republic of the Congo remains in conflict with smaller, less endowed but more coherent neighbors – Uganda and especially Rwanda – that intrigue with Congolese elements and covet its resources. There has been occasional talk that the Congo would be better off broken into smaller units, but nobody has proposed a plausible mechanism for doing so, while the ruling dynasty, aspiring warlords, and covetous neighbors profit by extracting what resources they can from places and peoples for whom they do not take responsibility. All have an interest in keeping the boundaries what they are, if only so that they can violate them. The international system, for its part, considers the Democratic Republic of the Congo to be a sovereign entity within a world of states.

Senegal: Managing the Gate

Senegal is a state with few natural resources; its most important export has been – literally – peanuts. Its history suggests that gatekeeping can up to a point be managed by an astute elite. Senegal's stability has depended on foreign assistance, providing a reasonably stable base for companies and NGOs working in West Africa, and on the desire of citizens who have migrated elsewhere to continue to send remittances to relatives back home. Its stability also depends on relations – neither domination nor subservience – with non-state institutions, notably Islamic brotherhoods.

Senegal, whose leading city, Dakar, was once the capital of French West Africa, lost its special position when the territories that had made up French West Africa went their separate ways with independence. Léopold Sédar Senghor's attempt to salvage a smaller federation by uniting with the French Sudan failed as leaders of both territories realized the risks they ran of challenges to their carefully built political machines in their home bases (Chapter 4). Senegal ended up a small, resource-poor country whose major assets remained its connections.

Senghor's rise to power had come from his understanding of the significance of the extension, in 1946, of French citizenship to all inhabitants of the colonies. By working through Islamic brotherhoods he had obtained the allegiance of former "subjects" in rural areas neglected by his urban rivals. He still appealed to educated Senegalese with a new vision of politics, simultaneously appropriating the best of European science and culture to aid economic and social progress and insisting that African culture had something of value to offer the rest of the world.

The territories of French Africa acquired territorial self-government in 1956, the status of Member States of the (French) Community in 1958, and independence in 1960. Senghor and the left-leaning Mamadou Dia, second-in-command of his political party, saw rural community mobilization as a new way forward.

They had little room for maneuver. Dakar's commercial establishment consisted of old colonial firms and Senegalese entrepreneurs connected to the Mouride Islamic brotherhood. These were conservative forces, and they fit poorly with Dia's "rural animation." Senghor's politics was one of drawing fine lines. Unlike Nkrumah, he did not seek to dismantle the organizations that had brought him to power, most especially the Mourides, and he did not want to break his French connections, which Senegalese were now in a position to take advantage of. Senghor moved back and forth between a politics that was at times authoritarian and at times open to dialogue, sometimes oriented toward mobilizing a population toward national progress, sometimes tending to rule by experts.

In 1962 Senghor, feeling threatened from the left, fired Dia and imprisoned him, along with some of his allies. From 1963 to 1976 Senegal was a one-party state, under Senghor's Parti Socialiste. In 1968 a wave of strikes by unionized and non-unionized workers, students, and unemployed youth – with episodes of stone throwing and sieges of government buildings – brought a harsh crackdown. The young demonstrators in the cosmopolitan atmosphere of Dakar knew of revolts and anti-imperialist agitation elsewhere in the world – notably against the ongoing war in Vietnam – and they sought a radical transformation of Senegalese politics and a break with France. But in the repression that followed the uprisings of 1968, the autonomy of trade unions was undermined and student organizations dismantled.

In 1974 Senghor was challenged from the rural areas, as Mouride leaders helped to organize peanut farmers to resist the government's setting of the purchase price of peanuts at a low level. The government gave in. The regime slowly returned to allowing a measure of debate and electoral contestation. Senghor allowed other parties to organize in 1976 and, in 1978, elections were finally held.

In 1980, in what at the time was one of Africa's few legal, orderly successions, Senghor retired in favor of his long-time protégé Abdou Diouf. Diouf had come up through the bureaucracy; he had built his legitimacy on claims to be a skillful technocrat and loyal follower, not the "father of the nation." He allowed – and won – elections in 1983, 1988, 1993, and 1998. The press was open enough to allow political debate but threatened enough by the possibility of censorship to keep the debate within limits. Although certain opposition leaders spent time in jail, some of them also spent time in Diouf's cabinet as he attempted to build coalitions. However, low peanut prices, poor harvests in Senegal's arid rural areas, and IMF-imposed structural adjustment policies limited the state sector when Diouf needed to strengthen his networks of clients. Opposition parties drew on students, teachers, health-care workers, and a few other public-sector employees with a message critical of the political old guard. Strikes, student rebellions, and peasants' periodic refusals to grow market crops kept up an oppositional ethos.

Until the 2000 election the state – and Diouf's Parti Socialiste – controlled patronage, so that, while competition at the level of ideas took place, only one political apparatus offered concrete rewards. Diouf's grip failed because the state's and the party's resources diminished in the era of structural adjustment and atrophied export markets. Economic relationships increasingly bypassed regulated structures. People had less to lose by voting for the opposition, and its criticisms of Diouf's ineffectiveness rang true. Whereas Diouf needed the support of the Mourides, successful Mouride traders had less need of the state, and they ceased to be a predictable source of support for a political apparatus that had lasted forty years under two leaders.

The victory of Abdoulaye Wade – a long-time, populist opposition leader, close to the Mouride hierarchy – over Diouf in the 2000 election seemed to signal a real change in politics. In the end, it did not. Wade turned out to be a demagogic leader, given to ostentatious public projects but unable to solve Senegal's basic problems. He managed to get reelected in 2006, but in the next election cycle he attempted to change the rules, first to get around term limits, then to allow the winner of a plurality of votes rather than a majority to be elected without a runoff. The perceived affront to democratic practices led the street to rebel. Youth played a prominent role in the demonstrations, encouraged by hip-hop singers who brought people out. Wade was forced to roll back his rule changes, and – to the surprise of many Senegalese – accepted defeat in an election that was conducted fairly. Macky Sall became President in 2012. His first term did not demonstrate an ability to deal with Senegal's poverty, limited agricultural possibilities, strained educational and medical facilities, a university (once one of Africa's best) beset by rebellious students and inadequate facilities, and a fishing industry – an important source of Senegal's food supply – threatened by overfishing by foreign factory ships.

The art of politics in Senegal is more about building connections than mobilizing ethnic or other forms of solidarity. The Islamic brotherhoods (the Tijanis as well as Mourides) cross lines of region and ethnicity for the 80 percent of the population who are Muslim. Moreover, the relationship of religious leader (*marabout*) to follower (*talibé*) is similar in some respects to that of patron and client – personal and long term, with broad mutual expectations rather than contractual ones, and with each having to take care to maintain the other's enthusiasm for the relationship. Political and socio-religious connections reinforce each other, but provide enough distance so that neither can impose its will on the other. The coexistence of these two sorts of vertical relationships has helped keep Senegal from the extremes of state efforts to exclude all non-clientage relations or of religious organizations to promote a fundamentalist alternative to Islam's role in society. A universalistic Islam, not linked to the brotherhoods, has a certain attraction for young Senegalese, and in the last decade or so there has been a lively and important debate about the place of Islam in a democratic republic. So far, the particular social and institutional structure of Islam in Senegal – more so than any specific doctrinal or ideological difference within Islam – has limited the influence of more radical or universalistic forms of Islam in Senegal more than in its neighbors.

The relationship between Senegalese remaining in Senegal and those abroad has also been important. Many young men from the arid regions of the country and from its inland neighbor, Mali, have migrated to Dakar and then onward to France, other European countries, or North America. Until 1960 these migrants went to France as citizens, and their right to do so was maintained for a time under the treaties between France and its former colonies. Along with North African migrants they became vital components of the French working class. Then France changed the rules, and since 1974 the entry of people from former colonies has been severely restricted, and harsh measures have been taken against illegal migrants, often deportation. However, a West African population is now well established in many European cities. This population is not cut off from Senegal – indeed, particular villages along the Senegal River Valley have close links to particular suburbs of Paris – and Senegalese abroad send regular remittances "home." Mourides have been at the core of a commercial diaspora extending – growing rapidly in the 1980s and 1990s – from Rome to New York, giving street sellers a strong social base in the cities where they work and strong links to Senegal. Dakar's peri-urban settlements are filled with houses paid for by migrants and remittances, built bit by bit out of durable materials, although the state's poor maintenance of roads, electricity, and water leaves entire neighborhoods with poor living conditions. The horizons of Senegalese are thus quite broad, and the contribution of expatriates to keeping their small and resource-poor country of origin going is a vital one, despite the pain of separation and the harshness of American and European immigration regimes. Whether such relationships are enough to maintain Senegal's particular socio-religio-economic order depends to a significant extent not just on whether Senegal can generate enough opportunities for its young citizens, but whether the linkages of Senegalese families to the Senegalese diaspora are more sustainable than possible linkages to Islamic networks that have become entrenched in other parts of Africa and the Middle East.

Nigeria: The Excesses of the Spigot Economy

Africa's most populous state has been doubly damned, first by an administrative structure of British design that turned its social and religious divisions into a politically deadly polarization, and then by the discovery of oil, a blessing that became a curse. Nigeria's educated elite had roots extending back to the nineteenth century and a cosmopolitan outlook from its linkages across much of West Africa and to Pan-Africanist circles in England. Its lawyers, teachers, and clerks had experience in state services for decades and familiarity with local, regional, and national deliberative councils, under the limited self-administration that Britain allowed. Nigerian cocoa farmers and commercial entrepreneurs, like urban lawyers, teachers, and clerks before them, were politically aware, with the means to support active press and political organizations. The human resources that Nigeria brought to independence were thus considerable.

By the 1950s the British policy of allowing African involvement in government at the regional, rather than federal, level was having divisive consequences (Chapter 4). In each region a single party, dominated by members of the majority ethnic group, obtained office and used it to provide services and patronage within its bailiwick. In each region oppositions developed, to some extent (notably in the north) as populist challenges to the governing elites, but most importantly among regional minorities.

This kind of politics took place both before and after independence in 1960. In the late 1950s and early 1960s exports of cocoa from the Western Region and a variety of other agricultural products from the Eastern and Northern Regions were sufficient to allow politicians to play their patronage games, for real progress to be made in education, and for Nigeria to build the symbols of its national independence. The modest powers of the federal government were, from independence, in the hands of Alhaji Abubakar Tafawa Balewa of the Northern People's Congress (NPC). All regional parties worried that their rivals would intrigue with other regional groups to gain solid control of the federal government. The east and west feared the north, which was populous and tightly controlled by an Islamic elite, while the north feared that east and west would gain control by insinuating their better-educated population into the bureaucracies that actually ran the government. For better or worse, Nigeria was lying atop one of the world's largest pools of high-grade oil, and by the mid-1960s it was coming into production.

Oil can turn a gatekeeper state into a caricature of itself. Requiring little local labor, with few linkages to the national economy and close connections to global energy corporations, oil defines a spigot economy: whoever controls access to the tap collects the rent.

Oil came from the Eastern Region, and potential oil revenues threatened a shifting regional balance. The diaspora of educated Igbo in Western and Northern cities was also a source of tension.

In January 1966 the Balewa government was toppled in a coup and Balewa was assassinated. General Johnson Ironsi soon took over from the coup leaders. Ironsi's government represented one of Africa's outbursts of military populism: a military elite, trained to get things done, perceiving a government of elected politicians to be self-interested, corrupt, and incompetent. The junta announced its determination to restore regularity to government and to work in the interests of the Nigerian people. It was not seen that way in the north, where Ironsi was less the national reformer than the Igbo power grabber. There had been anti-Igbo riots in the north in the 1950s, but the pogroms that broke out in the mid-1960s in the Igbo ghettoes in northern cities – with the connivance of local elites – killed thousands and turned many more into refugees. In July 1966 northern officers in the military instigated Ironsi's overthrow and assassination, and he was replaced by another officer, Yakubu Gowon, who was to rule for the next nine years.

In Eastern Nigeria the second coup was seen, in the context of the pogroms and the tensions over oil revenues, as anti-Igbo. Eastern autonomy seemed – at least to some of its top military and political leaders – the only way to protect the lives of Igbo and keep regional hands on the oil spigot. Eastern Nigeria declared itself independent and named itself Biafra. Only about half of Biafra's population was actually Igbo; most people in the oil-producing region belonged to other ethnic groups. What followed was a horrific war: a small regional army, convinced of its righteousness, fighting a larger one that claimed the legitimacy of the nation-state. Biafra had its outside supporters – France, most notably, but also South Africa – and as the war and the federal government's blockade had a devastating impact, particularly on children, the publicity generated sympathy for Biafra and deepened the image of Africa as a land of starving children victimized by wars that seem a product of irrational tribal enmity. That it was a war of maneuvering politicians, as much to do with geographic region as with ethnicity, was more difficult to convey than the stark images.

The federal government won the war, and Gowon tried to avoid a retributive peace. His government had earlier divided Nigeria into twelve states, blurring the correspondence of region and ethnicity of the British three-state system. The number of states would later expand to thirty-six. Each had its own governmental institutions, services, and educational system, creating numerous jobs and diffusing ethnic competition. The patronage structure was pyramidal, going down to urban neighborhoods, with the head of each pyramid jockeying for access to the next level. But the revenues came from the federal government's control of oil, so that Nigeria, as Nic Cheeseman (2015: 219) puts it, was "a centralised state in federal clothing."

At the heart of politics were vertical relationships, as individuals sought help from local "big men" who had access to information, jobs, and construction permits, and as brokers sought state funds for roads, clinics, and meeting halls for their areas. The possibility of using such ties provided alternative strategies to organizing horizontally – by the working class, for example – although there have been occasional general strikes. Patrons and clients tended to seek each other out within the same ethnic category, and the personal and exclusionary nature of their ties coexist uneasily with the sense of ethnic affinity that this kind of politics fosters.

Oil revenues entrenched Nigeria's government in its gatekeeper role. Instead of providing capital for the diversification and industrialization of the Nigerian economy, oil revenues were used above all for the primary task of the political elite: patronage. Having so much to distribute provided some political stability and a model of uneconomic spending. The building boom, focused on schools and roads, sent the cost of labor so high that cocoa farmers could no longer hire, and they themselves saw little reason to invest in developing their farms, when getting their children an education and contacts in the provincial or federal capital was more likely to bring them prosperity. Oil became the only significant export: the once-flourishing cocoa sector collapsed (see Figure 11, p. 149); industry developed in relatively narrow niches; port facilities, for a time, choked on imports; and the dream of a balanced, integrated economy was not fulfilled. With the fall of oil prices in the 1980s, Nigeria had much less money to throw around so inefficiently. It could no longer maintain roads, electricity, or hospitals; it became an oil producer with gasoline shortages. Its oil-producing zones, receiving little from foreign oil companies other than disruption, pollution, and heavy-handed security interventions, became discontented. There were periodic outbursts of violence, and regular efforts by local people to siphon oil from pipelines, sometimes with catastrophic consequences. The government's execution of the regional activist Ken Saro-Wiwa in 1995 dramatized to Nigerians and others the politics of neglect and repression in the oil-rich region. The marginalization of youth in both the oil-rich southeast and the economically struggling north has probably contributed to different kinds of ethnic and religious violence in these two quite different regions.

There was, however, no repetition of the Biafran war. Ethnic tension and violence there have been, most dramatically between Islamist groups and others, whether those practicing Christianity, a local religion, or a version of Islam deemed insufficiently rigorous. Tensions persisted over control of the gate through the ups and downs of oil prices and revenue. There were successions of coups, tentative attempts at civilian rule in 1979–93 – no less dishonest than the military variant – and reimposition of military rule. The military's annulment of the 1993 election was a bitter disappointment to the democracy movement, and the ensuing dictatorship of Sani Abacha was particularly harsh, brought to an end only by Abacha's fortuitous early death in June 1998. The Nigerian labor movement, especially during the huge general strike of 1994, was one source of organized opposition; the efforts of lawyers, doctors, students, and others in the Campaign for Democracy to forge links between Nigerian democracy activists and overseas human rights organizations were another.

Since 1999, with the election of former general Olusegun Obasanjo (who had run the country for a time after a coup in 1976), Nigeria has had a series of elections, none clean but not totally bogus. They produced a series of presidents who promised to clean up corruption and provide efficient government, and accomplished neither. Mohammed Buhari, elected in 2015, previously the author of a military coup in 1983, is the latest in this series. Lagos, the principal city, is chaotic, services unreliable and crime rampant, but Nigerian businessmen have become skilled in operating in such an environment, and Nigeria has produced entrepreneurs of great wealth, a substantial middle class – well educated and moving about in international circles – even as the majority of the population lives in poverty. Some manufacturing has developed; Nigeria has a significant film industry; communications have been revolutionized and great profits generated by cell-phone companies. Its educated population has provided the English-speaking world with some of its best playwrights (Wole Soyinka) and novelists (Chinua Achebe, Chimamanda Ngozi Adichie).

Nigeria also has the reputation as one of the world's most corrupt political and economic environments, a reputation not improved by worldwide internet scams run out of Nigeria. The line between patron–client relations – the expectation that it is normal and acceptable for a political leader to provide for his supporters and constituents and that it is normal and acceptable for him to do what it takes to obtain such resources – and the use of public office for private gain is a fine one. Corruption is not just a Western-imposed category, but one invoked by Nigerians, especially when politically useful against one's rivals. Reaction against corruption and the conspicuous consumption of an elite were factors behind the rise of groups in parts of the largely Muslim northern provinces to advocate since the 1980s a rigorous version of Islam and the imposition of Sharia law in their provinces.

The pyramidal structure of Nigeria's resource allocation – with oil revenues flowing directly to the top and then outward and downward – is complicated by the pockets of wealth that Nigeria's complex economy has produced. Basic problems remain unsolved, most visibly at this time the inability of the Nigerian military and police to contain the violence of Boko Haram, an Islamist terrorist organization that has murdered and kidnapped (including 300 schoolgirls in one raid) across a wide swatch of northeastern Nigeria, sowing so much insecurity that refugees have fled en masse, agriculture has declined, and urban dwellers live in fear of suicide bombers. The Nigerian military has itself committed atrocities that might well help Boko Haram's recruitment. As of now, progress against Boko Haram has been made – including by Nigeria's much poorer neighbors – but security has not been reestablished. Meanwhile, profound questions about the mutual coexistence of communities remain. Nigeria is both fractured along regional, religious, and ethnic lines and connected by networks of patronage, overseas linkages, and the differential allocation of resources.

Kenya: A Capitalist Alternative?

In the late 1970s some Kenyan and foreign scholars thought Kenya might be moving beyond the political economy of the gatekeeper state. They saw a Kenyan elite buying up farms, investing in industry and commerce, and founding joint ventures with multinational corporations. Some Marxist scholars thought that a property-owning, labor-employing – that is, capitalist – class was taking root. Market-minded observers applauded the elite's interest in land, for it seemed an antidote to a supposed urban bias in African government policies. Other scholars were skeptical of the "Kenyan exception." The relationship between political change and economic development has in fact been volatile.

With independence in 1963, Jomo Kenyatta had tried to reassure foreign investors that Kenya was not the land of Mau Mau. With British loans, elite Kenyans bought property from departing settlers and so acquired a vested interest in maintaining the security of private ownership of land and other resources. The government was challenged from the left, and alternated between co-optive gestures – making designated portions of land available in small units to the landless poor, bringing union leaders into the government, and providing a measure of services to poor urban zones – and repression – banning populist opposition parties, arresting or assassinating threatening leaders, suppressing dissident speech, and trying to paint opponents as "tribalists" standing in the way of national advance. Official political culture focused around meetings (barazas) where politicians made their distributive gestures in public: putting money into a school or road and encouraging local self-help projects.

The politicians around Kenyatta who were enriching themselves were largely Kikuyu. That made it unclear – to political activists at the time as well as academic specialists – whether they were acting as a budding capitalist class or as a state-centered clique. Disturbances in western Kenya in 1968 reflected both criticism of a class of wealthy Kenyans and concern – especially among Luo people – that they were being excluded from the riches Kenya was producing. Some Kikuyu responded to the challenge with an oathing campaign – with echoes of Mau Mau (Chapter 4) – to cement the loyalty of an ethnic base.

Doubts about Kenya's road to capitalism became stronger when Kenyatta died in 1978 and was succeeded by his vice president, Daniel arap Moi, who was from the Kalenjin ethnic group. Moi set about dismantling the Kikuyu-centered patronage system, enhancing the position of Kalenjin clients and working with other small ethnic groups to redress the regional balance. He had the disadvantage of doing this in a time of global economic contraction. His methods ran to the heavy-handed, including imprisonment and assassination as well as the use of security forces to remove Kikuyu from land coveted by Kalenjin. The Moi regime undermined the element that might (or might not) have become a more or less autonomous set of capitalists.

Moi's rule was opposed, especially from 1986, by Kenyan activists, notably in the legal profession and in established churches, as well as by international human rights organizations that began to work closely with Kenyans. International financial institutions, concerned with the regime's corruption and economic mismanagement, on occasion suspended aid. Student demonstrations and strikes were frequent; professionals, such as doctors and nurses, struck against the state's degradation of working conditions in public service. Kenyan businesspeople hurt by the reconfiguration of the patronage system helped to finance and organize opposition parties when they were legalized.

The government had to respond to internal and external pressure by gestures toward democratization, including the legalization of multiple parties and the holding of elections beginning in 1992. These elections were open enough that Moi won only a narrow plurality of the votes. The opposition was divided, largely because its factions were as much built around the personal networks of their leaders as was the apparatus of Moi himself. An old-style Kikuyu politician, Mwai Kibaki, managed to get elected President in 2002, but his reelection campaign in 2007 turned into a vicious conflict between Kibaki and Raila Odinga, himself the son of a leading (and leftist) politician who had challenged Kenyatta's regime in the 1960s. Kibaki's faction most likely stole the election, and the violence that attended the conflict resulted in over a thousand deaths and long legal battles over responsibility. For Odinga's Luo supporters the battle was in part over the fairness of election procedures, in part over policy differences, but to a significant extent over the claims of the once-excluded Luo and their allies that it was "our turn to eat."

The electoral contests were sharpening ethnic polarization. The violence of 2007, however, was enough for Kenya's politicians of different factions to pull back from the brink and avoid plunging the country into civil war. It has been governed since 2012 by Uhuru Kenyatta, son of Kenya's founding President, who had been accused (but not convicted) of complicity in the atrocities of 2007 and who beat back further attempts by Raila Odinga, in 2013 and 2017, to get a piece of the action. The last electoral round underscored Kenya's lack of consensus about the fairness and honesty of the electoral process. Odinga and his followers refused to accept defeat, successfully petitioned the courts that proper procedures had not been followed, then refused to participate in the do-over of the election that the courts ordered. So Kenyatta continues in power, but with many Kenyans unconvinced that his presidency is legitimate. Reminded frequently by civic-minded groups that violence is a dubious tool for fostering electoral democracy, both sides have so far avoided a repetition of the events of 2007, but it is not apparent that Kenya is any closer than at previous points in its history to solving the fundamental tensions over the procedures of democratic politics, over poverty and privilege, and over unequal access to resources across Kenya's regions.

Tanzania: A Socialist Alternative?

In the abstract, the leaders of African states had choices beyond those described in the narratives above. The very thinness of the social basis of the regimes – the absence of powerful pressure groups – gave leaders flexibility in how they could represent their goals. At some level, independence movements had been popular mobilizations. So "development" was a near-universal watchword, and building schools and clinics a near-universal policy. A number of regimes called themselves socialist, including some (Senegal) whose policies were not very different from those who represented themselves as "pro-market" or "pro-West." Even Jomo Kenyatta talked of "African socialism," by which he meant a capitalism that was truly African. The stakes of ideological positioning could be high, mainly because the Cold Warriors rewarded their friends and punished their enemies. But that did not necessarily translate into differences in how regimes actually operated domestically.

Recent research has made clear the extent and variety of thought that went into socialist projects in newly independent Africa. Students and workers who spent time in Europe read widely in Marxist literature and connected with leftists from other parts of the world, including Asia and Latin America. African students in France had in the early 1950s founded the Fédération des Étudiants d'Afrique noire en France (FEANF), creating a network for sharing political ideas and building a revolutionary spirit among young Africans, many of whom dispersed to their countries of origin. These activists maintained and continued to develop ideas for a socialist politics in an African context. They were behind numerous demonstrations and occasional insurrections in African cities in the decades after independence, especially in the 1960s and 1970s. Their chances for success, however, depended on finding allies in the military, and that happened in Dahomey, two years after Mathieu Kérékou had taken over in a coup, when he declared the "People's Republic of Benin" under a Marxist–Leninist banner. There is some doubt about Kérékou's convictions, but he was positioning himself in relation to leftist advocates in his country and pushed forward a Soviet-style version of scientific socialism. The self-proclaimed people's republics of Benin (1974–89) and Congo-Brazzaville (1970–91) and the revolutionary regimes of Mozambique (1974–92), Madagascar (1972–91), and Ethiopia (1974–87) developed programs of radical economic reform stressing state ownership of industries and commercial organizations, rural cooperatives or collective farms, the expansion of educational and health facilities, and attacks on the wealthy and on traditionalist chiefs. The "Afro-Marxist" states were not run by parties solidly rooted in working-class or peasant movements; the radical impetus was more likely to come from urban intellectuals, students, young soldiers, and bureaucrats.

The socialist governments were positioned differently from other African states in world politics. They sent students and industrial trainees to the USSR or East Germany rather than to France or the United States, and they received aid workers and military attachés from the Soviet bloc in their cities. African students sometimes brought back wives from Russia or Eastern Europe, and a variety of organizations cemented personal ties between Africa and the communist bloc.

But in their Marxist phases the policies of a Benin or Congo overlapped those of other gatekeeper states, with their tendencies to eliminate autonomous sources of wealth and power and to try to control key commercial institutions. They put more of what resources they had into education and health care. Some of them experimented in different forms of collectivized agriculture, rarely with success. They tended to advocate centralized administration on the grounds that building a national and socialist economy in the face of a rapacious capitalist world required a single authority structure, but other types of regimes had that tendency as well. African states, for the most part, lacked enough educated cadres to plan on a national scale or control production in a truly Soviet fashion. The Soviet Union and its allies provided little capital and questionable expertise, but for avowedly socialist countries it could be a necessary alternative to Western-dominated development agencies. The USSR also provided some of its allies with military support, particularly important in the cases of the MPLA in Angola and the Derg in Ethiopia.

The fate of the Afro-Marxist states overlapped with that of other gatekeepers. The salary bills of a large state sector were hard to pay;

state enterprises run by clients of the leaders did not necessarily function well. As Benin and Congo-Brazzaville ran out of money, they had to turn to the same international financial institutions as other countries, and the conditions imposed were inimical to continuing the socialist agenda. A leader such as Denis Sassou-Nguesso in Congo-Brazzaville had few compunctions about turning his ideology upside down as long as he could maintain his power – as he has done to this day.

One of the most attractive of Lenin's ideas to African rulers was one of his worst: the single-party state, popular in the 1970s and 1980s (along with the no-party state of military rulers). It provided a historically based justification for rulers' desires to delegitimize and stamp out opposition, a trait not limited to Afro-Marxist regimes. The rationale for one-party rule lost its appeal, if only nominally, under domestic and international pressure beginning in the 1990s.

For some African leaders a Maoist focus on the peasantry made sense, but they had more trouble dealing with actual African rural dwellers with their diverse social structures than with the abstract category of the African peasant. These versions of socialist ideology – with their insistence on a singular "people" in whose interest the government or the party was to act – fit a little too comfortably with the tendency of African leaders, of different ideological stripes, to conflate themselves with the nation.

There was still another alternative: to work out an ideology and a program that were original and focused on conditions in Africa and that might resonate outside the universities and capital cities. Tanzania's "African socialism" was a notable example of such a quest, positing "self-reliance" against the trade-and-aid model of development and emphasizing the engagement of rural communities with a national project. Whether in the form of rural cooperatives or consolidated villages, the solidarity of the rural community – or rather an elite's vision of an African rural community – could be seen as the alternative to the domination of foreign corporations and financial institutions that had seemingly moved into the space once occupied by colonial rulers. African socialism was rooted, in this conception, as much in the African past as in the socialist internationalism of the twentieth century.

Tanganyika, before it joined with Zanzibar in 1964 to create Tanzania, had a few zones of export potential: the sisal-growing area inland from the coast and, above all, the coffee-growing area near Mount Kilimanjaro and other highland regions, surrounded by much larger areas where a culturally diverse population lived in resource-poor environments. Tanganyika was led into independence by a former schoolteacher, Julius Nyerere, a small educated elite, and a modest trade union leadership. In the few tense years before independence, Nyerere's party, the Tanganyika African National Union (TANU), forged ties with a variety of rural movements, particularly those aggrieved by heavy-handed British development and soil-conservation programs. At first TANU's development policies were close to the orthodoxy of Western experts. Given Tanganyika's spread-out resources, it was not attractive to investors.

In 1964 Tanganyika negotiated its union with the island nation of Zanzibar, which had recently undergone a revolutionary struggle that threw out its substantial landowning class of mainly Arab origin, and installed a radical, self-consciously African regime. The new Tanzanian state set out to build a nation of citizens. In both official and popular discourse the notion of citizen implied a polar opposite, expressed in Kiswahili by the contrast between *wananchi*, patriotic citizens, and *wanyonyaji*, blood suckers, who could be capitalists, foreigners, or, most strikingly, people of South Asian origins, many of whom had been active in commerce. The truest *wananchi* were the farmers, although city-dwellers could be exempt from the wrong side of the dualism if they performed useful functions and lived modestly. The government undertook several rounds of expelling apparently non-useful city-dwellers to the countryside.

The state was ambivalent about just how nationalist Tanzanians should be, for it wanted to connect to radical Africans elsewhere on the continent and in the diaspora, and at the same time to construct a specifically Tanzanian national culture. Officials and TANU supporters wanted to insure that Tanzanian culture was disciplined and proper, and campaigned against young women who wore mini-skirts and anyone who exhibited other manifestations of what might be considered decadent, bourgeois, or Western culture.

Taking stock of the post-independence years in 1967, President Nyerere argued that trying to base development on "money" had failed. We will not get the money, he concluded, and moreover, the danger of eroding fundamental African values was all too real. Nyerere's Arusha Declaration (after the city by that name in inland Tanzania) called for togetherness and self-reliance, a strategy based on the allegedly communal nature of African society. The state, and the party in particular, would breathe dynamism into Tanzania's communities, and they would bring shared values to the nation.

FIGURE 28 A "village of solidarity" (*kijiji cha ujamaa*), Tanzania, 1974. Women hoeing a communal plot. These villages were promoted by the socialist government of Julius Nyerere as a way of integrating farmers into the fabric of the nation, but farmers resented being forced to move into them, and they were soon seen as a new form of state imposition. Economically, they proved to be a failure. AFP/Getty Images

The new plan entailed nationalizations, particularly in banking and commerce. The government improved education and tried to emphasize rural clinics over fancy urban hospitals. At the heart of its strategy was the building of *vijiji vya ujamaa* – solidarity villages. The program envisioned bringing people who were living in scattered homesteads into villages that could be provided with schools and clinics – and party offices. TANU promised peasants a voice within the single party. By 1976 the large majority of the rural population had been incorporated into the *vijiji vya ujamaa*.

The results were disappointing. Many – probably most – peasants did not want to move. The government was able to force them into villages, but not to make them grow crops in accordance with its plans. Implementing villagization depended on intermediaries, mostly young TANU activists, for whom the policy was congruent with their ideals of building a new African society and an opportunity to exercise a small degree of power, not necessarily with the same goals as the government. In any case, bringing the people of the Tanzanian countryside closer to a political party that was losing favor did not necessarily make them more active participants in "self-reliance."

The nationalizations in the commercial sector – including efforts to push South Asian merchants out of the roles they had long played in East African countries – had negative results, so that Tanzania fell into a pattern of de-development – less production, less trade, less availability of consumer items, less integration into a truly national economy. The standard of living fell, in some calculations, by 40–50 percent between 1975 and 1983. Self-reliance never meant what the words implied: heavily supported by Scandinavian countries and even the World Bank, Tanzania became one of the world's biggest per capita consumers of foreign aid. In retrospect, the *vijiji vya ujamaa* bore a resemblance to colonial programs of "villagization," intended to bring dispersed rural populations under closer surveillance.

Nyerere, architect of the one-party state imposed in 1965 as well as of socialism and self-reliance, had the wisdom to recognize that things had gone wrong. Having done his share of arresting opponents and stifling dissent, he was one of few heads of state who willingly passed on the torch (in 1985), remaining as party head and elder statesman. In 1990 he was willing to admit that the one-party state was not a good idea. Multiparty, competitive electoral politics was reinstated in 1992. Tanzania also backed away from its collectivist economic strategies. With the loosening of control of production and prices a semblance of economic order returned, coffee exports rose, and a wider range of goods became available. Cooperating with the IMF's structural adjustment strategy, Tanzania allowed its budget allocations for education and health to be cut, and literacy rates fell. Tanzania's economy came back from its low point; it slowly returned to being a conventional impoverished country.

Conflict across Borders

States confronted not only internal challenges but networks that connected elements within to elements in other African states. That ethnic groups were not neatly bounded and that kinship, trading, and religious networks wove together people across borders complicated governing elites' task of focusing political ties and loyalty on themselves and their nation-building efforts. Such networks could expand the opportunities of people to earn a livelihood via trade and make cultural and religious connections that could enrich their lives. But cross-border connections could also foster violence, not only against an established state but against populations living in zones where the weakness of state power left a vacuum.

We have already seen an example of cross-border connections spiraling out of control in eastern Congo/Zaire. That people related to the Tutsi of Rwanda lived across the border in Zaire, among other ethnic groups, was not in itself a cause of conflict, but after the 1994 genocide, Hutu, including perpetrators of the genocide, crossed into Zaire and threatened Zairian Tutsi. But now a Tutsi-led government controlled a state and an army in Rwanda, and the Rwandan military intervened in Zaire. Uganda and Rwanda also had interests in Zaire's mineral wealth, contributing to the proliferation of militias engaged in a mixture of ethnic mobilization, predation, and resource extraction. In this cauldron, Laurent Kabila was able to put together his rag-tag army that eventually, with Rwandan help, took over the country, setting off further episodes of cross-border alliances and clashes. Some have referred to the fighting, still flaring up after nearly twenty-five years, as Africa's world war. That may be an exaggeration, but the conflagration cannot be understood apart from this complex and shifting relationship of cross-border networks, militias, state power, and the plundering of resources.

Even murkier were the connections within a region that embraces Liberia, Sierra Leone, Guinea, Burkina Faso, Côte d'Ivoire, and Libya. In 2012 Charles Taylor, a Liberian warlord and briefly the internationally recognized ruler of that country, was convicted by an international court of crimes against humanity for fomenting civil war in neighboring Sierra Leone. The story that brought Taylor before international justice begins in the nineteenth century, when Liberia was founded under the sponsorship of Americans, who were both philanthropic and racist, as a place to send freed slaves and their descendants away from the United States. It soon became an independent country under the rule of the descendants of African-American settlers, who came to be known as Americo-Liberians. The indigenous population was in effect colonized. As African countries came to be self-governing, Liberian halls of government and business were dominated by a small group of families many of whose members had married women from indigenous ethnic groups but whose self-identification followed the male line and hence emphasized their distinctiveness from indigenous communities. The economy was dominated by a huge rubber plantation owned by an American corporation and by iron mines controlled by multinationals, leaving most of the country in poverty.

This political structure came to an abrupt end in 1980 when a coup led by Sergeant Samuel Doe, from the Krahn ethnic group, took over the government, murdered the deposed President, and set about dethroning the Americo-Liberian elite. Doe hung onto power through a phony election, a failed coup attempt, and deteriorating economic conditions. In 1989 Doe's regime was attacked by a rebel army led by Charles Taylor, a man with a US college degree, who had served for a time in Doe's government, been accused of corruption, fled to the USA, escaped prison while waiting to be extradited, and installed himself in Côte d'Ivoire. There he recruited a gang of soldiers, mostly from ethnic groups overlapping the Liberia–Côte d'Ivoire border, many of whom had suffered under Doe's rule. Many of his soldiers, some of them children, were recruited by force. The government of Côte d'Ivoire connived with Taylor, largely because of President Houphouët-Boigny's personal connections to the regime that Doe had overthrown.

Doe's government no longer had the means either to provide enough to citizens to gain their support or to supply enough patronage to maintain the loyalty of followers. Taylor's dubious army crossed Liberia and attacked the capital, Monrovia. ECOWAS – the association of West African states – tried to mediate the conflict and restore peace, although its neutrality was questioned by some owing to the connections of Nigeria's President Ibrahim Babangida to Doe. In 1980 a sometime ally of Taylor captured Doe while he was trying to visit ECOWAS headquarters. He was tortured and killed. Taylor's National Patriotic Front of Liberia (NPFL) became the dominant militia faction, but others organized themselves too, with connections to Guinea and other neighboring countries.

Taylor began to extend his reach into Sierra Leone, where armed conflict had begun. A rebel group, the Revolutionary United Front (RUF), had taken a part of the country's diamond-rich territory and was using trafficked diamonds to finance its attack on the government. The RUF recruited youth who saw no future either in the communities of their parents or the national economy, but their anger at the status quo did not necessarily translate into a specific ideological or political agenda. Taylor supplied the RUF with arms in exchange for "blood diamonds," and witnesses accused him of recruiting soldiers and directing some operations for the RUF. Taylor also developed close ties to the leader of Burkina Faso, Blaise Compaoré, who had taken power earlier in a coup (with help from Liberian exiles), and Compaoré also had links to Côte d'Ivoire's president Félix Houphouët-Boigny. These connections at the top were underscored by cross-border networks that trafficked in arms, diamonds, and other commodities and which recruited young men. Through Compaoré, Taylor's NPFL, along with the RUF in Sierra Leone, made connection to Muammar Gaddafi, President of Libya, whose oil-rich economy gave him the capacity to intrigue in sub-Saharan Africa to extend his own influence and to counter that of "the West." The Liberian civil war was thus intricately tied, in more ways than one, to an anti-state movement in Sierra Leone and to state leaders in Côte d'Ivoire, Burkina Faso, and Libya.

Taylor, like the warlords who opposed him, was recruiting and operating in a region that had long been criss-crossed by trade routes, and these networks could be harnessed by warlords. The often-youthful foot-soldiers equipped themselves with amulets and prayer books, hoping that both local religions and Islam would protect them. Taylor himself was initiated into one of the most important of the secret societies that were widespread in the Liberia–Sierra Leone region. Rape and plunder were part of the daily activities of Taylor's men, as they had been of Doe's.

ECOWAS kept trying to broker peace, although its agents, and part of its Nigerian-led officer corps, were also trafficking commodities out of Liberia. In 1997 ECOWAS helped to arrange an election in Liberia, which Taylor won, undoubtedly with the votes of people who thought that the only way to avoid the depredations of the most powerful of the warlords was to give him the state authority that he wanted. Indeed, the ambiguity between seeking state authority and fighting against it was one of the driving forces of conflicts in different parts of Africa. The Liberian conflagration, in some estimates, resulted in over 200,000 deaths and a million refugees.

The fight among warlords entered another phase in 1999–2003, with groups organizing themselves in Guinea and Côte d'Ivoire against Taylor's regime. The fighting was eventually brought to an end by the armed intervention of forces put together by ECOWAS, the UN, and the USA. As these international actors tried to install a government, Taylor was exiled to Nigeria. He was eventually extradited to The Hague, tried before an international tribunal, and in 2012 convicted and sentenced to fifty years in prison for war crimes and crimes against humanity.

By then, and with much help from outside, Liberia had come back from the brink. Its internecine wars had ended; it had experienced elections, and in 2006 it had chosen Africa's first female head of state, Ellen Johnson Sirleaf (who had once been a minister in the legal phase of Taylor's rule). After her term was up in 2018, a relatively peaceful election was held, and she gracefully exited power. Liberia, however, was only slowly recovering from the mass uprooting of people and the collapse of infrastructure and administrative organization. That situation, particularly the collapse of rural health services, was one reason why the Ebola epidemic of 2014 was as severe as it was in Liberia, as well as in its neighbors, Sierra Leone and Guinea, which had been caught up in the interlocking episodes of violence.

Sierra Leone's war was not entirely the offshoot of Taylor's machinations in 1991; it was rooted in youthful alienation and blood diamonds. Government forces were no less predatory than the rebels; at one point the government hired a South African-based mercenary force to fight on its behalf – paid for with promised access to diamonds. Some armed men became known as "sobels," government soldiers by day, rebels at night. RUF leader Foday Sankoh could claim to be leading a "people's armed struggle," but the rhetoric was far from the horrific reality. The RUF became notorious for cutting off the hands of people who would not join. Over the complex ups and downs of the relationship of the Sierra Leonean state, the RUF, and ECOWAS, Sankoh, like his sometime ally Taylor, managed to make himself part of the government, but he ended up before an international criminal tribunal as the war wound down in 2002. He died before his case could be completed.

Violence like this is organized. It takes place in a context, but a Charles Taylor or a Foday Sankoh has to put together the elements that make it possible – followers, arms, connections across national territory and across borders – and exploit the weaknesses of national and international structures that in other circumstances regulate conflict. That the conflicts in Liberia and Sierra Leone – and one can add Somalia and Rwanda/Zaire – began in the 1990s puts it in the context of the economic devastation caused by the recession of the 1980s exacerbated by structural adjustment in the 1990s, leaving states with limited capacity to make either civic institutions or patron–client relations work for them. The abandonment by rival Cold War powers of the need to support (and discipline) their African allies, the expansion of worldwide arms markets, the willingness of international commercial networks to traffic in diamonds and other high-value commodities, and the ineffectiveness of international organizations charged with keeping the peace are part of the picture.

In the end, African institutions, ECOWAS most notably, and international organizations did intervene. In some circumstances, former colonial powers deployed force in cooperation with ECOWAS or African governments to stop a civil war (Britain in Sierra Leone in 2000) or avert a threat from an Islamist terror network to an African state (France in Mali in 2014). European intervention has played its role in exacerbating conflicts, through Cold War rivalries that fostered violence across the Ethiopia–Somalia border in the 1970s and 1980s or France's aid to the Habyarimana regime in Rwanda in the years before the genocide of 1994.

Although most cross-border networks and violence did not lead to changing borders, it did so in two instances: through the secession of Eritrea from Ethiopia in 1993 and of South Sudan from Sudan in 2011. Both secessions followed bitter wars that produced the kind of ethnicization that is sometimes seen as the cause of such conflicts. Ethiopia had itself been an empire, and the struggle of Ethiopians to free themselves from monarchy in the 1970s overlapped with that of Oromo, Eritreans, Somali, and others to free themselves from Ethiopia. Eritrea's independence produced neither a democratic expression of its people's will – it is a repressive dictatorship that has driven thousands of its citizens into exile – nor regional stability, for border wars with Ethiopia over seemingly marginal bits of territory have erupted periodically.

The secession of South Sudan seemed for a time to be a positive response to sustained violence organized by a state – dominated by an Arab elite intent on fostering its own interests – against non-Muslims (practicing both Christianity and indigenous religions) in the southern part of the Sudan, a conflict made worse by the discovery of oil in the contested region. The guerrilla movement in the southern region gained enough international traction to pressure the Sudanese government into negotiating. The upshot was the creation of an internationally recognized state, South Sudan. But shortly after liberation a civil war erupted between two factions of the new state's governing elite. The violence, like so many clashes in Africa, didn't originate in conflict between two ethnic communities, but became ethnicized as the rival leaders mobilized Dinka and Nuer followers in their struggle for power. Displacement and famine have been the consequences of this as-yet-unresolved confrontation. The episode should serve as a warning that the logic of self-determination – the idea that each self-styled people should have its own state – does not necessarily have limits, and quests for self-rule are subject to ever-finer definitions of who represents the authentic collectivity that should govern itself, unless other means are found to resolve the tensions within differentiated societies.

In the last two decades another kind of cross-border network has come into view, even if its antecedents are much older – networks working on a large spatial scale for Islamic *jihad*. Islamic networks, going back to the early centuries of Islam, reached with some intensity across the Sahara into western Africa and along the Indian Ocean coast, and from there into the interior of central Africa. In the late eighteenth and early nineteenth centuries Islamic reformers with close links among themselves, particularly along networks pioneered by Fulani pastoralists, advocated and fought for a more rigorous brand of Islam than practiced in the Sahelian states of West Africa. The post-*jihad* states became wealthy – partly on the basis of slave labor and subordinated peasantries. They fought the colonizing drive of Britain and France at the end of the nineteenth century, but the emirates of Northern Nigeria later made their peace. To the west the larger states were broken up, but Muslim elites remained in place, and they made their accommodations with French rulers.

During the decades after World War II Islamic West Africa was on the whole conservative, its elites trying to keep lower-status parts of the population in their place and maintain their own position in the face of challenges from more radical, more populist elements in the region. There was always considerable movement around the Sahel and between the Sahel and adjacent regions, so that people knew what was going on elsewhere. Sean Hanretta (2010) has related the story of an Islamic scholar from Mauritania with a substantial following who ran afoul of French administrators and later turned up in Côte d'Ivoire, where he and his community established good relations with French administrators, prospered, and formed useful ties to the very Christian Houphouët-Boigny; such was one trajectory of Muslims into a wider society, in this case one accepting of them. The connections of Islamic scholars across Africa and to Cairo and Mecca were part of what shaped the social field of West Africa.

By the early 2000s some of these connections were bringing to Sahelian Africa, along with financial support from Saudi Arabia and Kuwait, new versions of a rigorous Islam, claiming that a particular reading of the Koran and the Sharia was the only legitimate one. This argument met with an uneven reception in much of sub-Saharan Africa. Where things became complicated was the development in the Sahara Desert itself of new jihadist organizations, largely Arab in personnel, and linked to al-Qaeda, the violent network of Saudi origin responsible for the 9/11 attacks on New York and for much conflict in Afghanistan and parts of the Middle East.

These groups developed ephemeral and not-well-understood links to Tuareg networks that had for generations plied the Sahara, engaging in commerce and traffics of various sorts. In the nineteenth century this included the slave trade, but in the twenty-first narcotics were a key item. Tuareg groups, with their nomadic life, had tense relations with the Sahelian, as well as North African, states, and some of them in the 2010s wanted to carve out a separate state in the northern part of Mali which they called Azawad – a rather territorialized way of thinking for nomadic people, but apparently the only way to claim status in the nation-state system as it now exists. For a time, the Tuareg groups formed an alliance with the al-Qaeda affiliates despite their divergent moral codes. Drug trade and kidnapping were financing the assertion of fundamentalist Islam. Those alliances were never very solid, but they were threatening, and by 2014 they were too much for the government of Mali, itself in dire straits, to handle. Fearing that Islamists would take over Mali, if not the entire Sahelian region, France intervened militarily and drove out the militants, to the apparent approval of many Malians. The Mali government has tried to reconstitute itself, with an uncertain future; the Tuareg–al-Qaeda alliance no longer appears to function; and both Tuareg groups with their long-distance connections and unclear demands and jihadists hiding out in the desert edge remain active in the region.

Islamist networks have also implanted themselves in Somalia, and have carried out terror operations in neighboring Kenya. The near-complete collapse of the Somali state in the 1990s, after years of meddling by both Cold War rivals, gave space to different attempts at claiming not only the territory that was once the Somali state but

Greater Somalia, parts of neighboring states where ethnically Somali people were an important minority. One of these groups, al-Shabab, claims affiliation to global jihadist networks and continues a campaign of terror of varying effectiveness in both Somalia and Kenya, fighting other Somali factions, Kenya, the African Union, and the United States. The conflict has displaced enormous numbers of people. There is no one "Somali" vision of the future, but rather divergent but sometimes overlapping claims to a territory of one's own, to a recognized place in a diverse state such as Kenya, and to close relations with a Somali diaspora found in North America and Europe as well as Africa.

The Sahelian/Saharan networks, al-Shabab, and Boko Haram pose a challenge to the state structure which was the outcome of the way decolonization unfolded in sub-Saharan Africa. They stand little chance of actually governing significant portions of the continent, especially given the willingness of outside powers to be sure that they do not do so. But they are capable of causing serious violence, and they are a moving target, difficult to pin down.

On Reform: Possibilities and Limits

The limits on the capacity of nation-states to exercise effective power and capture people's political imagination has given an opening to such networks. Outside intervention contributed to the problem through various forms of meddling in African affairs, including attempts to recruit Cold War allies before the collapse of global communism in 1989 as well as the enforced austerity of the structural adjustment programs of the 1980s and 1990s. In the 1990s international organizations came to recognize the seriousness of the problem, if not their own complicity in it. The World Bank, the IMF, and a wide range of NGOs have engaged with issues of human rights, legal reform, women's empowerment, and ecology. Outside pressure helped bring about some of the political reforms in African countries.

Internal pressures were important to the debates over democracy and good government in the 1990s as well: key categories of African societies, notably professionals and students, found their paths to the future blocked and little outlet for their talents. Workers and the urban poor have in some times and places taken to the streets to demand economic and social reforms. The availability of youth, which enabled warlords to recruit, also brought young people into the streets to demonstrate for democratic reforms. Popular mobilization was a factor in moves toward electoral democracy in Zambia and Senegal. Civil society organizations were a factor in Kenya from the 1980s through the present, strong enough to keep in place formal electoral institutions, not strong enough to bring to power the kind of democratic, rights-oriented regime those movements advocated.

In the 1990s there were more elections – some of them offering genuine choice – than in any time period since the early days of independence, and several countries adopted new Constitutions that contained, on paper at least, safeguards against an overmighty executive. Yet the hope that some political observers had for a "wave" of democratization in the 1990s does not describe Africa's last two decades. The point to stress is the unevenness of both democratic reform and effective government. One can point to examples over the last two decades of elections where incumbents lost: Ghana, Senegal, and Zambia for instance. Somalia, the Democratic Republic of the Congo, and the Central African Republic are at the other end of the spectrum. Incumbents turned the office of head of state into a decades-long sinecure in Angola, Gabon, and Equatorial Guinea, but long-entrenched rulers have been pushed out in Burkina Faso, Gambia, and Zimbabwe. Liberia and Sierra Leone have come back from long-lasting civil war in the 1990s and early 2000s. Côte d'Ivoire became fragmented after the end of Félix Houphouët-Boigny's thirty-three years in power in 1993, culminating in a civil war in 2011, but it has been relatively calm since then, although it is not clear that the factions that once fought regard each other as legitimate.

In several instances, rulers were able to manipulate the rules of electoral politics to give the opposition little chance, and in some instances – Kenya in the 1990s, for example – opposition movements were themselves too divided to topple the regime. Countries such as Uganda and Rwanda have been facade democracies, with long-serving rulers who brook no serious opposition. Nigeria has had seriously contested elections but cannot get itself to a place where a government actually governs effectively in the name of the people.

Just as the revolution that overthrew colonial rule came about not as the bottom overthrew the top but as interaction became more intense and the path of change less controllable by rulers, the uncertainties within African regimes seemed to promise an unfolding dynamic of political restructuring. Movements for multi-party elections and increased freedom of speech can be infectious; a contested election in one country suggests a possibility in another. Although it is a familiar axiom among students of politics that democracies are less likely than tyrannical regimes to suffer internal violence or instigate external aggression, democratization is a more volatile process. Introducing elections into a conflict-ridden society, especially where the incumbent ruler acted under duress, might well exacerbate political instability. The Kenyan election of 2007 (p. 263) is a case in point.

Even where elections come to be a feature of politics, it is uncertain how deep democratization can be unless ordinary citizens have a reason to believe that they have something to gain from their citizenship. There has been a tendency, in Benin and Zambia for instance, for victorious oppositions to replicate the regime they replaced. Nigerian political scientist Julius Ihonvbere (1997: 374) fears that "elections and more elections" have "recycled" old leaders, old ideologies, old political styles, and old suspicions. They have neither ended the politics of patronage and suppression of dissent nor put in place governments capable of addressing fundamental problems, and problems of poverty, ill-health, and poor communications facilities are not easy to solve.

At first glance, pressures to "liberalize" politics – to reduce rulers' arbitrary power, foster electoral competition, and encourage debate – may seem congruent with pressures to "liberalize" economies – to reduce the size and power of government, privatize public enterprises, and stimulate market competition. But the effects of such double liberalization can be contradictory. Decreased government services, under pressure from the IMF, are not the best selling points for democracy. Thandika Mkandawire (1999: 122–30) fears that without more resources African states will become at best "choiceless democracies." Privatization of state enterprises may not release assets into an open "market" but put them into the hands of leading politicians and their clients, who in their "private" capacity as businessmen do what they did as "public" managers. Indeed, the private–public distinction is a misleading one where politics depends on the "big man" who controls a range of resources, from money to kinsmen to clients to state office. Downsizing the state might do less to reduce clientelism than to reduce the effectiveness of those institutions, including the civil service, that provide services to the population as a whole, making the search for a patron all the more necessary. At an extreme, public service can collapse altogether and the "state" loses control of even the gate, leaving in place a series of power brokers who acquire followers and weapons and transform themselves into warlords. This happened most clearly in Sierra Leone and Somalia in the 1990s, and was resisted where state institutions retain at least some respect and effectiveness, as in Senegal or Kenya.

At the positive end of the spectrum is Botswana, where a relatively coherent leadership, with traditional legitimacy, education, and business acumen, has maintained a strong civil service, governed through recognized institutions rather than personal deals, allowed room for debate and decision making at the district level, bargained firmly with foreign corporations to insure adequate state compensation and control of key resources, aided private enterprise, and insisted that state enterprises be commercially viable. Electoral democracy has remained intact, and Botswana has maintained one of Africa's highest rates of growth – although the distribution of income and wealth is highly unequal. Even more of a limitation on Botswana's place on the good side of the democracy ledger is the exclusion of people outside the Tswana-speaking agriculturalists – mainly pastoralists and hunter–gatherers – from full and equal membership in the body politic.

The relationship of democracy and economic growth followed yet another pattern in Ethiopia. After the overthrow in 1991 of a dictatorial regime that claimed to be following a Marxist line, the Ethiopian political system opened up for a time, and even experimented with federal structures to take into account the diversity of its population. But political liberalization only went so far, and the regime became increasingly authoritarian. The increasingly illiberal political situation did not stand in the way of Ethiopia's achieving some of the highest rates of economic growth in the continent, attracting important investments from China, including textile factories and a railway linking Addis Ababa to the coast.

The election to the prime ministership in April 2018 of Abiy Ahmed, from the once-marginalized Oromo population, has given some hope that Ethiopian politics might be moving beyond the authoritarianism and ethnic conflict that have been so difficult to transcend. The accession some months later of a woman, Sahle-Work Zewde, to the presidency gives additional hope that barriers might be falling. But it is too early to tell.

That change takes place across a certain spectrum should not be surprising. The historical pattern of global inequality that gave rise to gatekeeper states in the first place has not fundamentally been altered, and the political economy of an African state cannot necessarily be remade by an act of will of even the most enlightened leadership. But the fact that economic and political reform have been debated and attempted in different African countries is itself of great importance. Such debate has, perhaps in a way unseen since the 1950s or early 1960s, enhanced among ordinary citizens a sense that citizenship entails multiple possibilities: that officials can be held accountable for their actions; that constituencies for reform can be built; that associational life and public discussion can be enriched; and that trade unions, women's associations, and political parties can be organized.

Other Africas: Popular Culture and Political Critique

One of the mistakes of Western critics of African governments and their policies, coming from journalists and international financial experts alike, is to think that they were the first to diagnose problems. The fact is that African intellectuals became aware of fundamental difficulties within their countries while most of their Western counterparts were still celebrating the arrival of Africans in the "modern" world. In city after city and village after village, even under oppressive conditions, popular discontent has found powerful forms of expression.

A revealing moment in the emergence of a critical intelligentsia was the publication in 1968 of Ayi Kwei Armah's novel *The Beautyful Ones Are Not Yet Born*. Armah evoked the disillusionment of young Ghanaians who had been captivated by the idealism and dynamism of the new state, only to see their classmates and families caught up in the greed and corruption of the new order. The book ends with the chaos of a coup, in which the hero helps his corrupted former classmate escape, an ending which evokes the shared humanity of people whose political and ethical decisions differ and which opens the possibility that a new generation will have another chance. Other novelists and playwrights of that era – Mongo Beti, Chinua Achebe, Wole Soyinka, Ngugi wa Thiong'o, for example – developed a politicized fiction written for Africans literate in French or English and for foreigners as well. It brought out the moral dilemmas of people who had struggled against colonialism and were facing new struggles. Other writers refused to be typecast into the mold of writing political fiction and saw themselves opening up a wide variety of imagined worlds, as writers in many contexts have done. Equally important were the efforts of intellectuals familiar with a variety of oral and written literary forms to perform in ways accessible to a wider populace. The emergence of a Yoruba popular theater in western Nigerian cities is a case in point, as was the performance of plays in Kikuyu by Ngugi wa Thiong'o, an effort which, unlike his equally critical writing in English, landed this distinguished writer in prison.

Critical artistic creation took more forms than the literary. The Nigerian singer Fela Ransome Kuti, the scion of a family active in the Nigerian nationalist movement, developed a politicized and highly popular musical style in Lagos, for which he was harassed and detained by the police. In Kinshasa, renowned for decades for its musical creativity, a subtle form of criticism of Zairian society under Mobutu crept into what at another level were love songs and dance music. The café/club/bar scene was entertainment, but it was also part of forming new kinds of sociability, which as in the 1940s and 1950s was not without political content. Zairian musicians – including Papa Wemba and Franco – were influenced by African-American jazz and Ghanaian high life, and they in turn influenced music throughout Africa, Europe, and North America. African-American hip-hop and rap influenced a newer generation of African singers, whose own innovations spread across other regions of the world.

So, too, with visual art. Kinshasa was the home of a vigorous community of painters, Chéri Samba and Kanda Matulu Tshibumba the best known of them, who were influenced by comic-book art as well as by formal schooling in painting to create a style that was in part moral lesson, in part political critique, and in part a colorful, visually appealing form of self-expression. Their creativity developed "right under the nose of the Mobutu regime," writes Sarah Van Beurden (2015: 193), noting that the government preferred instead to put "traditional" works of art in state museums, portraying itself as the guardian of African cultural authenticity, all too reminiscent of the colonial government's custodial view of its relationship to African culture. In apartheid South Africa, the production by Africans of any sort of beauty was an expression of defiance, as Daniel Magaziner (2016) shows in his study of an art school intended by the regime to train people in line with its view of "African art" but which was turned by the students into a more vigorous expression of individual creativity.

African writers, artists, singers, and filmmakers have long debated what it means to "decolonize" African culture as well as to distance the artist from the rigidities of post-colonial successor states. Does it mean rejecting European ideas of what constitutes a novel, a painting, or a film as much as refusing Eurocentric content? Does decolonization mean searching for some sort of African "authenticity"? Or does it mean that the artist is open to whatever influence he or she wishes to turn to, to whatever themes he or she wishes to engage? The Nigerian novelist Chimamanda Ngozi Adichie, for example, has explored in fiction (*Americanah*, 2013), the life of a young woman moving between Nigeria and the United States, a novel that illuminates the peculiarities of race and culture in the Unites States as much as gender relations in an African country.

It would be a mistake to see African urban culture, in Kinshasa, Lagos, or elsewhere, as simply a popular, critical form standing in stark opposition to "the state." Power is much more ambiguous than that. Achille Mbembe (2001) finds a culture of "vulgarity" in African cities. The "big men" of the regime are seen to "eat" the country, to have huge sexual appetites as well, to flaunt their wealth and power. Popular culture is at one level angry at this kind of display, but at another level desirous. The vulgarity itself marks both an evil – dangerously close to witchcraft, for supernatural forces are also seen to "eat" their victims – and a sign of power, something deeply desirable as well as immoral.

The insight is especially valuable when one is not limited to seeing society divided into categories – elite versus popular classes or ethnic, racial, or gender divisions – but rather stresses relationships, and in particular vertical relationships. Rich and poor see each other not just in terms of antagonism, and not just via the desire of the latter to become the former, but by interaction and mutual expectations between the two. The poor seek access not just to wealth, but to the wealthy. The rich have access to many of the poor – who can provide political support, muscular action, and cheap services – while poor people have limited access to the rich. The jockeying for access gives rise to both connection and antagonism and gives African political culture, particularly in cities, a high degree of volatility. Outbursts of popular rage, whether riots against price increases in Zambia, strike action against the Abacha regime in Nigeria, or for that matter violence against foreign Africans in South Africa, coexist with periods when patron–client networks offer at least a possibility for vulnerable members of society to get something – even if most will end up disillusioned.

The importance of the quest for a rich relative, a *marabout*, a former classmate, or a well-placed fellow-villager is thus incorporated into popular culture, even as patron–client relationships are also crucial to the very summit of power. Patron–client relationships are part of any political system, but a particularly big part of African polities – not least because of how much is at stake in the degree to which different people have access to the economic, educational, and cultural resources of the world beyond Africa. Writers, artists, and musicians both experience these inequalities in their own lives and can try to come to grips with the complexity of the moral universe of which they are a part.

Africa and Africans in the World

As emphasized in previous chapters, the national focus of African elites at the moment of independence represented a shrinking of spatial perspectives. Léopold Sédar Senghor, for one, had a broad perspective on what it meant to be African, and regretted for both philosophical and practical reasons the narrow territorial focus that politics took on. Kwame Nkrumah, by hosting the All-African Peoples' Conference in 1958, tried to revive Pan-Africanism, which had lost ground to territorial politics after the Manchester Congress of 1945. Pan-Africanism, however, was becoming a relationship of states, not of people. Nkrumah's dream of a United States of Africa achieved little support from African leaders intent on protecting the sovereignty they had so strenuously fought for.

State-centered Pan-Africanism became institutionalized as the Organization of African Unity (OAU). Representatives of its member states met regularly, discussed common action on various fronts – above all seeking global economic policies more favorable to developing countries – but its possibilities were constrained by what it was: an assembly of African heads of state, many of whom were part of the anti-democratic trends of their own countries. It had no judicial institutions. Early on, the OAU proclaimed that African states would not question each other's borders, artificial as they might be. Over time, the OAU failed its most obvious moral test: to act in the name of values shared across Africa against those leaders who were their most egregious violators.

In 2001 the organization reconstituted itself as the African Union, a takeoff on the European Union, which had come into existence a few years earlier. In discussing possibilities for the Union, some African leaders brought up Kwame Nkrumah's proposal of 1958 to create a United States of Africa, but the outcome was less ambitious. The AU has an assembly, a semi-annual meeting of heads of state, a secretariat, and a number of specialized organizations, such as the Economic, Social and Cultural Council. Its stated goal is to insure peace among African states, promote cooperation among them, foster development, promote the African Charter on Human and Peoples' Rights, and work with governments and international organizations to improve the lives of African peoples. In principle, the AU claims the right to intervene in the case of a member state that engages in egregious human rights abuses or endangers regional stability. What it has little of is power, considerably less than its European counterpart.

Economic cooperation, as described in Chapter 5, had its failures, such as the East African Community, and also moderate successes in regard to tariff reduction, shared banking institutions, and other inter-state arrangements, notably ECOWAS in western Africa. Economic cooperation has been facilitated by the Economic Commission for Africa, a UN-sponsored body (one of five regional commissions worldwide), founded in 1958. Its primary mission is the collection and sharing of economic data as well as writing reports, coordinating action among its fifty-four member states (including North Africa), providing advisory services, and providing mechanisms for governments to reach consensus on important issues and to promote African interests in world forums. Whether the AU will be able to realize its aspirations to develop a more ambitious African Economic Community in the 2020s remains to be seen.

Regional organizations, notably ECOWAS, can also provide a political and military component. ECOWAS performed credibly, if not disinterestedly, in its interventions in Liberia and Sierra Leone. The OAU and the AU have a weak record, particularly where they (alongside international organizations) should have done the most: to contain the border-crossing conflict and cross-border trafficking of resources. The AU has taken on an active peacekeeping role in South Sudan and Somalia. But it has not had a notable success there, and it remains to be seen whether it can act over a range of important issues as a coherent expression of "Africa."

Since the Congo crisis of 1960, African states have been regular targets of intervention from outside. Their need for periodic financial bailouts has made it hard for them to pose alternatives to IMF policies. Africa has been the focus of operations by refugee and famine-relief organizations, whose services have been desperately needed. International humanitarian organizations such as Human Rights Watch and Doctors without Borders have given Africans a means to find allies in their struggles against abusive regimes, in obtaining support for sustainable agriculture, or in combating AIDS or Ebola. The danger that the prominence of international NGOs entails, however, is to define the problem in terms of African helplessness – its need for benevolent intervention – rather than as a question of a common effort to address issues of injustice and impoverishment.

At the same time, Africans have actively participated in international organizations which address the continent's problems. A Ghanaian, Kofi Annan, headed the UN from 1997 to 2006. The United Nations Development Program (UNDP), where Third World economists and other specialists play important roles, has been instrumental in keeping alive the idea that growth and structural change in Africa require the participation of its citizens in the process. The United Nations Educational, Scientific, and Cultural Organization (UNESCO), which for many years was directed by Mochtar M'Bow of Senegal, called attention to the diversity of historical and cultural contributions of peoples throughout the world, and while opponents have criticized it for wastefulness, intellectual and cultural innovators have made use of its resources to promote the idea that not all literary, artistic, and musical contributions fit within canons derived from European experience. It has promoted education and cultural preservation in Africa as in the rest of the world. The UNESCO-sponsored history of Africa has its virtues and its flaws, but the fact that members of its editorial board have spent time in detention or in exile reveals that African intellectuals can both argue for specifically African perspectives and criticize the nation-states that claim to embody Africa's particularity.

To the extent that there is any such category as a Muslim world or a Christian world, Africa is part of both. Chartered planes leave African airports every year for the pilgrimage to Mecca; in earlier decades Muslims crossed the desert on foot or camel to join this ritual. Islamic scholars from Africa have joined others in centers of scholarship in North Africa and the Middle East, shaping circuits of Islamic knowledge. Financial support from Saudi Arabia, Kuwait, and before its collapse Libya has paid for the construction of mosques and teaching centers in sub-Saharan Africa. Islam, as in Senegal, may mean participation in a brotherhood deeply rooted in local social and political relations, while it can also mean participation in a universalistic faith with adherents around the world. Christian churches, whether the Catholic Church, established Protestant denominations, or pentecostal churches, involve Africans in important transnational linkages. Priests of African origin are today in charge of churches in France, where local recruitment of clergy is insufficient – a notable change of direction in the movement of clerical personnel since the colonial era. Numerous Africans who have obtained higher education in Europe and North America, who participate in international professional organizations, and who work for NGOs, animate worldwide networks. The extent of labor migration and the fact that African communities are now well established in European and North American cities shape other sorts of connections.

All this suggests that political imaginations of Africans, from poor migrants to sophisticated professionals, have multiple roots and draw on multiple connections. They may provide alternative models for changes. Some forms of political organization have been – permanently, one hopes – excluded from the realm of possibility: the colonial empire and the white supremacist state, for instance.

How wide the circle of the possible can be remains to be seen. Basil Davidson, a stalwart supporter of African nationalism in its heyday, later (1992) saw the nation-state as the "black man's burden," an imposed institution inappropriate to the conditions of Africa. We have, however, seen something worse than the nation-state: its absence. The collapse of state institutions in Somalia, and their weakness in the face of warlordism in Sierra Leone, Liberia, and Congo/Zaire, reveal how much, in today's world, we depend on state institutions to regulate conflict and provide basic infrastructure. Anthropologists can celebrate the ability of the Somali clan structure to balance the relative strengths of different kinship groups, foster equality among males, and settle conflicts within the kinship system itself, but once – following the cynical manipulations of the United States and the Soviet Union – Somalis got access to AK-47s and truck-mounted artillery, clan conflict took on an altogether different aspect.

Seeing the possibility of actually dominating others, clan leaders carried warfare to a more devastating level, tearing down state structures. It is too simple to lament the "Western" character of the state, for states as they exist throughout the world reflect a history shaped by the struggles of once-colonized people, and state institutions take new forms when they are used in different contexts.

States can and should be judged on whether they can perform such basic tasks for the benefit of the large majority of citizens. But states consist of people, and people build networks. The institutional strength of states and the networks of its most important leaders may reinforce each other or stand antagonistically to each other. A political leader may benefit from fostering economic growth in which many people share, adding to his political capital, or he may try to deny potential rivals access to resources and insure control by eliminating alternatives. One process fosters institution building and resource generation; the other weakens institutions and consumes resources. Both are rational strategies, and both are used by leaders of African states in various combinations. Nothing guarantees that the virtuous circle will triumph over the vicious one. Historical reflections should not simply assign blame to past actors but deepen discussions of accountability. We see how governments, oppositions, and concerned citizens made their choices, and how those choices had consequences. Perhaps that will help us think through the consequences of choices we make today.

The history of decolonization did foreclose alternatives that were once the object of attention – supra-national federations and Pan-African unity – and it put in place a particular kind of state as well as a ruling elite conscious of its own fragility. The devolution of sovereignty by European states was accompanied by a denial of responsibility for the historical process that had put this institutional nexus in place. This history leaves the question of whether in the future the range of possible forms of political action can be expanded as well as constricted. The key question is not whether Africa should maintain or abolish the nation-state, but rather what kind of state can be constructed, what kinds of relationships can be forged across state borders, and what kinds of recognition within states can be given to the variety of forms of affinity to which citizens subscribe.

In the immediate aftermath of independence most African rulers seemed to be pushing aside the possibilities their political struggles had opened up: of a citizenry choosing its leader; of a socially conscious citizenship, in which education, health services, and other services are seen as a duty of government; and of cooperation across borders against the injustices of imperialism and for recognition of Africa's contributions to global culture. That states are units of electoral politics and territorial administration does not preclude a politics of larger and smaller units, of activism across borders or allowing local collectivities more room to act in the interest of local and regional concerns. While some see sovereignty as a barrier against any questioning of the good or evil done within borders, others argue that it is a part of an effort to share the planet, and that the abuse of any nation's sovereignty abuses that of people everywhere. Many African states may well remain stuck within the limitations of the gatekeeper state – with its brittle and heavily guarded sovereignty – unless states in Europe and North America as well as Africa acknowledge a shared responsibility for the past that shaped them and the future to which they aspire.

A full bibliography for this book may be found on the website of Cambridge University Press at www.cambridge.org/CooperAfrica2ed.

Bibliography

Armah, Ayi Kwei. *The Beautyful Ones Are Not Yet Born*. Boston: Houghton Mifflin, 1968.

Barber, Karen. *A History of African Popular Culture*. Cambridge: Cambridge University Press, 2017.

Bayart, Jean-François. *The State in Africa: The Politics of the Belly*. 2nd ed. Cambridge: Polity Press, 2009.

Branch, Daniel. *Kenya between Hope and Despair, 1963–2012*. New Haven: Yale University Press, 2011.

Bratton, Michael, and Nicolas van de Walle. *Democratic Experiments in Africa: Regime Transitions in Comparative Perspective*. Cambridge: Cambridge University Press, 1997.

Callaghy, Thomas. *The State–Society Struggle: Zaire in Comparative Perspective*. New York: Columbia University Press, 1984.

Cheeseman, Nic. *Democracy in Africa: Successes, Failures, and the Struggle for Political Reform*. Cambridge: Cambridge University Press, 2015.

Davidson, Basil. *The Black Man's Burden: Africa and the Curse of the Nation-State*. Oxford: James Currey, 1992.

Diouf, Mamadou, ed. *Tolerance, Democracy, and Sufis in Senegal.* New York: Columbia University Press, 2013.

Ellis, Stephen. *The Mask of Anarchy: The Destruction of Liberia and the Religious Dimension of an African Civil War.* New York: New York University Press, 1999.

Hanretta, Sean. *Islam and Social Change in French West Africa: History of an Emancipatory Community.* Cambridge: Cambridge University Press, 2010.

Hutchinson, Sharon. *Nuer Dilemmas: Coping with Money, War and the State.* Berkeley: University of California Press, 1996.

Ihonvbere, Julius. "Democratization in Africa." *Peace Review* 9:3 (1997): 371–78.

Lal, Priya. *African Socialism in Postcolonial Tanzania: Between the Village and the World.* Cambridge: Cambridge University Press, 2015.

Lynch, Gabrielle. *I Say to You: Ethnic Politics and the Kalenjin in Kenya.* Chicago: University of Chicago Press, 2011.

MacArthur, Julie. *Cartography and the Political Imagination: Mapping Community in Colonial Kenya.* Athens: Ohio University Press, 2016.

Magaziner, Daniel. *The Art of Life in South Africa.* Athens: Ohio University Press, 2016.

Mann, Gregory. *From Empires to NGOs in the West African Sahel: The Road to Nongovernmentality.* Cambridge: Cambridge University Press, 2014.

Mbembe, Achille. *On the Postcolony.* Berkeley: University of California Press, 2001.

Mkandawire, Thandika. "Crisis Management and the Making of 'Choiceless Democracies'." In Richard Joseph, ed., *State, Conflict, and Democracy in Africa.* Boulder: Lynne Rienner, 1999, 119–36.

Mustapha, Abdul Raufu, and Lindsay Whitfield, eds. *Turning Points in African Democracy.* Woodbridge: James Currey, 2009.

Pierce, Steven. *Moral Economies of Corruption: State Formation and Political Culture in Nigeria.* Durham, NC: Duke University Press, 2016.

Reno, William. *Corruption and State Politics in Sierra Leone.* Cambridge: Cambridge University Press, 1995.

Reyntjens, Filip. *The Great African War: Congo and Regional Geopolitics, 1996–2006.* Cambridge: Cambridge University Press, 2009.

Smith, Lahra. *Making Citizens in Africa: Ethnicity, Gender and National Identity in Ethiopia.* Cambridge: Cambridge University Press, 2013.

Straus, Scott. *Making and Unmaking Nations: War, Leadership, and Genocide in Modern Africa.* Ithaca: Cornell University Press, 2015.

Van Beurden, Sarah. *Authentically African: Arts and the Transnational Politics of Congolese Culture.* Athens: Ohio University Press, 2015.

Weitzberg, Keren. *We Do Not Have Borders: Greater Somalia and the Predicaments of Belonging in Kenya.* Athens: Ohio University Press, 2017

CHAPTER 8

Twenty-First-Century Africa

In 2000 a cover story in *The Economist* was entitled "Hopeless Africa." In 2011 a cover story in the same journal read "Africa Rising." In 2016 a *New York Times* headline read, "'Africa Rising'? 'Africa reeling' may be a more fitting slogan these days." In each of these instances the journalist made two of the most elementary errors in the social sciences: turning a partially valid point into a false generalization and looking at the future as a linear projection of the recent past. Looking back at Africa between 1940 and the present, one sees major differences across space and across time. In a continent that contains different ecological zones, different connections to the outside world, nearly fifty distinct nation-states in its sub-Saharan regions alone, varied languages and belief systems, and different historical trajectories, it is hardly surprising that Africa should not share a single fate. Yet in the eyes of much of the outside world – and in many African eyes too – Africa is a singular entity, defined by different criteria: by race, by a colonial past, by poverty. Such visions have gone along with the idea that Africa should follow, or should have followed, a singular path through time, whether it is called development, modernization, or liberation.

The very prevalence of such conceptions creates a certain truth: one cannot avoid writing a history of Africa in relation to concepts of political liberation and economic and social development, because those concepts have shaped the way African governments and opposition movements, international agencies and their critics, talk – and sometimes act. But if homogenizing stereotypes and linear projection are part of the history of Africa, they do not frame it, and we need to analyze alternative and often conflicting visions of what any part of Africa is and should become, and the divergences as well as convergences of historical patterns.

There have been times when convergence seemed to be the main story, even if one recognized complexities and exceptions. Between 1945 and 1960 colonial rule was transformed from an ordinary and generally accepted place in the world's repertoire of political organization into a symbol of oppression and backwardness, and African political movements played a major role in effecting this transformation, encouraging each other and turning holdout colonizers into pariahs. But it still took until 1979 for the Portuguese colonies and Zimbabwe and until 1994 for South Africa to come out from under white domination. Observers thought that those countries, with their histories of revolutionary mobilization, might follow a different trajectory than the states that had followed an earlier and less violent route to independence, but the distinction between early and late – largely peaceful and significantly violent – decolonization does not correspond to the most important similarities and variations.

As the colonial option shut down, it became less and less clear whether the sole criterion for its exclusion from the global repertoire of political organization was that colonial rule meant "foreign" or "white" domination, or whether the issue that concerned much of the world should be political repression, economic exploitation, and discrimination in whatever context they took place. Such questions had indeed been raised by liberation movements before they took power.

In the 1940s the major colonial powers abandoned their insistence that colonies must pay the costs of their own economic advancement – and even the costs of their own oppression – in favor of a new politics that went under the name of development and entailed commitment of funds by the wealthy to the poor. Even the Portuguese empire and South Africa claimed to join the development project, not that they acted to raise black Africans' standard of living. Elsewhere, what began as a colonial project became a national project, supported by international organizations and the aid agencies of former colonial powers and new entrants into the game – now with the goal of integrating new states and different peoples into an international order based on nation-states but riven by antagonistic power blocs and animated by fears of disorder and conflict.

One can in this general sense speak of a development era running from roughly 1940 to 1975, even though what development was to signify and who would benefit from it were not so clear. There were dissident voices, coming from both the most orthodox of economists, who saw violations of the principles of market economics, and the most radical of political activists, who saw development as another form of Western (or perhaps Eastern) imperialism. There were serious attempts at following a socialist line of development, but the goal was still the transformation of African economies into something that could be considered "modern." If there was convergence at the level of development as a worldwide project, there was divergence on the ground – indeed, a wide range of policy initiatives – and for some Africans development meant loss of land and even the minimum of subsistence they could expect to enjoy.

The development consensus fell apart in the 1980s, with influential economists and powerful international financial institutions claiming that, compared to the free market, development initiatives were doing more harm than good. Whether these institutions were simply writing off Africa – insisting that governments impose austerity so that they could give priority to their debts – or trying to make African economies "sound" is debatable. Aid in fact continued to be provided, but often in the form of debt relief or more generally partial – very partial – compensation for the large decline of revenue following upon the world recession of the late 1970s. Investment in Africa, which market-friendly policies imposed by international financial institutions was supposed to unleash, fell by half between the 1970s and the 1990s.

The effects of structural adjustment were variable, since some African leaders privatized state institutions to themselves and gave priority to maintaining patron–client relations. At their most devastating, the new policies reversed those that had previously had the most positive effect: improving education and health services, maintaining a decent standard of living and a measure of security for workers in the most essential sectors. To the extent that they did what they were intended to do, the imposed policies pushed people out of stable jobs into precarious ones.

By 2000 international institutions and some economists were changing their minds again, and development projects and development funding were now touted as the Millennium 2015 plan or the Poverty Reduction Strategy. The switch in policy fashions overlapped, without notable foresight, a much stronger trend: the increase in demand for African raw materials largely driven by the ferocious pace of industrial production in China, and to a lesser extent India, as well as the uneven recovery of European and North American markets. Here was the origin of the Africa rising narrative.

However, if we break with the assumption of linearity, the pattern is consistent with the past: a cyclical view of African economic history, of growth spurts that came and went, driven by specific demands for exports: slaves early on, cocoa, coffee, cotton, copper, and gold in the early colonial period, and a wider range of agricultural and mineral products in the 1950s and 1960s. Because the high degree of responsiveness to primary-product demand did not lead to the creation of diverse or industrialized economies, the spurts eventually exhausted themselves. We now stand at an ambiguous point. The growth spurt of the 2000s, largely based on oil and other minerals, driven by the addition of new actors in the world economy, might either continue, as the Africa rising thesis would have it, or peter out, as the growth-spurts model suggests. The latter is more likely, but only the future will tell.

What we have seen since the 1990s isn't just an Africa-wide pattern, but unevenness across space. A few countries, Ghana and Botswana most prominently, have impressive records of both political stability within the framework of competitive elections and substantial economic growth, despite the inequality and residual poverty that is still evident in these countries. Other parts of Africa – Somalia, the Central African Republic – have experienced both political breakdown and economic decay. Many countries fall in between these two poles.

Politically, there was a negative convergence from the 1960s to the 1990s: not a single African head of state left office because he was voted out. There were one-party states and no-party states, civilian and military rulers. Some countries were relatively peaceful and others extremely violent, but the strongman sticking as best he could to his place in power was a common thread, with some exceptional voluntary "retirements" such as those of Senghor and Nyerere. In the 1990s this pattern broke apart. There have been from then to this day elections where presidents or prime ministers were voted out of office: in Benin, Cape Verde, the Central African Republic, Madagascar, Malawi, Senegal, and Zambia. And there were presidents who stayed on and on: Mugabe in Zimbabwe until December 2017, and Museveni still in power in Uganda. The contrast between relatively calm transitions in power and those where power is contested by violence is striking. African politics, since the 1990s, has been moving in different directions.

One can point to further contrasts: the successful mobilization of young Senegalese or young Burkinabé to demand fair elections in 2012 and 2014 with the sorry spectacle of Mugabe's thugs beating up opponents to extend his overlong presidency; the innovations and resilience of East Africa's coffee growers with the thousands of people from Sahelian West Africa who risk their lives to cross the Mediterranean to seek precarious jobs in Europe because they have no alternatives in Africa; the continued insecurity in the desert-edge parts of Mali with the ongoing recovery from horrendous civil war in Liberia and Sierra Leone. Angola, Equatorial Guinea, and Gabon epitomize oil economies that look good on paper but not in practice, run by kleptocratic elites with callous attitudes toward the welfare of their populations. Nigeria has squandered so much of its oil revenues since the 1960s – producing extreme wealth and a significant middle class, while leaving much of its population in poverty – and remains so badly governed that it is hard to project a future very different from its recent past. South Africa is a bigger unknown, having transcended a system of racial domination that had seemed deeply entrenched and brought a small number of blacks into the ranks of the wealthy and more into a respectable class of civil servants, skilled workers, and small-scale entrepreneurs, while leaving a large portion of the working-age population unemployed. Politically, South Africa has remained formally democratic since 1994, but with doubts about the lack of transparency and unchecked clientelism within a political party that allows opposition voices but monopolizes power.

The period covered in this book is characterized by high degrees of extroversion that leave African economies dependent on the vagaries of markets in a narrow range of raw materials and – since the 1960s – fragile states trying to come to grips with difficult economic, political, and social conditions. They are also vulnerable to internal intrigues, to cross-border networks, and to the direct or indirect interventions of outside powers. With the end of Cold War, the increasing presence of militant Islam, the diffusion of arms traffic, and the multiplying of commercial channels, the effects of Africa's connections to the rest of the world have become harder to predict. In the last two decades more than ever, it has become evident that the capacities of some states to manage, if not to supersede, the circumstances in which they exist are shaped by complex historical patterns. South Africa and the

Democratic Republic of the Congo are both mineral-rich countries with considerable agricultural potential; their historical trajectories have been very different.

The transformations that have been the principal subject of this book took place in a longer context of Africa's relationship with the rest of the world. Africa was systematically conquered, but not so systematically ruled. The pre-1940 colonial system was able to function because it had limited transformative ambitions. Colonial power was a combination of gatekeeping, bastion building, episodes of repressive violence, and the state's effort to make itself into the patron of patrons, particularly of chiefly elites who brought coercion and the distribution of rewards to the village level. Chiefs and commoners found numerous niches and crevices in the system. Trading diasporas, labor migration networks, associations of school graduates, churches, mosques, and shrines cut across "tribal" territories and territorial borders, even as islands of wealth and influence developed among cash-crop producers in several regions. Mining enterprises and European-owned plantations created islands of wealth extraction, dependent on labor from surrounding regions deliberately kept from expanding their own resources.

By the 1940s the reality of Africans in dynamic agricultural systems, in wage labor, and in cities could not be contained within this system of rural power and patronage. The custodial and extractive colonialism of the 1930s became the developmentalist colonialism of the 1940s and 1950s. As they played out, the claims of developmentalist colonialism – that it would revolutionize the backward ways of African economies, creating a new type of African as much as new wealth – translated into a focus on those more bounded areas of the economy that the state could actually remake. Politically, the developmentalist state tried to look away from provincial and chiefly administration. It turned to civil servants with technical and bureaucratic knowledge rather than to white men who "knew their natives" or chiefs who knew their traditions.

Much of this scenario applied to the different colonial powers, but with variations that would have important consequences. Belgian Africa took the lead in stabilizing and providing a minimum of social service (health, primary education) concentrated on the people it needed to work the copper mines, while keeping a tight lid on political activity and trade union organization. Portuguese Africa had its version of development that brought Europeans to its colonies to fill roles occupied by Africans in French or British colonies, while allowing political freedom to neither whites nor blacks. South Africa followed a policy of "separate development" that for Africans put the accent on the separate, not on the development. Within each imperial bloc there were more variations, depending on the prevalence of settlers, access to ports or intra-African trade networks, the relative importance of African export agriculture, and many others factors, playing out over time in even more ways.

After the collapse of the European empires, the constraints on new countries were not those of "colonialism" per se, but of an entire process, including the form of African political and social mobilization. This was true in a double sense. First, the shift in the colonial state toward an activist, centralizing, modernizing direction presented a particular target to the political activists of the 1950s: the possibility of an activist, centralizing, modernizing project that Africans could control themselves. The leaders of parties challenging colonial rulers sometimes partook of the same arrogance toward peasants and small-scale entrepreneurs as their predecessors, but they were more concerned with the implications of development for patron–client relations, with providing resources to people loyal to them, and, once they took power, keeping resources away from potential opponents. Second, the first generation of leaders knew from their own experience the potential of claims made on the basis of citizenship. The reformist colonialism of France and Great Britain had been beset by demands – for equal wages, equal social services, and an equal standard of living – based on a notion (explicit or implicit) of imperial citizenship; their successors faced such demands from mobilized groups on a national level, and they had more meager resources with which to meet them. They faced the need to demobilize their populations, to channel workers into tame trade union federations while co-opting or eliminating the most effective leaders, and to limit the autonomy of farmers' associations.

The national idea has had an ambiguous place in contemporary African history. Although Senghor, Sékou Touré, Nkrumah, Nyerere, and others had during their years of mobilization against colonial rule made "Africa" an ideal above that of the individual nation, the territorial nation is what they got. For all their ideological differences, these leaders made the most of the national configuration of power. The governments of most African countries tried to instill a sense of national belonging and national purpose. Their success in doing so has been mixed, and the excitement of independence – of people controlling their own destiny – has been hard to sustain when forces beyond the control of an African state have such powerful effects on economic and social possibilities and when government leaders seem to act in their own interest rather than that of the people they represent. Patriotism can still take the form of protests calling for the accountability of rulers, but national ideals are at times replaced by a bitter sense of betrayal.

People may instead try to find a patron inside the governing elite who can send some of the fruits of the gatekeeper state in their direction. Or they might focus their collective imaginations on neighborhoods and religious affiliations, on kinship relations, and on other sorts of personal ties. Such affinities had been important all along. But for a time, claims could be made as citizens, in the name of common interest. The very process of claim-making had helped to define a national imaginary. The repressive actions of African leaders, starting with Nkrumah, not only damaged associational life and expression, but the very national ideal that the leaders themselves asserted. But the ideal of the citizen as an active agent of his or her destiny keeps coming back, in young demonstrators against electoral manipulation or corruption, less positively in episodes of violence against migrants from other African states.

The first generation of African rulers inherited from colonial powers the institutions of state: bureaucracies, armies, customs houses. The sovereign state gave leaders access to international resources. Heads of state could draw on the intellectual, moral, and financial resources of the United Nations, international financial institutions, and the development agencies of industrial states, who were concerned with making the international system at least minimally functional. Rulers such as Mobutu proved skilled in manipulating Cold War and other international rivalries. Whereas state elites tried to guard the gate, regionalist movements, smuggling networks, and rebels tried to get around it, and the complexities of international business and rivalries of nations, as well as the possibilities of cross-border networks within Africa, made gate evasion a feasible possibility – at least if the rebels had resources that somebody might want to buy. What was crucial was the struggle to control the nodes in a pattern of resource movement.

Gatekeeping strategies thus emerged out of a particular history of colonization and decolonization. The history of decolonization, for better or worse, gave rise to a series of states which stood at critical junctures in a highly unequal world.

Were there alternatives in the past? Are there in the future? If colonial regimes had put more money and effort into development in the 1950s, could they have overcome the burdens and neglect of pre-war colonialism? Or would a more market-oriented approach in the 1950s have let Africans take fuller advantage of favorable economic conditions? The most likely answer to both questions is, probably not. It is not clear that the goose which the trajectory toward gatekeeper states killed was capable of laying golden eggs; indeed, the obstacles facing development within a capitalist world economy were themselves an important reason why state leaders tried to find other means of expanding national (or their own) wealth.

Even before colonization, Africa had presented unfertile ground for capitalist expansion. It offered many places where people could survive and if necessary hide; it offered closely woven social networks that could foster movement across certain routes and solidarity in certain places; and it offered relatively few places where an elite could try to exclude all others from access to crucial assets – notably land – and thereby create a permanent workforce subordinated to its task. African kings frequently faltered in their quest to turn power into systematic extraction from their own populations, and looked to external connections – trade, conquest, and enslavement – to set themselves apart. The would-be capitalists of the colonial era, with the notable exception of South Africa, were able to go only so far. They could build islands of wage-labor capitalism, and, outside of instances of extremely brutal extractive economies, mostly lived off less direct extraction from peasants who were both spread out geographically and connected to each other socially. Colonial capitalism focused on the export of a few commodities and on the building of narrow commercial structures, not on wide and inclusive commercial interaction or diversified and long-term investment.

The rulers of independent Africa found themselves in a similar bind, so that their takeover of the development project of late colonialism also failed to produce systematic transformation of production and exchange, but instead reinforced narrow channels which rulers could try to control, and much larger areas which they could not. By then, countries exporting primary products faced an international economy dominated by powerful corporations with a wide choice around the world of where they could find primary products, cheap labor, and investment opportunities.

From the late 1940s through the early 1970s, expanding crop and mineral exports plus development efforts in their most expansive phase seemed to promise more varied economies. Some cash-crop producers, despite the tendency of states to confiscate a significant portion of export earnings, acquired significant wealth. The best-organized workers achieved better wages and the possibility that a career could provide a family with a decent house, education for the next generation, and a pension.

These hopes fell victim to world economic trends that turned viciously against primary-product exporters in the late 1970s and 1980s. But even in the best years of export growth, few African countries got much beyond increased primary-product exports and import-substitution industrialization. The most successful, such as Côte d'Ivoire, faced steep declines later on when crop prices fell. Neither the most market-oriented African economies nor the most nationally focused achieved notable breakthroughs, even if for a time many were able to finance substantial improvements in education and health. Internally, African states had already run into the limitations posed by gatekeeper elites who feared both the claim-making capabilities of organized farmers and workers and the danger that pockets of wealth could produce regionally based opposition. Small-scale entrepreneurs, from market women to cross-border traders, were often harassed by African governments, as they had been by colonial regimes, unless they could be incorporated into the leadership's patron–client structure.

Such restrictiveness contradicted governments' desire to promote economic activity in their national territories, and the balance between these tendencies varied greatly. But the absence of long-term trends toward the emergence of strong business communities and the reversal of the 1950s pattern of developing a stable, decently paid labor force reflected back on the political process itself, making politics more of a winner-take-all situation, where both wealth and power depended on keeping control of the central government. Local and regional government were discouraged, leaving little space for those out of power to retain a stake in the system independent of the patron–client system. States discouraged the activities of civic as well as political organizations, from unions to women's associations to organizations advocating ecologically responsible development. This historical sequence, a limited opening followed by a narrowing of political and economic possibilities, trapped African states in a vicious circle: the resources of the gate had to be all the more protected because resources were so limited. Such a situation encouraged intrigue – in the army, among regional power brokers – to take over the all-important institutions attached to sovereignty and linkage with the outside world. The rash of *coups d'état* of the late 1960s in Africa revealed the extent of the problem.

Some gatekeeper states possessed civil services and state institutions that functioned moderately well, and they allowed a degree of debate and civic organization. In quite a few states, including Kenya, Senegal, and Nigeria, the media and public debate became more open in the 1990s, and have by and large remained so. The internet and the cell phone have made it more difficult for governments to control information.

In a number of countries the weakening of state economic control, under pressures of structural adjustment and leaders' realization of their own policy failures, has led to expanding entrepreneurial possibilities, misleadingly labeled "informal," and this has produced a rather different sort of market economy from that imagined in the 1960s, one where artisans and women traders play a bigger role and male wage workers a smaller one. At the other extreme, a few governments have become little more than the most powerful warlord among others, each trying to keep together a set of followers and reward them with the spoils of certain export revenues or predation.

Do the expansive years between 2000 and 2015 suggest that new trajectories are opening up? Chinese-built railroads from coast to interior – such as the recently opened Djibouti–Addis Ababa and Mombasa–Nairobi lines – will make more efficient rather than transform the pattern established by colonial transportation policy. Export zones provide employment and earn foreign exchange, but they encourage more focus on specific commodities demanded outside than on a broad range of economic linkages. Building communications parallel to the coasts rather than perpendicular to them would help the cause. So would regional common markets, something ECO-WAS and the African Union recognize and are trying to implement.

It is nevertheless hard to see, in this day and age, how a redirection of economic initiative is possible without external support. Good schools, reliable electricity networks, and responsive health facilities are all necessities for a balanced economy. Few African countries have the resources to undo the damage done since the 1970s. Is Niger ever, on its own, going to be able to educate its population and provide high-quality training to the cadres needed to run effective enterprises? What African countries can afford to make the investments needed to turn their export orientation into horizontal linkages of African economic regions with each other?

Because Africa is the poorest of the continents, the vicious circle of lacking the resources to obtain resources takes an extreme form. The breakthroughs that some countries in Southeast Asia have made suggest that escape routes from vicious circles do exist. However, the dual myths of markets as optimizing agents and nation-states as the unit of economic action stand in the way of creative action. African economic problems have long been co-productions; they have been shaped by the interaction of very different sorts of systems, horrifically so in the era of the slave trade, with more mixed effects in the years after World War II.

Sharing of responsibility for the consequences is another story: to talk about "African" economies as if they were truly African, while international financial institutions and transnational corporations are "givens" to which Africans must adjust, is to stifle thinking about economic change from the start. At the same time, African governments have not been much better than Western ones at listening to what small-scale cocoa farmers in Ghana or market women in Nigeria or the people who mysteriously supply Kinshasa with food have to say about economics. They might have learned a few lessons.

Are there more constructive ways of broaching the reform question? Here follow some suggestions, not for prepackaged solutions, but for historically based ways of thinking about the future.

First, to think realistically, we need explanations. It may be true that most African states are ineffective, prone to corruption, and follow unsound economic policies; but such observations mean little without explanation. Gatekeeper states do, in fact, have something to fear from networks or collectivities able to pose a challenge or from African cultivators who use social connections to make the state irrelevant. This leaves the question of whether certain kinds of policies by governments or outside institutions can encourage "going with the flow" – taking advantage of social systems that keep options open – instead of imposing yet another single-minded solution. What can states and outside agencies do to encourage small-scale producers rather than to assume that the model of agro-business can be imposed on Africa? Artisans and small- or medium-scale entrepreneurs can be encouraged not just by minimizing procedures to register a business but by providing security, electricity, and communications facilities.

Second, we need to think more subtly than the opposition of state and market or of a dichotomy between state and civil society. Some political economists have pointed out that keeping a market economy functioning requires more state capacity than maintaining a centralized economy; the latter may work badly, but it functions in the interests of the rulers. Shrinking government may do less to shrink the capacity of bad rulers to steal than to weaken the basic institutions that permit workforces to be trained and to stay healthy, or to provide the predictable services that domestic and foreign investors need. Patronage politics blurs the line between public and private resources and depends on the vertical relationship of an elite and the individuals and groups that make up society; privatizing ownership may redirect rather than reduce the importance of patronage. Indeed, all systems, not just those in Africa, contain mixtures of personal connections and institutions that play by a set of rules. The problem is to make institutions rule-bound and transparent enough that all citizens can obtain services or make claims upon them, while avoiding their becoming distant and alienating.

Rejecting the state in the name of civil society or the market is likely to be no more effective than assuming that the state can solve all problems in the name of the people. All this requires careful attention to the institutional capacity of states; it requires thinking in the long term. Whatever the failings of African governments that claimed to be "socialist," a democracy that is not in some sense "social" will garner little support. Voters need to sense that their decisions will bring them predictable services and opportunities that improve their lives.

Third, we need to ask what the implications are of the fact that "African" problems are actually Afro-Euro-American co-productions, emerging from a history that included the slave trade, colonization, and international support for even the most self-aggrandizing of African rulers. In both the literal sense (the indebtedness of African countries) and in a more figurative sense (the accumulation of bad habits and the failure to solve basic problems), the burden of this co-production lies heavily on Africa. We are caught in a dilemma: on the one hand is the fact that young Africans are saddled with the multiple costs of the illegitimate rulers who built up big debts and bad structures, as well as the stifling colonial systems that preceded them. On the other hand, the writing off of debt encourages irresponsibility. The international system recognizes the latter danger, but not the former; even Mandela's South Africa was expected to pay the debts that the apartheid state had incurred to oppress its African population. If a new generation of Africans is to get out of the difficulties that their elders – with lots of help from outside – got them into, international agencies need to take a more balanced view of responsibility.

Let us realize that international banking, transnational corporations, donor agencies, and international institutions are not some impersonal embodiment of the "world economy" but are specific institutions, particular kinds of power relations. They should be scrutinized just as carefully as the behavior of African politicians. International corporations and foreign aid can help or harm; they – not just the behavior of Africans – deserve examination. Africa has been told endlessly what it should do to conform to the world market; the more difficult question is how the institutions that constitute the world market can be restructured to give the world's poor and excluded more of a chance.

From the days of anti-slavery movements to opposition to colonial rule to mobilization against apartheid, successful political action has depended on the resonance between the concerns of "local" people and their networks of supporters in other regions and in other countries. Such connections have turned slavery, colonialism, and racial domination from facts of life into political anathema. Political change does not come simply from well-meaning outsiders getting their way or from authentic local communities bringing down the all-powerful. Time and time again, change has happened by interaction. Africa has its scoundrels who speak in its name as well as its thoughtful critics who were the first to warn that governments were failing to live up to their promises, well before Western journalists and academics made their transition from credulous to judgmental. Outsiders need to know the difference: to listen and to think about what they hear. The future of purely "Western" intervention is likely to be no better than its past, but the prospects of thoughtful cooperation remain open. As the experience of past cross-national social movements makes clear, the possibility that large-scale institutions can be changed is not entirely a utopian one.

Africa, under colonial rule or independent administration, has not had the opportunity to develop multiple, diverse, and dense economic linkages to the rest of the world. Its conquerors wanted certain things from it, and they constructed an infrastructure and incentives for them to be delivered. Colonial regimes, until late in the game, were not interested in systematically transforming African societies, and they weren't capable of moving beyond a patchwork of zones of exploitation, zones of neglect, and zones where African enterprise could achieve a modest prosperity. Faced with these forms of colonialism and capitalism, Africans struggled to hold them at arm's length. They had considerable success and paid a frightful price for it. Are Africa's choices between the poverty of marginalization and the devastation of exploitation? Or are there other ways to organize agricultural production, small-scale industry, and regional markets? Are the moments, from the 1940s to the 2010s, when Africans demanded the benefits of citizenship, doomed to be fleeting, as rulers fearful of the tenuousness of their own power repress forms of association and communication that might counter their singular hold on limited political and economic resources? Or do the experiences Africans have had over the past seventy-five years in forging associations and alliances among themselves, of imagining new forms of religious, cultural, and political action, offer possibilities for the future?

Index

40 Age Group, 97

Abacha, Sani, 198, 260, 283
ABAKO, 112, 246
accountability, 239, 281, 288, 298, 302
Accra, 44, 67–69, 111, 181, 243
Achebe, Chinua, 260, 283
Action Group, 88, 91, 101
Adichie, Chimamanda Ngozi, 260, 283
Afghanistan, 276
Africa
  as defined by race, 15–16
  asserted unity of, 4–8, 17, 94, 105, 107,
    283–85
  connections within, 17, 32, 63, 77–78,
    80, 105, 270, 272, 275, 285, 288,
    295, 298, 300
  and diaspora, 16–17, 24, 32, 35, 125,
    190, 238, 244, 256, 267, 277, 297
  diversity of, 14, 17–18, 39, 181, 240, 286
  images of, 17, 22–24, 30, 35, 48, 51,
    87–88, 94, 101, 113, 125–26,
    258–59, 287, 291
  international connections of, 12–14, 17,
    19–21, 64, 113–14, 117–19, 190,
    192, 234, 238, 298–99
  population and demographics, 17–18,
    117–18, 121, 133, 135, 161–65
  sub-Saharan
    and North Africa, 15
  see also African Americans, and Africa;
    international opinion; Pan-Africanism

"Africa rising," 8, 120, 291, 294
African Agricultural Society, 61
African Americans, and Africa, 14, 17, 32,
  34, 80, 222, 282
African Development Bank, 156
African Mineworkers Union (Southern
  Rhodesia), 99
African National Congress (ANC), 13–14,
  74–77, 198, 213, 215, 219–29,
  231
African National Council of Southern
  Rhodesia (ANC), 200, 202
African Union, 156, 277, 285, 301
Africanism (South Africa), 75–76, 144,
  221
Afrikaans, 218
Afrikaners, 43, 71–72, 223
agriculture
  African initiatives in, 22, 28–31, 97,
    130, 302
  biofuel production, 140
  collectivization of, 138, 265, 268
  and European export firms, 30, 88, 192
  failures of, 140, 266
  growth of, 28–32, 92, 119, 130, 135–38,
    294, 299
  and plantations, 22, 82, 139, 210–11,
    271, 296
  and rural political mobilization, 10, 61, 65,
    79, 95–97, 130, 199, 202–3, 211
  and rural wealth, 28–31, 89, 130–37,
    242, 299